Crash & Burn

AJ NICOLE

3rd Edition

Published by AJ Nicole

Cover Designed by Sherri, wildlovedesigns

Edited by Paige Conway

PLAYLIST

Burn- Ellie Goulding
Fragile- Prince Fox, Hailee Steinfeld
Burn Break Crash- Aanysa, Snakehips
Headstrong- Trapt
Crashing- ILLENIUM, Bahari
i'm yours- Isabel LaRosa
EAGER- Britton
Good Thing- Jake Miller
Baby- KINGDM, Kevin Garrett
Close- Nick Jonas, Tove Lo
As Long As You Love Me- Justin Bieber, Big Sean
As The Worlds Burning – Able Heart, Alyson Mary
Replay- Zendaya

For Paige,
This is as much yours as it is mine.
For All My Badass Booktok Babes,
I hope this lives up to the hype.

It's okay if you crash and lose your spark.
Just make sure that when you get back up,
you burn like the whole damn fire.
-Unknown

A NOTE FROM THE AUTHOR

This story contains depictions of a car accident, mentions of drunk driving, cancer, and a very light intro into elements weaved into spicy and graphic scenes of mature intimacy.
This story is intended for audiences of 18 years and older only.

THE PROLOGUES

Sterling

"I have a medium iced chocolate-cherry latte on the bar for Lisa!" I shout as I place the drink on the bar.

I turn around and start steaming more milk. There's a line of people waiting to have their order taken and a crowd begins to form around the bar as others wait for their drinks to be made. It's busy at the café for a Thursday.

"This was supposed to be hot." Lisa approaches the bar, a look of annoyance crosses over her resting bitch face as she speaks condescendingly to me.

"I'm so, so sorry. Let me remake that for you." I attempt to reach for her cup, but she pulls it back toward her.

"I don't want you to remake it for me. I want you to make it right the first time. I've been waiting for like seven minutes and this is the third time you've gotten my order wrong this week!" I smile at her before turning my back and rolling my eyes to the ceiling. I take a breath and grab a hot cup and then turn to face her as I start pumping syrup into the cup.

"I'm sorry. But again, the café is pretty busy so it's normal to experience a wait time, but I can get that drink remade for you right now." I put on a fake smile.

"Did you hear what I just said? Or are you stupid?" Lisa comes in every week and calls someone stupid. Why? Because she's an entitled bitch. But more often than not, I'm the one who takes the brunt of her verbal attacks. Half of the time, her order isn't even wrong. She just likes to get free drinks and she thinks throwing a temper tantrum will get her there, and most of the time it does. But tonight, I'm feeling brave.

"Hello?" She sets the drink down to wave her hand frantically in front of my face. "Anyone there?"

It takes me a moment to realize that everyone is staring at me and jumping over the counter like an animal at her isn't an option. I'm not a violent person, but the fantasy forms in my head regardless. Instead, I settle for a snarky remark.

"Listen, Lisa. You can come in here and act like a child to every barista in here if you want. Or you can be a decent human being and take the iced drink, because that is what you actually asked for, and leave." I feel a relief take over as I get some of my aggression out in words to this slimy human. But I also feel a knot form in my stomach because I normally don't let myself get vocal like that.

"Ugh!" Lisa shouts and suddenly I'm drenched. The sound of the clap her hand makes against the cup as it connects and flies at me from the counter makes me jump out of my trance.

Ice and espresso soak my shirt and seeps through the fabric to my skin. I guess I should be glad it wasn't hot.

"Who even hired you?" she shouts, as she turns to walk out of the café. "The incompetence!" She hits the door hard with both of her palms as the bell rings above, and I look up to see a very angry Giselle – my boss – staring at me, hands on her hips.

"Clean it up! And this is coming out of your paycheck!" she demands. And of course, I obey. But I flinch at the mention of a paycheck deduction. Especially because she's sipping on an iced matcha that she didn't even pay for.

I pick up the ice and soak up the liquid with a rag, I realize my white shirt is bleeding with a chocolate-colored liquid, and I smell like milk and cherries. I guess it could be worse. I bend over to pick up the cup and toss it in the trash, then lean into the sink to rinse the coffee off my clothes, when there's a voice behind me.

"Are you okay?"

I flip around quickly, almost jumping at the words.

"Oh, I'm sorry. I didn't mean to scare you," he defends, but I'm not scared. I'm in awe.

I mean, he's handsome. He's got a few visible tattoos and dirty blonde hair to match mine, spiked over a little to the side. His dark eyebrows and honey brown eyes contrast perfectly with his light hair, and though I'm drenched with ice and cold milk, my body starts to feel hot.

"Umm, no I'm-" But I look down at myself and realize my shirt is see-through from the liquid and my red bra is exposed. I suddenly feel somehow even more embarrassed, and I lose my voice.

"What the fuck happened here?" Dakota says as she comes out from the back. "I leave for ten seconds to get changed and you've already made a damn mess?" She laughs as she hurries over to the napkins to help me clean up. She's always been a great friend.

"It was Lisa," I say, and Dakota rolls her eyes.

"That crazy lady who stormed out of here just a second ago?" the man says. I almost forgot he was standing there, still staring, probably at my chest.

"Who are you?" Dakota asks.

"Name's Tom." He shoves his hands in his pockets, looking briefly at Dakota to answer her question but then focuses right back on me.

"Hi, Tom. Nice to meet you. Are you just gonna stare at my friend or did you need something?" Dakota says in a bold tone.

She's always been straight forward, where I'm a bit more reserved up front; she has no problem spitting her sass at people. Whereas it takes me a minute to open up to people before they get that side of me.

"Yes, well I did come in for a coffee. But I think I'll just take a tall drink of her instead," he says, answering Dakota, but his eyes are glued on me. And suddenly my bra isn't the only thing that's red, my cheeks burning in evidence.

Dakota starts coughing frantically and I look over at her to see she's holding her throat like she's about to die. I reach for her arm, not knowing what to do. And suddenly she pulls me down to the ground.

"What the hell?" I demand.

"Shush." She pulls a finger up to her lips. "I think you need to let tall, dark, and handsome over there drink you up tonight," she whispers as she pretends to be cleaning up invisible liquid. Sure, we're ducked behind the counter, but I'm fairly sure what's-his-face can still see us.

"I really don't know if that's a great idea," I whisper back.

"C'mon, Sterling. You haven't gotten laid in like a year and it might relieve some frustration from...ya know..." Dakota points to my shirt drying with coffee stains.

She's right. It's been a while, but I've not had the best experience with one night stands or dating, sex, and relationships in general.

I roll my eyes at her before I pull myself up from the floor and Dakota follows.

"She gets off in an hour," she speaks for me, not even giving me a second to think.

"I'll just wait outside then." Tom turns on his heel and leaves the way he came. Leaving me shocked *and* wet. Wet from the drink that was thrown at me, of course.

We get to his place. I follow him into a garage and pull in behind him. It feels awkward to get out of my car, not really knowing why I agreed to this. *Living on the wild side*, as Dakota would say.

Once we're inside, he hurries me into his room and his jeans are practically already on the floor. Everything is so rushed. Stripping. Kissing. The foreplay. No foreplay, actually. If one didn't know better, they'd think that we have been teasing each other all day and couldn't wait to sleep with each other. But the truth is, it's just a rushed one-night stand. Just like the rest.

He struggles to unclip my bra; *must I do everything myself?* I reach behind me to unhook it and he grips his erection before moving his head toward mine. He goes in for a kiss, but I avoid it by asking a question.

"Do you have a condom?" I'm on birth control – for no good reason other than to control the cramps – but I'm not taking any chances.

He nods and pulls it out from the side table. We hit the bed, heads bumping awkwardly as we do. It hurts a little, but neither of us care because the heat of the moment is hot. *Is it really hot though? Or am I being desperate?*

Dakota was right. It has been a while.

I don't do this much. I hate admitting that every one of my sexual encounters have been one-night stands. Yet here I am about to give it up to some random dude; someone who came into my job and announced that he wanted to *drink* me. Whatever the heck that means.

I try to study his facial features a bit, though it's dark and he's moving around so much. We're both down to nothing but our underwear. He takes off his boxers and my eyes are immediately gifted with... well, it's *decent.* I take my turn taking mine down and now I'm exposed.

"Fuck yeah," he says as he flips me over onto my back. And the way he says it kind of turns me off, like he just finished first place in a *Grand Theft Auto* race.

He doesn't waste any time before throwing himself into me. It's big, but not too big to hurt. He thrusts and I join making the bed rock back and forth. He tries to lean in for another shot at a kiss, but I lean my head back and pretend to moan instead because I've decided that I don't want to give this man the intimacy of kissing me – not that sex isn't intimate already.

We rock back and forth for a few more seconds, and unexpectedly, he starts shaking. Silently. He buries his face in my neck and shivers into my body. Then he pauses.

He finished?

Not the *Grand Theft Auto* race.

In me.

He's done?

Are you fucking kidding me?

It's been...all of two freaking seconds.

I push him off of me with a frustrated huff. I can't believe I just let this guy take spot number four on my list. Not that I'm keeping any sort of physical list, of course. But the thought is embarrassing and I hate myself for allowing this to happen the way it has.

I find my clothes and pull them on quickly, avoiding eye contact with the loser still recovering on the bed beside me.

"I'm so sorry. I just- you're so hot and..." But I don't let the asshole finish, throwing my hand up to silence his lame excuses.

Why am I even mad? Because I thought this might feel good for a night. Though it might take my mind off all the bad luck that's been following me around the past three years. And honestly, I've never had an orgasm before. I definitely thought hot-café-guy might do the trick. But damn if this isn't embarrassing, for him, sure, but for me the most. Because at least he got to finish.

"Wait!" he yells from the bed as I'm halfway through the door. "Can I at least get your number?"

I can't help but let out a small laugh at his desperate plea as I swing the door shut behind me.

See you never, *Two-Second Tom.*

Callan

"Happy thirtieth, son," my dad says as he hands me a stack of paperwork.

"Seriously?" I question dryly, but really, I wouldn't expect any less from him. He's a workaholic, and running a company requires loads of paperwork. Though you'd think he'd give me a break for once, since I do everything as his office manager.

Every year for my birthday, we come to the same fucking restaurant. We come here because the owner is a client and *business is business*, in the words of my father. But I've never been one to really celebrate my birthday, I'm just here because my mom looks forward to it every year.

"I need these signed by tonight." He's very bland with his words. My father believes in two things: success and manhood. Being an emotionless motherfucker is his definition of being a real, true, *man*.

"Can it wait till tomorrow?" I ask.

"My lawyer has already drawn up a contract and dated it for today. I need you to sign it now," he pauses. "You are now David Dealership's new owner and CEO." He looks over at me with an ever-so-slight smile attempting to curve on his lips, as he puts his napkin down nicely in his lap.

"What did you just say?" I look over to my mom, whose face is lit up with excitement.

"Your mother and I have decided, it's about time to hand down the business. It's all yours. You just have to sign the paperwork." My mom reaches over for my dad's hand. He almost doesn't take it, for whatever reason, but joins her as she smiles bright and wide.

I look down at the stack, it's true. He wants me to sign the paperwork to gain ownership of the dealership. But I don't want it. *Do I?*

I look at my mom, who's practically crying because she's so happy for me. I can tell this means a lot to her; she wants this for me. My mom has always been my number one fan. But shit, if she knew of my extracurricular activities, maybe she wouldn't be. Though, I'm not sure she doesn't know; I was a rough kid for as long as I can remember. Always getting into trouble and causing problems.

My father's beady little eyes watch me. He can see the gears turning in my head, my thoughts forming. *Is this what I want?* I mean, this was the end goal, right? But I like my life the way it is. The money. The women. The parties. I thought I'd be settled down and married by the time I came into ownership, just like my dad. But maybe this isn't so bad. Because honestly, would I really even *want* a wife? Running a dealership, I can handle, but relationships are a commitment that I'm not built for.

"Callan, this is important to the family. You're the only one who can take over, and your mother and I want to start settling down for retirement," he insists as he takes a sip of wine.

I don't mind disappointing my dad, though he'd be fucking pissed. It's my mother I can't bear to see upset. I need to excuse myself, take a breath, before I sign anything.

"I'm going to use the restroom. I'll be back in a moment."

"And then you'll sign?" my mother asks in optimistic anticipation. I give her a reassuring smile as I nod and walk away from the table.

I walk down the hall toward the bathroom, trying to relax and calm my thoughts. I don't know why this irritates me so much, but it does. Maybe it's the pressure of it all and following in my father's footsteps. He didn't even discuss this with me. I already have everything I could ask for. Though the thought does excite me a bit; being able to control the company and never having to answer to my father's dumb ass requests ever again.

As I turn the corner, a young woman with a black apron bumps into me from the side, drinks spilling off her tray and over my shoes. She immediately leans down and starts picking up the mess.

"I'm so sorry." She pauses as she looks up at me, and her eyes widen as she takes me in. "Callan," she whispers my name under her breath.

"Apologize," I demand, even though she already did.

"I'm-" She can't get the words out. So, I help her.

I grab her by the hand and yank her up so that she's standing with me. Her cheeks flush with pink as I maintain eye contact the entire time. Her black hair is tossed into a ponytail, a pen tucked neatly into her hair tie. Her collared shirt is buttoned all the way up except for the top one, giving me the perfect view of her cleavage as I tower almost a foot taller than her.

I pull on her chin, forcing her mouth open with my hand. "I said, say you're fucking sorry, Desiree." I throw her up against the wall, her back pressed firmly against the brick. I remove my hand from her mouth and reach for her ponytail, gently tugging on it.

"I'm so sorry, Callan," she gasps. "I didn't mean to be a bad girl. I promise I'll make it up to you," She finally pleads out behind bedroom eyes. And now, we're back to our old ways. Desiree reaches out a hand toward my crotch, but I smack it away. She once told me she liked it rough and I didn't mind that one bit. It's like roleplay for her, for me it's just a game.

"You know the rules." I burn my words into her skin. "Now, are you going to clean up this mess?" I pull a little harder on her hair and she lets out a whimper.

"I, I-" She tries to find words. I take my hand out of my pocket and run my fingers down her neck and over her cleavage. She quivers under my touch. "I'm just so sorry," she whispers up at me, now behind pleading eyes.

"How sorry?" I breathe into her neck; I can almost feel her pulse. But I don't give her time to speak before I yank her by her hair, pulling her off the wall and down the hallway, into the women's restroom.

I kick open the stall at the end and push her down to her knees. She's practically begging me to taste me. But she doesn't call the shots.

I don't do relationships. In fact, Desiree is the most consistent fuck I've had. Otherwise, it's strictly one-night stands. But every year like clockwork, she's here waiting for me. It doesn't mean anything, at least not for me. It *never* means anything to me.

I pull her up off the floor and back her into the wall, locking the stall behind us. I take my hands and place them just inside the opening of her collared shirt before ripping it open and exposing her breasts. No bra. *Figures.* For the last three years, it's been the same damn thing.

"I'm so sorry," she pants. I hike up her skirt as she reaches for my belt, but I smack her hand away before she gets there.

"The rules," I huff. She doesn't touch me unless I permit. I am in charge, and she obeys. Those are the rules. I yank her underwear down to her ankles and rip my belt off. I turn her over, face to the wall.

I turn her back over, pulling my dick out of my pants. I take a condom from my wallet and slip it on before thrusting into her.

"Yes, daddy!" she screams, and I'm immediately grossed out. I hate that. *Why do women think we want to be called daddy?*

I flip her over back into the wall and position myself behind her. But as I do this, like I have done successfully in years prior, I realize something isn't right. I'm going soft and I'm so out of sorts, even having this girl willing to submit to me feels off. So I pull away from her, and she sighs in annoyance.

"What the hell?" She turns to face me.

"This shit has become way too predictable. I'm over it." I can tell my words insult her, but I don't really owe her an explanation.

I live life in the dull areas, the areas that are darkest where not a lot of light shines through. Why? You can blame that on my dad. It's all I know. But surprisingly, I've been okay with it. I don't know how to do anything except to take what I want. And usually, it's on my terms. But something about this lifestyle I'm choosing to live just doesn't feel right anymore.

"Callan, come on. Don't you like a little role play?" she pleads, and I usually do like roleplaying, but I feel sick looking at what I'm doing. It doesn't feel right to keep doing this. Almost like I'm too old to be fucking around this way.

I roll my eyes as I pull my belt back through my pant loops and unlock the stall, leaving her there breathless as I walk away.

But then I remember something. I turn back around and approach her again. I lean into her and take the pen from her ponytail before leaving the bathroom. After all, I'll need something to sign the paperwork with.

Business is business.

ONE

Sterling

ONE YEAR LATER

I can't get my shirt off fast enough. Why did I decide to wear a full-blown button up today? The buttons keep getting caught; I try to fish them through the holes, but they just won't budge. I take heavy breaths, trying to pull the material away from my skin, I'm hot and sweaty. Unbuttoning a shirt is a lot of work and I decide that I don't have time for this, so I yank the blouse from my chest. Fabric tears against my skin and the buttons start flying into the air. Finally, I'm free.

"I'm so sorry," she says, looking at me behind puppy dog eyes, "I can't believe I did that."

I look over at the twelve-year-old girl, her brown eyes looking back at me behind tears, her cheeks flushed. "I didn't think I would puke," she cries.

"It's okay, Sara. But I did tell you to slow down on the candy. I told you it was going to make your stomach sick." I did tell her, but as most pre-teens on a mission to prove someone wrong, she just didn't listen.

I realize I still have vomit on my chest, almost vomiting myself from the smell; sour patch kids and rotten milk, curdled in Christmas colors.

I take Sara over to the shower and start the water. She apologizes again.

"It's okay. Let's get you cleaned up." I help her into the shower and make sure she has a towel before leaving her to clean herself off.

It's Friday night, and while I should be out with friends, maybe at a party or a club, I'm here working, because really, that's all I have time for. For the last year I've been babysitting Sara most weekends and I'll be honest, I prefer it over the party life. I've never been one to have a ton of friends and life took a sharp turn when I decided to leave home. I have to be an adult now, but I'd be lying if I didn't say I feel like I'm missing something. Like I missed out on life after high school.

I look at myself in the mirror. *Pathetic.* The only time I get to rip off my clothes is when a twelve-year-old pukes on me.

I walk over to Mrs. Chen's closet and grab an old shirt that I know she won't miss, because her closet is worth more than my entire apartment and I know she doesn't even wear half of this crap. I use a hot washcloth and some of her fancy body wash to speedily clean myself over their bathroom sink. I pull the Yellowstone National

Park T-shirt over my head and steal a spritz of perfume before heading downstairs.

I pull out my phone to text Dakota, my only friend.

Hope you're having a fun night! Be safe.

She's at a club tonight celebrating her boyfriend's birthday. I'm supposed to be with her, but when Mrs. Chen sent me a frenzied text at the last minute, asking if I could watch Sara tonight, I agreed. I need the extra money far more than I need a night out of getting hit on by sweaty, drunk dudes.

Thanks, bestie! Wish you were here.

I can hear my best friend's sincerity when I read her message in my head. She's always been so effervescent, and based off the selfie she sent me earlier, she definitely looks it too.

She's wearing ripped up jean shorts, paired with a black mesh, see-through long sleeve shirt which exposes her black bra. She topped off her outfit with an oversized jean jacket and knee-high, black boots. Her fiery, red hair is pulled up into a high, tight ponytail and her green eyes gleam into the camera lens as she smiles with her bright white teeth and holds up a peace sign.

I look down at my own outfit, a borrowed t-shirt, and leggings with a pair of mismatched patterned socks. Even if I hadn't just been thrown up on, my outfit would be a real embarrassment next to Dakota's stylish, put-together ensemble.

Dakota and I met when I was out looking for jobs after leaving home. She had also just left home, but for other reasons, and was new to Colorado when we met. She was working behind the counter at the café when I went in for an interview and we've been inseparable ever since.

I'm happy to know I have someone like her in my life, she's always been so supportive of me and cheers me on. Though sometimes, I feel a bit envious toward my best friend. She's got a boyfriend, a career, and she can still go out and have fun on the side. It just reminds me that I really need to get my shit together.

Sara comes down after a few moments, her long black hair still sopping wet. She has on her pajamas, they're covered in tiny JoJo Siwa heads. She looks cute, not like the little brat who decided that shoving fourteen sour candies in her mouth at once was a clever idea.

"I'm so sorry again, Sterling." She's upset with herself; her big brown puppy dog eyes are the telltale sign. "I should have listened to you about the candy. I'll never eat another sour patch kid again, I swear it." We both laugh as I bring her in for a hug. But our moment of sisterly bonding doesn't last long before she makes her first snide remark of the night.

"Can I be honest with you?" she asks and I nod my head.

"I think you need more friends," she deadpans; it's almost funny how she knew exactly what I was thinking but then it's not funny because she's right.

"Why do you say that?" I ask her as I get up from my chair and go to pull an overpriced sparkling water out of the fridge.

"I don't know. I just feel like you're wasting your time here with me, when you could be out there exploring your heart's desires." I take her dramatic tone as a joke, but I can tell she's trying to be serious. Honestly, her words sound somewhat inspiring, even coming from a twelve-year-old. But they also sound like a line from a movie that she's now repeating back to me. I laugh internally, knowing that she's trying her best to be motivational.

"Sara, if I wasn't here *wasting my time with you*," I say motioning quotation marks, "you would be home alone and there would've been no one here to hold your hair back while you puked your brains out." I laugh at her, and she rolls her eyes at me.

"I could have called my boyfriend." She sticks her nose up in the air, her brown eyes shining from the light of the crystal chandelier that hangs above.

"You're twelve, you don't have a boyfriend," I remind her, hinting that she's too young to have a boyfriend.

"You're twenty-two, you don't have a boyfriend," she articulates while mimicking me, and welp, she's not wrong. I can count on one hand the amount of guys I've dated...or more so just slept with. I don't know what it is about me. Dakota says I have the looks but lack the confidence and she told me I couldn't get offended because we're best friends and she has an obligation to be honest to me. But I wasn't offended more than I was confused...lack the confidence?

I'm not sure if I blame that on my inability to flirt very well, or rather it's the lack of wanting to flirt because guys these days just miss the mark, or if I blame my parents' relationship for not truly showing me what love and happiness should look like.

Theirs was a relationship of toxins and passive aggressive arguments.

When my dad left, my mom turned to alcohol to fill the void, and in turn, she stopped being a mom. I was about Sara's age when he left, maybe a year or two older. But she went downhill almost immediately and after three years of seeing my mom turn into someone I didn't even recognize, I needed to escape. She stopped paying bills; my brother had to drop out of college and work two jobs just to keep our lights on. She stopped caring. The whole dynamic of family changed for us. And not only did my dad leave me, technically, so did my mom.

I don't blame my mom, not at first. But as time went on and she started to become detached, it became unbearable to handle for me.

Once my mom became a belligerent drunk, her words aimed to hurt and her actions of motherly love were nonexistent. I tried so hard to have a relationship with her, but the second I turned eighteen, I threatened to leave, and her response was what ultimately ran me out the door.

No one wants you here anyway.

My brother, Graham, hated me for leaving. Or so that's what he made it feel like...hate. But Mom made it clear, I wasn't wanted. He thought I gave up on her too soon and for that, he cut ties with me too and that hurt just as bad because I like to think we were somewhat close.

So maybe my lack of confidence comes from feeling like I was never good enough. And even four years later, the past affects me and no matter what I do, I can't seem to figure this thing called life out. Though, I'm not sure I can blame anyone but myself at this point.

I look over at Sara and I'm reminded that I actually do have someone. I've grown to love this little brat. Sara is the closest thing to family I've got right now, and she looks at me like I'm her big sister. I love that for us. I pull her in for one last hug as I kiss her on the forehead, letting her know that I will get my life together once I'm done watching over hers and she just giggles. I tell her goodnight before sending her off to bed.

I make my way over to the Chen's living room and sit on the couch, velvety blue with a gold-woven blanket draped over the arm. I take a look around, and notice nothing has changed about this room, about this entire house, since my first day here almost a year ago. I don't know how they do it. If it were me, change would be needed weekly. I get bored often and living in the same house for your whole life, looking at the same never-changing walls would drive me insane. Maybe it's because we moved around so much when I was a kid, but I really prefer a change of scenery from time to time.

I stare at my phone. It's fifteen minutes till ten, so the Chen's will be home any minute now. I should probably get up and start gathering my things, but this couch, the velvet. *So comfy.*

I turn on the TV and start scrolling for a show to watch. I land on a reality dating show. The idea of these shows are ridiculous to me. People go on a show to find love in strangers all while trying to win a cash prize? It's like a bribe to find love.

Though I guess some people really do find their soulmates on these silly shows. I guess you can find love in the craziest of places. And it gets me thinking...what if my true soulmate is out there somewhere and what if I never meet them because they live a thousand miles away? *What if my soulmate is on this TV show right now?*

I laugh at the idea. These shows are stupid. And I guess I'm okay with not finding *the one* because in all honesty, I need to get my life together before I even think about bringing someone else into the mix.

Suddenly, I feel myself dozing off. The soft knit of the blanket wraps me into the smooth velvet couch as my eyes drift to the frosted window, snow gently falling outside.

"Sterling?" I hear a faint voice enter my head as I try to open my eyes. "Sterling, honey?"

I open my eyes to Mrs. Chen's long, beautiful legs standing in front of me. I immediately bolt up and frantically start to apologize.

"I'm so sorry, I must have dozed off." I stand up and start folding the blanket, trying to shake off the sleepiness.

"It's okay," she chuckles. "It happens to the best of us." She helps me to my feet and hands me my phone, which had fallen to the floor. "I've fallen asleep plenty, back in my babysitting days." She tries to make me feel better.

"I'm so sorry I'm getting home later than planned but thank you again for being available to watch Sara tonight. Your coat is by the door and your payment is tucked safely in your purse," she adds.

I check my phone and realize it's almost midnight. I'm glad I slept a little, knowing I have to be back at the cafe tomorrow at 8am. As I put on my shoes and coat, I ask Mrs. Chen how her night was. She tells me it was pretty uneventful. Like last time, I notice that her husband did not follow her home which is weird, considering it was supposed to be date night.

"It started snowing pretty heavily, so please be careful. I'll see you next week." She opens the door and waits for me to get to my car safely before closing it behind me.

I hurry to my car trying to avoid getting snow in my hair, as it frizzes like a troll when it's wet. I close the door to my 1998 Chevy Cavalier, hoping and praying that it starts. Half the time it gives me trouble just because it's cold outside, so I have low expectations right now, as it's snowing like all hell.

I turn the key, and it makes a rattling sound but doesn't turn over. Figures. I try again, this time cranking the key harder, and again, nothing. I throw my head back and sigh heavily. "Please, universe. Don't do this to me," I whisper into the air, my breath leaving steam in place of my words. I try my hand at the ignition again and miraculously, it rumbles over, and the engine gives life. Thank God.

The roads are bad. The plows obviously haven't been out yet and it doesn't help that the snow covers my windshield faster than my wipers can fight back, leaving my view fogged and frosty. Winters in Colorado are the worst. We're in the middle of what everyone calls "second winter" because it's the beginning of March and we're still getting blizzards, while the rest of the country is preparing for spring.

I vividly remember a similar snowstorm, years ago, that my parents swore wasn't as bad as it looked. I was six and my brother was about eleven. My parents took us to *Chuck E. Cheese* that night; I think my dad actually slid through a four way stop on the way there, but he said nothing would stop the Cooper family from having an adventure. We ate pizza and played games. We worked together to win as many tickets as possible. The ball drop was my favorite, I even figured out the timing to drop the ball straight into the jackpot. Graham would climb up the ramp to Skee-Ball and throw the ball into the one-hundred-thousand slot when the workers weren't paying attention. My mom and dad faced off shooting hoops on the basketball game, laughing at one another when they missed a basket. We used the tickets to buy the silliest little prizes like cheap-ass slinkies, a stuffed animal that looked like a mix between a cat, a racoon, and a goat, and I remember Graham bought ten packages of jacks, but we didn't care. We were just having fun. On the ride home, I remember falling asleep in the back of the car to the sight of my mom and dad holding hands in the front seat. It was bliss.

Suddenly, I'm forced awake by a blaring horn and bright white lights. *Shit.* I fell asleep at the wheel. I swerve out of the other lane, avoiding a head on collision with the car speeding at me. My car spins several times before stalling, then coming to a complete stop in the middle of the road. My heart is pounding uncontrollably. Jesus, that could have ended much worse.

I try to turn my car back on but this time, there's no noise. It doesn't rumble, stir, or growl. Nothing. I attempt to gather my thoughts and figure out what to do, when another pair of headlights comes barreling down the road straight toward me. I don't have time to think before impact. I'm thrown back with force, the airbags come bursting out of my dashboard, the horn starts blaring, and through the snowstorm, smoke fills the air. I hear glass shatter, my safety belt is locked, and my legs are trapped under the steering wheel. My head starts to feel heavy and finds its way crashing down to the steering wheel; my eyes fall shut and now the only thing I see now are the back of my eyelids.

TWO

Callan

My driver, Gerald, drops me off and I walk through the double glass doors of my all-too-familiar childhood home. I head straight to the bathroom, turn on the faucet and notice that my hands are shaking for the first time in my life. I splash cold water over my face and look in the mirror. I don't even recognize the person staring back at me.

I grip the sink with my hands as I take a deep breath. I've never felt so out of control before. My whole life has been made up of rules and regulations, like a damn contract handed over by my father.

I have cancer.

As I stare back at my reflection, my eyes are clouded with dark circles and my deep brown hair is a scrambled mess. I think about why I acted out when my father called me and told me he has cancer, why what he said angered me so damn much.

I have cancer.

He said it like it didn't matter to him. Like it didn't matter to me. And maybe it doesn't. Maybe I don't care. Maybe I'm just pissed because he knew we were celebrating a big night tonight, my first since I've been in control of the company and as usual, he needed to steal the spotlight.

I look back down at my hands, and I can't stop them from shaking. I'm so pissed off that this situation took a turn for the worst. So pissed, that it causes me to throw my fist into the mirror.

The glass shatters, spilling all over the counter, shards glistening with the running water. It doesn't shock me when I look up and see my dad standing in the doorway, staring back at me behind unamused eyes. He turns back into the hallway. I reach over for the hand towel and clean up the blood from my knuckles before joining him.

"What's your problem?" My dad takes a seat at his desk and motions for me to do the same as I follow him into his office. The dark cherry wood of his desk seems darker than normal as the blackout curtains are pulled shut, leaving only the sconces stuck in the wall to provide dim lighting around us.

"Are you fucking kidding me?" I shout in question without thinking.

He shuffles his position in his chair.

"Don't play dumb. You know what you did." I try to keep it together, but I can't control my irritation. This is probably exactly what he wanted to happen. He wanted me to need him for something.

"Callan. I understand this may seem-"

"Fucked up," I finish his sentence.

"Yeah, sure. But you have to understand-"

"Fuck that. Don't tell me what I have to understand. Do you have any idea how fucking selfish you are?" My father is always one to try and weasel his way out of owning up to anything. And even if there wasn't a bigger picture here, I'd still make a big deal about it. He's always trying to make everything about him; springing his illness on me on one of the biggest nights of my life is a prime example.

"Are you mad at your carelessness or that I have cancer?" His question ticks in my ear. "Son, I didn't ask for this disease. But you sure as hell didn't need to lose control like that. You should be thanking me."

"For what? For being a fucking hero and saving the day?" I lean in my chair, loosening the tie around my neck as I huff in frustration.

"Everything is taken care of," he answers as he lights a cigar that he pulls from his stash.

"That's all you're going to give me?" I question, getting up from my chair.

He stops as he drags the cigar to and from his mouth, blowing a cloud of smoke into the air. "Callan, this can't get out to anyone. Me being sick is bad enough. But you're the CEO now, the owner of the business. If this got out..." He trails off and it takes me a second to process what the fuck just happened. I start to realize that all I can do now is move on. What's done is done, and the sooner I accept that, the quicker I can get the hell out of here.

I get up from my chair and dust off my pants.

"What kind of cancer?" I look toward the hallway with my back turned to my dad as I wait for him to answer.

"Lung," he says on a sharp exhale.

I scoff as I notice he's still sucking on his cigar.

"You know," I start, "you really ought to at least pretend you like your family. Soon, you'll be laying in a hospital bed and I'm not too sure you'll have anyone by your side to mourn you while you die." I imply how much of an asshole he's been to all of us. "And maybe quit smoking," I add before walking away. I don't wait to hear his response because I don't care.

I pass a family portrait of the four of us hanging on the wall as I stride through the hallway. My mom, my dad, my little sister, Virginia, and I all stand together happily smiling at the photographer. Even my dad has a smirk on his face. Anyone else looking at this photo would see a happy family, but I know it's just a façade, because eventually we were bound to be broken. You don't put people like my mom and my dad together and expect happiness. He's a morally gray asshole, I guess that's where I get it from. And my mom is a saint. She's beautiful inside and out. How did these two complete opposites end up together?

I know my mom loves my dad. Why? I'm not sure. I imagine they loved each other at some point but once his business took off, money and success became his top priority. His only priority.

I remember the first time I asked him if I could help out around the dealership. I was desperate to get to know my dad, and as cliché as it was, learn how to be a man. He was hardly home, so it was the only chance I had. I worked on engines with him in the mechanic shop and for once, we'd have actual conversations.

One day I told him about a crush I had on a girl at school. I was nervous but finally built up the courage in hopes that we could bond over something real. He said to me, "*That's not worth your time. Love doesn't take you as far as money.*" And that's when I knew he'd stopped loving my mom. The older I got, the more like him I became, and now, I fear I'm more like him than I care to admit. He's a hardworking man, but that's all there is to him.

I don't hate the idea of family. But I do hate the idea of sticking around with each other just for the hell of it. There was a time when our family was truly as happy as we looked in that photo. But something changed in us along the way, and it seems like we've been playing pretend ever since.

I'm so fucking tired of pretending.

THREE

Sterling

My head is pounding as the harsh light from my phone screen beams onto my face. I immediately drag the brightness down before checking my notifications. Five missed calls, and three new text messages, all of them from Dakota. Except for one text from Mrs. Chen, checking to make sure I got home okay - which I obviously did not - but I don't have the energy to explain that to her right now.

I'm exhausted and hazy. One glance at the clock on the wall confirms that it's nearly three in the morning and I feel sick to my stomach.

What the hell just happened? Was it all a dream?

I notice a white envelope out of the corner of my eye and the realization of what actually happened hits me hard. I wasn't dreaming.

The car. The smoke. The red and blue lights. The hospital. The IV drip still stuck in my arm. The headache. And then there was *him*. The man in a black and white suit offering up the envelope that now sits at my bedside. He handed it to me and apologized for the hit and run. The entire interaction was clouded by whatever painkiller was running through my veins.

I notice no major injuries on my body, but I feel a scrape above my eyebrow as I run my hands along my face, slowly, fearfully. I see a few small bruises forming on my legs, once I lift the hospital bed sheets.

"Hello, Miss Cooper." A voice comes from the doorway as a middle-aged, ashy-haired woman in scrubs enters the room. "I'm Jackie, I'll be your nurse this evening. I'm so glad to see you're awake," she speaks with a gentle Australian accent as she pumps sanitizer on her hands, before walking closer to the bed.

"What happened to me?" I ask worriedly. I think I know, but I don't want to believe it.

"You don't remember anything?" she answers me with a question.

"Yeah, I do but-" The sight of that stupid little envelope stops me mid-sentence. I can't let anyone see it. I wait till she turns her back to fill out the patient checklist tacked to the corkboard on the wall, snatch the envelope and shove it under my ass.

"I remember the car accident. But not much since," I finish my sentence as she turns back to face me.

"The good news is, we see no signs of broken bones or fractures. But I do want the doctor to check you for a concussion before we release you," she explains.

I swallow and nod.

"Don't worry dear, I reckon the doc should be here in just a few moments. Are you able to arrange for a ride to pick you up once you're released? We know that your car was totaled, and we don't have an emergency contact listed for you. Oh, and I'll need you to update your billing address on these forms as well, so we know where to send the bill to. Unless you have an insurance update?" She hands me a clipboard and pen.

I shake my head as I write down my address. My mind spins like a tilt-a-whirl, trying to take everything in. I sure as hell won't be able to afford a hospital bill whenever it comes, but I fill out the paperwork anyway and hand the clipboard back to her.

"I'm so sorry to hear about the accident by the way. Must've been a bloody big deer to cause that kind of damage," she states and my heart jumps to my throat.

"A deer?"

"Yeah. Said it jumped right out in front of you, in the middle of a snowstorm, nonetheless! So glad you weren't seriously banged up, dear." She starts to leave.

"Wait. Did anyone stop by and visit me?" The question comes out so fast and I almost regret asking. It's not like my family would visit even if they knew I was here.

"No, dear. No one's been in to visit you. Sit tight and I'll get the doc right in."

I shift nervously in my hospital bed as an uncomfortable amount of bile makes its way up the back of my throat, and I have to swallow hard to get it back down. I pull my phone back out, knowing I need to figure out how I'm going to get home from here. Seven percent battery life. *God, I hope Dakota answers.*

"What the flying fuck happened?" Dakota stands at the frame of the door leading into my hospital room. She's changed out of her club clothes and is now sporting gray sweatpants and an oversized T-shirt.

"I got into a car accident." My answer is short as my voice almost cracks, holding back tears.

"Well, obviously. But are you okay?" She approaches me almost frantically before she holds out my arms to inspect me as I'm sitting in the chair in the corner of the room, trying to put on my shoes.

"I'm okay. The concussion exam came back clear, and they said there were no breaks or major injuries. So, I'm fine physically. Mentally, I don't know yet," I admit. My head is still scrambled. Like someone literally cracked it open, took an electric mixer to it, then glued it back together.

"Are you sure you're okay? Are you sure there's no-"

"Dakota, I'm fine," I cut her off and she takes a deep breath.

"I'm sorry. You know how I am with freak accidents," she sighs. I look over at my best friend and feel immediate guilt over my annoyance with her questions. She's asking because she really cares about me. And she's right, after hearing about what happened to her dad, I'd be panicking about any kind of accident too. I should feel lucky just to be alive and okay, but I'm really starting to get annoyed with the whole one step forward, three steps back, routine.

"How did this happen?" she questions after calming down.

"They said I hit a deer."

"A deer?" She looks at me like I'm speaking a different language.

"A deer," I repeat with no emotion.

Dakota studies me as I gather the rest of my belongings.

"You don't believe that do you?" she asks, seeing the hesitation on my face.

"I'm not sure. It was snowing pretty badly, and I might have fallen asleep." I pull the envelope from my back pocket to shove it into my purse.

"Sterling, what do you mean you fell asleep? What's going on?"

"I don't know," I sigh, but I know I'm tired. Tired of not getting anything right. I feel like I make decent progress, then something stops me in my tracks and pushes me back.

"Someone came by my room earlier. A man. And he gave me this." I decide to hand Dakota the envelope instead of trying to hide it. She takes it and looks at it for a second before looking back at me.

"What's in it?" Her eyes scan over me.

"Open it."

She opens the flap, and her eyes grow wide.

"What in the world, Sterling," she whispers. "Who gave this to you?"

"I don't know. I've never seen him before. And I was pretty loopy, but all I remember is a man in a suit and he had these dark, unapologetic eyes. But that's all. He mumbled some things to me," I say as I focus hard on the memory, remembering bits and pieces as I do. "He told me that he needed the accident to be kept quiet. Said that someone he loves will be destroyed if I speak out about being hit," I continue. I try my best to remember the conversation, but my heart is pounding so hard I can't hear myself think. "He didn't say much else. He apologized again, for my car being totaled, gave me *that* and then walked away," I finish.

"And did you ask the nurses who he was?" she asks.

"I did. But they said no one had been in to visit me. I know I didn't hit a deer. I know I definitely didn't imagine that man being in my room. And I know it was a car that hit me, Dakota." Saying it out loud sends a chill across my body. I'm still trying to wrap my mind around this insane situation.

"What are you going to do with it?" she asks as she hands it back to me. I blow out a shaky breath before stuffing it in my purse.

"I don't know, Dakota. I mean, I could use it to pay this damn hospital bill. God knows I don't have health insurance. Or I could use it to buy a new car. Maybe something that starts on the first try." I think of all the things twenty grand could do for me right now. I've been struggling for years on my own, even while living with Dakota, who covers half the costs.

"Sterling, I know your situation is tough right now," she says in a gentle tone. "I'm always here for you if you need anything, I'll help out as much as I can. But taking that bribe, that could be just as bad as the man who gave it to you." She shifts in her stance, leaning down to help me get out of the chair.

She's right. I know that taking this money is so wrong. But I'm tired of not being able to provide on my own, and the money is already mine technically. It's not like I can track this man down and give it back to him.

"Let's get you home so you can get some sleep, okay? We can talk more about it tomorrow if you want." Dakota wraps an arm around my shoulder as she walks me out of the hospital.

It's been a week since the car accident. The doctor suggested I rest for a few days before going back to work, so today is my first day back. My boss, Giselle, was not thrilled to hear about my car accident. Not that she was concerned about me at all, she just hates when people take time off.

I spent most of my days in bed, the white envelope on my nightstand haunting me. I thought about everything I could do with that kind of money. Buy a plane ticket and move somewhere new. Buy a fancy new car. Pay the hospital bills that have already started coming in. Or maybe take Dakota with me and blow it on a weekend in Vegas. But ultimately, I decided to shove it back in my purse and cart it around with me on my way to work. I'm second guessing my choice now, as I sit on a bus full of strangers, wondering what they would do if they knew of the contents of my purse right now.

I feel so relieved when I finally make it to the café. I'm more than an hour late though because I really don't know the public transit system yet. The bus didn't show up on time, it took me the wrong way and then I realized I actually got on the wrong bus.

"Hi, Giselle!" I frantically run behind the counter and reach for my apron. "I'm so sorry I'm late. I tried calling the store, but the phone gave a busy sig-"

"You're fired," she speaks, not looking up from her books.

I laugh, a little panicky because I can't tell if she's being serious or not. The café is booming with business. Bri is taking latte orders for a line of six customers, while Josh is cleaning tables for people waiting to sit. There's no one preparing food by the ovens for bakery items, which would have been Dakota if she hadn't graduated nursing school and quit her job here.

"I can work late if you need me to. I'm so sorry." I continue to wrap my apron around my waist as I start to clock in at the register.

She reaches in front of the register, blocking me from punching my time in. "You're fired," she repeats, in a sharp, whispered tone. She waves her hands at my apron, directing me to take it off and give it back to her.

"Giselle, you can't be serious." I don't move, but she continues holding out her hand and staring at me unblinkingly.

"Drop your apron, I'll write you your last check now. That way I don't have to worry about you being late to pick that up too," she snarls.

"Giselle, please," I beg as I unwrap the apron from around my waist. "I really can't afford to lose this job right now."

"Well, you obviously can't afford to keep it either, because you're always late!" She throws her finger up in the air as she walks into the backroom, the backroom doors swinging past each other aggressively after her. Giselle is tough and doesn't take any bullshit. Even though she can be sweet, she has a firm 'three strikes and you're out' rule.

I've been late two times in the four years I've been here. Today makes three.

Returning in minutes with a check, I try to bargain with her. Beg her not to do this.

"Giselle," I plead one last time. My entire body cringes when I notice that everyone is watching me.

"I have a business to run, and it's no longer benefiting from you," she says. Her words come out harshly, stinging me as they hit. I'm reminded of my mom's words. *No one wants you here anyway.*

I don't see the point in arguing anymore. I try to hold back tears as I reluctantly hand her my apron, take my final paycheck and head for the door, avoiding eye contact with every customer on my way out.

I reach into my purse for my phone, planning to request a rideshare, when I see it staring at me. That stupid envelope, stuffed with cash. My mind races in circles yet again, thinking of all the ways I could better my life with this kind of money.

It takes me a minute to process my thoughts; *is this something I really want to do?* Do I want to take this stranger's money and use it to right his wrongdoing? Two wrongs don't make a right. But for the first time in my life, I feel like I actually have the power to take control of my future. Call it fate or destiny or a fucked-up joke from the Cosmos, but this money practically landed in my lap, and I get to decide how I use it.

Instead of requesting a car to take me back home, I type in an address to the nearest car dealership, and patiently wait for my ride.

FOUR

Callan

"There's a new client coming in, Mr. David." Cora nudges me with her elbow as the automatic doors glide open. Her jab at my side immediately annoys me, even though I know she's just doing her job. I guess my employees pride themselves on recognizing new clients from existing ones.

Cora has been at the dealership for about five years now. On her first day here, I couldn't deny my attraction to her. We were both in our mid-twenties and I'd spent the day training her. Her golden-brown hair springs into natural curls and has big, light gray eyes. But as soon as I got to know her personality, the attraction faded. When she's not complaining or gossiping, she spends her time sucking up to the boss, who was my dad at the time and he loved the adoration of his employees, but now I'm the boss and I see right through her act. She's made several pass attempts at me, all of which I've declined. When I'm at work, professionalism is my main focus, especially now that I'm running things.

"How can I help you, sir?" she asks as the new client approaches the receptionist counter. She looks back at me and winks slyly, making sure he doesn't see her, before she continues. I roll my eyes as I turn away, leaving her to work her charismatic magic with our new client.

Bits and pieces of the other night still haunt me as I stand in my lobby surrounded by the bustle of business. I'm still so angry with my dad, but I hate that I'm missing parts of that night. Having most likely blacked out after I threw my fist through the fucking mirror, which is still minimally bandaged and slightly aching in pain.

But as I take a look around at my staff, my lobby, my business, I realize this is, in fact, all mine. At the age of thirty, who can honestly say that they have an empire of this magnitude that is all theirs? Few. Yet here I am. I didn't want any of it, though. At least not at first. But now that I have it, it feels fantastic and I know I can't let anything ruin it. Not even my own stupidity.

I walk around the receptionist desk and start heading to my office when I hear the front doors slide open yet again. Cora's ridiculous knowledge has me curious, would I be able to tell the difference between an old client and a new one? I turn my head toward the door and stop dead in my tracks at the sight of *her*. This is *definitely* a new client. As beautiful as she is, she looks out of sorts; definitely not fit for the millionaire lifestyle most of my clients live. Nonetheless, I head her way.

I notice my sales lead, Jax, starts to walk over to her as well. His eyes look like they've just set sight on dinner. I almost stop to let him take the business, but then I realize he'd be going after the wrong business. It's funny, he's also one of my closest friends, so I probably shouldn't cock-block him, but I can't help myself right now, professionalism first.

I keep walking, and wave him off the moment I grab his attention. He throws his head back in disappointment but then chuckles under his breath as he turns around.

"Good afternoon, Miss. Welcome to David Dealership. What brings you in today?" I question as I finally reach her. She's way more attractive up close. Her hips are hugged in a pair of light-wash skinny jeans and she's wearing a red short-sleeved blouse which doesn't do much to hide the curve of her cleavage. Her skin is smooth like cream, her eyes a delicate blue, like the lightest parts of the ocean. Her dirty blonde hair is thrown up in a messy bun.

She looks up at me behind long, dark lashes but doesn't say anything. Her eyes wander across some of the indoor inventory. Up front I have the bright blue De Tomaso P72 next to the all-black, roofless McLaren Elva. Toward the back sits the sleek red Hennessey Venom GT and a Bentley Bacalar in a beautiful forest green. Only then, after she scans a few of the high-end vehicles that occupy the lobby, does she look back up at me.

"I think I'm in the wrong place," she admits as she holds her purse closer to her side and goes red in the cheeks.

"I'd be happy to point you in the right direction. First, can I get you something to drink?" I ask, trying to make her feel more comfortable. The commotion surrounding the lobby dies down as the interaction between us seems to play out in slow motion.

"Umm, I don't think so," she starts, "I mean, I came looking to buy a car, but I don't think I can afford anything here," she finishes. Before I can open my mouth to respond, she turns around and starts walking toward the door.

"Well, maybe I can help," I express, trying to keep up with her pace and not stare at her ass as she walks away from me, because she does have a nice ass.

There's an air about her that entices me a bit. I'm so used to the type of attention that comes with the entitled women I'm normally surrounded by. Seeing this beautiful girl in her bashful demeanor, seemingly uninterested in me, throws me off guard a bit.

"We do offer used cars." I decide to offer, because if we stand here any longer, the awkwardness filling the space between us, I'm going to lose my patience.

She stops and faces me again. "Can we look at some of those?" she asks, and I take her to the back lot outside, where I house all my used inventory.

As we walk to the used car lot, I can tell she's uncomfortable and out of place. She looks sort of rattled and I kind of find that attractive about her, almost like a challenge.

I've helped plenty of clients before. Usually they come in here knowing the price point and they know what they're looking for. Obviously, this one has no idea what she just walked into.

"Before we start looking, do you have a budget?" I ask, like I do with all of my clients.

"Yeah, it's-" she pauses, and I can tell she's hesitant. A gust of wind blows between us causing a few strands of her bun to fly free and fall in front of her face. She takes her fingers to pull the wavy hair behind her ears as she bites down on her bottom lip shyly. The gesture is so innocent yet so sexy. I clear my throat in an attempt to refocus on the task at hand.

"You know what, never mind," she says, turning back around and this time practically running through the doors.

I stay standing in the middle of the lot, watching her put distance between us as she disappears back into the lobby. It's not like I'm going to chase her down. She's pretty and all, hell she's alluring even and a hell of a lot prettier than any of the girls I've fucked with, but I don't chase anyone. Not clients. Not women. No one.

Jax starts walking in my direction. "Damn, boss. What'd you do to her?" he chuckles.

"Nothing worse than what you would have done to her."

"I would have taken great care of her, boss. Would have made all her dreams come true." He nudges me.

"Grow up, Jax." I give him a disapproving laugh before leaving him behind, though I'd be lying if I said I wasn't thinking the same thing.

It's been a hectic day at the dealership but we're finally close to closing time. I start packing up some of my things and realize what a shit-show my office has become. Nothing is organized and there are papers all over the place. It's only been about a year since I've been sole owner of the dealership and I didn't realize how much added work came with the promotion. When I was the office manager and assistant for my dad, everything felt so much easier to keep up with. But since going almost a year without an assistant of my own, things are getting out of hand.

I pull out manilla folders, planning to stay late to take care of some organization, when there's a knock at my door.

"Come in," I shout.

Cora enters the room and shuts the door behind her. She does this a lot. Cora doesn't take no for an answer, but I've also made it noticeably clear that I want nothing from her. I don't date coworkers. But her response is always, "*We don't have to date, we can just fuck.*" And my response is always, "*I don't fuck coworkers, either.*"

"Someone is here for you," she says as she holds her hands behind her back.

"Who?" I ask, not looking up from my papers.

"I don't know, but I think it's that girl from earlier. The one who ran out of here like a manic dog. She said she wants to speak to the hiring manager." She smacks a piece of gum between her teeth as she pulls a strand of hair between her fingers and twirls it.

"Why did you close the door to tell me that?" I shuffle more papers out of the way in an attempt to clear my desk, but there are So. Many. Papers.

After I took over the dealership, it's been a nonstop whirlwind of paperwork and a very sad excuse of a system to manage it all. I'm still trying to figure that part out.

"We're both adults, Callan. I think we both know why I closed that door. Wouldn't it be hot to get a little frisky while someone is outside that door, possibly listening to the noises you can get out of me?" She attempts to entice me as she leans against my desk, exposing the top of her cleavage.

"Cora, please exit my office and invite my guest in. And button up your shirt. Goodbye now." I wave her off and while she looks disappointed, she doesn't argue. Before I know it, the blue-eyed beauty from earlier is standing at my door frame.

"How can I help you?" I ask. I've stopped fucking around with the papers by now and stand up from my chair, feeling the need to provide her with all my attention.

She seems different this time. Not so panicked and lost but still slightly reserved. She shifts at the doorway, and I get a good look at her whole body from a new angle. From her heart-shaped face and her slightly rounded chin to her soft pink lips that puff out in the slightest. Or how she stands only about five-foot-six to my six-two. How her lashes are the darkest part of her and her hair shines golden in contrast against her pale-colored skin. And the fucking perfection behind her straight smile, bright whites biting down on her lip out of nervousness.

Let me tell you, I'm fucking *mesmerized* by the look of this girl.

"I wanted to apologize for the way I acted earlier." Her tone is timid and soft.

"You don't have to apologize," I tell her. "But I do wonder if I did anything wrong. You ran out of here pretty fast." She walks into the room a little further and I can tell she's thinking about shutting the door, but she doesn't.

"I just panicked is all. I'm not sure why. I've just, I've got a lot going on." The way she's holding her elbows tells me how nervous she is, and something in me softens when I see her close her eyes in disdain.

"What's your name?" I ask, wanting to change the topic.

A strand of hair falls into her eyes, and she tries to swipe it away, but it falls right back into place. It's kind of cute how annoyed she gets.

"Sterling," she nearly whispers.

"Sterling," I repeat, the name rolling off my tongue like ice. I get up from my desk and meet her where she's standing, reaching my hand out for a handshake. "Hi, Sterling. I'm Callan David."

Silence falls over the space between us for a few moments, then she finally decides to give me her hand and her palm is soft against mine as I squeeze it lightly in a gesture of greeting. I find myself studying her while she looks apprehensively back to the ground and pulling her hand away.

"Anyways, I just wanted to say sorry. I won't be needing that car after all so I should probably get going." She chucks her thumb over her shoulder waiting for my approval.

"Wait, Cora said you might be interested in a job?" I query, stepping back to lean against my desk.

"What?" She looks at me innocently as she pulls both of her palms to her cheeks holding her face in her hands and I immediately think how her skin would feel against my hands. How her skin *did* feel against mine, just moments before when we shared a handshake.

"Oh, yeah," she says before pursing her lips. "I actually got fired from my job today." She drops her hands to her side. "On my way out earlier, I noticed the hiring sign. I guess I just wanted to see if I could apply."

She seems sweet enough, but I know just by looking at her that she's probably not interested in the janitorial position that we're hiring for. And I wonder what kind of backlash I'd get if I even interviewed someone who wasn't remotely qualified for a different position, just because I liked looking at them.

Then I look behind me and see the mess on my desk.

So.

Many.

Papers.

"Why did you get fired?" I decide to ask.

"Because my boss is a bitch," she states and immediately I can tell she regrets what comes out of her mouth. "Oh my gosh, I didn't mean to say that out loud. I just mean that she fired me over something stupid. It was because I was late." She rubs her elbow sheepishly while I lock my eyes on her, not knowing if I should laugh or pretend that I wasn't fazed by what she just said.

"Well, I've got a position open for an assistant." I lie, I don't. Or I didn't, because Cora was going to get the promotion due to seniority and she was really the only one who was interested. But I guess she's no longer running unopposed.

"But seeing as I'd be your boss, I don't know how I'd feel about you calling me a bitch behind my back." She looks at me for a second, her eyes finally catching mine. She's been avoiding direct eye contact all day. And until now, I didn't know what it felt like to want to drown in someone's gaze. Her eyes are like elusive crystals, brilliant and rare. I see a small grin thaw on her face.

I continue to watch her with great interest and wait for her response. But she doesn't give one. She just forces her stare back to the ground.

I stay leaning on my desk, allowing her the time she needs to reply to me, but also allowing me the time I want to keep eyeing her. I mean it when I say I've never seen someone so attractive. Maybe it's got to do with the way she's acting. The girls I'm used to are stuck up, entitled, and rude. She doesn't seem like that at all.

"On second thought, I don't think I'd qualify for... this." She waves her hands in the space around her, breaking the silence.

Suddenly the lights behind us all power down as the team closes up shop for the night, leaving my office as the only room still illuminated. She looks over her shoulder, caught off guard by the sudden change.

"I have to say, I'm not used to women running out on me. And today, you'll have done it twice." I straighten the watch on my wrist as her face turns red.

"An interview won't hurt," I tell her as I walk over to meet her at the door frame and wait for her to make her way fully inside my office.

Am I wrong for entertaining the idea of possibly making this girl my assistant? Not because she has me hanging on to every word, the little that she gives. No, that's not why. It's because she just lost her job and I feel sorry for her. At least that's what I'm telling myself.

You don't date coworkers. I remind myself, but then she lets out a small hum as she takes another step inside my office and like clockwork my mind starts wondering what other sounds that pretty mouth of hers could make.

"I guess you're right," she agrees, breaking me from my dirty thoughts.

I motion her into my office and close the door behind us, stopping my mind from spending any more time debating between right and wrong.

FIVE

Sterling

I watch Callan as he prints out the job application. I can tell he doesn't think I'd qualify for this job; I can see it on his face. Maybe he's just being nice. But honestly, I'd clean toilets at this point. I just really need a job.

He hands me the papers, still warm from the printer, and tosses me a pen.

"I'll be back in a few moments, I have to make sure everything closed down okay," he says, "Fill out what you can, and we'll go over it together when I get back." He turns to leave the office and closes the door, leaving me by myself in his fancy ass office.

I look over the application and start filling in the blanks. I get all the way down to the job experience and reference sections freeze. I've held one legit job, the café. Other than babysitting, I don't have anything else to put down. And references? You can forget it. Giselle would laugh and Dakota, well of course she's going to praise me, she's my best friend. But I feel silly listing my one and only friend as a professional reference.

I stare at the paper, the ticks of the clock loud and present reminding me that time is of the essence. The fact that I even came back here surprises me, as if I didn't make the choice myself.

After I panicked and ran out of the dealership earlier, I took a bus back into town. I didn't walk far before I was standing on a bridge, looking out at the river below. I hesitated for a second, thinking about dramatically throwing myself into the water first. I laughed at the thought, knowing the river is only a few feet deep and my fear of heights would never let me make the jump even if I actually wanted to. So, I tossed that stupid envelope of money over the edge, instead.

Yeah.

All of it.

I know, it was stupid and probably really irresponsible but I concluded that I'm not the kind of person who wants to live with the fact that I took a bribe. It stung to watch the money flutter in slow motion down the wavering river, but I never want to know what the consequences could have been, what my karma could have been, and it almost started feeling like the money was controlling me. That's not who I am.

Callan comes back into the room and sees that I'm struggling.

"Everything okay?" he asks, standing over the desk from behind me, his body towering over mine as I stay seated. I can feel the heat from his body, and it makes me squirm uncomfortably in my seat.

"Thank you so much for the opportunity, but I think I'm gonna go." I pick myself up from the chair and start to head for the door, but he grabs me. By my wrist. His fingers are touching my skin. *Did someone turn up the heat?*

"Are you hoping that the third time's the charm?"

Callan has muscles in all the right places, not too much but just enough. He's lean and toned and his skin is perfectly sun-kissed. His eyes are a melty pot of hazel dreams. I've never seen greens and browns blend together so seamlessly. His hair was slicked back classically earlier, but now the curls have let loose, and his dark brown locks fall effortlessly over his head, longer on the top and faded slightly on the sides. I've never seen a man so ship-shape, so well suited and professional. But staring at his body with his fingers locked around my wrist feels anything but professional and I also wonder if he's got a naughty side to him.

"I'm sorry. I just-"

"That won't be necessary," he says as he gently lets me go.

"Listen, I'm not sure what you're getting out of this," I express. I try, but fail, to free myself from the invisible imprint his grasp left behind...his touch lingering on my skin gives me exciting chills.

"Out of what?" he questions.

"Entertaining the idea of hiring me, knowing damn well that I'm not qualified for this. But I do appreciate the thought," I breathe out. Suddenly I feel a loss where his warmth once wrapped around me, the lingering sensation no longer present.

He smirks down at me. "Entertain me," he practically whispers, and my body shuts down for a hot second while I melt under his tone. His words send a shockwave over my body. How in the world did this man just bring me to my knees with two freakin' words?

He leads me back to the desk with his palm placed on the small of my back, a feeling of dizziness overcomes me.

"This is the job offer," he starts, assuming that I'm willing to play along with this crazy idea. "The job pays thirty dollars an hour, you'll be guaranteed at least two days off a week, and we are closed on Sundays." He leaves me standing in the middle of the office, takes up my unfinished job application and sits down at his desk. "We can go over scheduling needs and there's an employee handbook that I'll need you to read and sign."

"I don't understand. I didn't even finish the application," I state obviously.

"Thanks for pointing that out, Sterling Rose Cooper." He smiles as he reads the paper and turns back to his computer, typing. "Take a seat, I have some new hire paperwork for you to sign." He motions me back to his desk, but I physically cannot move. I think I'm experiencing some form of shock right now.

"What makes you think I want this?" I examine him carefully.

"You wouldn't have come back a second time after embarrassing yourself the first time, now, would you?" He doesn't even look up at me when he answers and something about that annoys me but attracts me at the same time. I really don't want to admit that he's right.

Clearly, I'm not fit for the job. But how am I supposed to turn down thirty dollars an hour? Especially after throwing that envelope of cash into the river earlier. I would be stupid to throw away this opportunity, I just hate the way my potential boss is already under my skin. I'd love for his touch to be *on* my skin again. *Jesus, Sterling, pull yourself together.*

Callan interrupts my thoughts as he stands up, walks over to the chair on the opposite side of his desk and pulls it out for me.

"Miss Cooper." He waits for me to sit.

My legs manage to move, and I approach the chair, sliding in between him and the desk to take a seat.

"You'll start Monday. We can go over availability then." He continues to hover over the back of my chair as he explains the papers laid in front of me. "I just need you to sign here." He reaches over the back of my shoulder and points to the dotted line.

But my hand doesn't move to pick up the pen. My mind is still spinning, because he's too close and I feel hot all over. *Seriously, someone needs to turn down the heat.*

"Sterling." He lowers himself to my level, bringing his lips down to my ear, as he reaches over my shoulder to grab the pen. The smell of him makes me nervous; cedar and whiskey and moss wrap around me like a warm blanket. He brings the pen up to my hand and whispers, "All you need to do is sign, and the job is yours."

I jump back at the heat of his voice trailing over my ear, electricity shooting to my stomach. I accidentally bump into Callan; he stumbles back a bit, and a chuckle escapes his lips. I stand and turn to him. My composure is anything but kept at this point.

"Are you okay?" he asks, dusting his hands down his shirt.

I don't know what's wrong with me. The way he looks at me does anything but reassure me that I am not attracted to this man. No. He looks at me like I *should* be attracted to him, like I have no choice. His eyes are low, and his lips are slightly curled. His five o'clock shadow taunts me as his jawline peeks through. *Breathe, Sterling.*

"I'm so sorry, I'm just a little jumpy from-" But I don't finish. What I want to say is, *I'm a little jumpy from the car accident I just got into a week ago.* Which would be a perfect explanation. But I can't say that, not without going into further detail and looking like a charity case. The only person who knows about the accident right now is Dakota and I plan to leave it that way, indefinitely.

"You're nervous." He fills my mouth with words, showing off his full lips as he smirks almost nefariously at me.

"Why are you doing this?" I force myself to ask. He's near the door frame, after I accidentally pushed him back.

"You need a job and I need an assistant," he states, a shrug raising on his shoulders.

"Shouldn't we be doing some kind of interview then? What's the catch?" I question, turning to look down at the contract on the desk.

"No catch, Miss Cooper." He wanders over to where the pen had dropped to the floor. As he leans over to pick it up, I can't help but look at his ass. It's like it was chiseled by the gods.

"Like what you see?" Callan asks as he stands, forcing my gaze back up to his eyes. I shake my head from the thought. *Shit. What is wrong with me?*

"The job offer," he says, pretending that he didn't just catch me staring at his ass.

"Oh, um, yes," I stutter. Taking the pen from his hand, I lean down to sign the job offer, choosing not to think about it any further. What do I have to lose? Before I can pick up the paper to hand it to him, I'm surprised by the sound of a knock at the door.

I recognize the woman standing in the doorway, she's the one who brought me into Callan's office earlier, but she's not wearing her work attire anymore. Now she's in a pink, floral dress and heeled sandals, her beautiful curls bouncing around her perfectly round face. She must have gone home to change. I look at my phone and realize it's just past seven thirty. I've been here for over an hour and a half. I'm surprised Dakota hasn't called me yet; she must be staying as Asher's again.

"Cora?" Callan looks at her and cocks his head. I look back and forth between the two of them.

"I forgot something." She waves her phone in the air. "Oh, she's still here?" she asks, eyeing me up and down. She looks nice, but she doesn't sound it. In fact, she kind of sounds demanding, like a jealous girlfriend. *I'm so stupid.* Of course, he has a girlfriend.

Suddenly I feel totally embarrassed by the thoughts I've been having; about how dreamy Callan is and how nice it would be to have a hot boss. I'm totally out of my league here.

"Cora, this is Sterling. My new assistant." He throws one hand in his pocket as he motions the other toward me. Cora looks at me more intensely and I feel like her gaze could burn a hole through me.

"Hey," I offer meekly, trying to assure her I'm not a threat. She doesn't give anything back.

There's silence for a moment and my brain can't take it.

"Are you two dating?" I blurt out immediately, hating my mouth for having a mind of its own.

"I don't do relationships," Callan says darkly, and Cora crosses her arms with a huff as she sends Callan a pouty look. All at once, I feel the awkwardness thicken in the room while Cora stares at Callan, Callan stares at me, and I stare at the ground.

"Callan, can I please talk to you, *alone*?" Cora slices the silence as she sneers at me before turning her attention to Callan.

"Miss Cooper," he says as he studies the contract I just signed, "I'm going to finish up some things here in the office, I'll see you Monday morning." Callan walks over to his desk to grab the contract and filters it into a file, then hands me a business card. "Here's my contact information if you have any questions. Otherwise, I hope you enjoy your weekend." He gives me a smile. A small one, but a smile that melts the discomfort that fills the room.

"Thank you," I respond quietly to Callan as I turn to leave the room, avoiding eye contact with Cora on the way out.

"Oh, and Miss Cooper?" Callan stops me before I'm completely gone. "Don't be late." He winks at me before Cora rushes to close the door behind me, leaving the two of them alone in his office, and me alone with my thoughts. My crazy and sinful thoughts.

SIX

Callan

"So, who's this new employee you hired?" My dad sits at the island in the middle of our family's kitchen.

It's Saturday morning, the sun peeks into the kitchen through a window as I walk over to the fridge and take out the butter per my mom's request; she's whipping up her famous peanut butter pancakes. I have to admit it's been nice enjoying some homemade meals while I've been staying with my parents. My penthouse is undergoing a remodel and as much as I love waking up to the sound of power tools, staying here hasn't been as bad as I'd imagined.

"I finally got around to hiring an assistant," I say as I start to set the table where Ginny sits with her phone in her face.

"I thought that Cora was going to be your assistant?" my father asks, skimming through a newspaper and I know where he's going with this. He's still trying to have some kind of role in the dealership.

I think back to the conversation Cora asked to have with me after I had Sterling sign the new hire paperwork. She demanded that I reconsider hiring a new girl for the job because she worked hard for that promotion. And she did. But the fact of the matter is, it is my decision and I decided to give the job to Sterling.

Why? Not a fucking clue.

"She was." I sit across from dad at the island. "But I found someone who was better qualified." I lie, because I know Sterling has zero qualifications so, really, I'm not sure why I offered her the job. Something was pulling me to her, and I didn't want to let her walk away. Besides, how hard could an assistant position be? I'm sure she'll learn the job just fine.

"Hopefully, she's a good fit." My father takes down his paper and stares directly at me.

"Virginia, why don't you head upstairs and pack your things for cheer camp. We need to be leaving shortly after breakfast." My mother intervenes and Ginny rolls her eyes.

My phone starts to buzz on the counter next to me.

"Sounds like my remodel is almost done." I share with my family after opening the text.

"Already?" My mom sounds disappointed as she walks through the kitchen, placing a plate full of pancakes in the center of the table. "I like having you around."

"Yeah, seems like it." I put my phone back in my pocket.

"Must be nice to be able to come and go when you please," Virginia sneers from the doorway of the kitchen as she drags her suitcase over.

Virginia is a teenage girl through and through. She was a teenager before she was a toddler. But the last couple of years have been tough with her, she doesn't really let anyone in and it's hard to be the big brother she needs when she doesn't want it. It does make me a little upset that I don't have as close of a relationship with her as I'd like. But there's only so much I can do.

She glares at me behind big, deep brown eyes that match her hair and I shake off her mean-mug with a chuckle.

"Don't be rude to your brother, Virginia," my mom says to her calmly.

"Ha. You're one to talk." Ginny rolls her eyes at my mom before running out of the kitchen.

"What's wrong with her?" I ask.

"Just being a teenager," my mom defends. "You were one too, ya know." She reaches in to hug me before walking out after my sister. "Don't forget to call us!" she yells back before she's fully disappeared.

"Son?" my dad calls at me as I'm walking to head out of the kitchen. He coughs, trying to be quiet about it, but instead it comes out harsh. "Don't forget about the annual auction gala coming up," he says after recovering from his cough attack. We lightly dance around the fact that he seems to be getting worse. Cancer isn't a subject we're used to in the house. And I honestly don't know how to approach it, so I don't.

"Next weekend," I add on, reminding him that I'm fully aware of all business events.

"I won't be able to make it, for obvious reasons, so you'll need to find someone else from the dealership to go with you. Maybe your new assistant." He sits back down in his chair, needing to catch his breath. The thought hadn't crossed my mind, but it would make sense to have Sterling tag along, that's what assistants do. I was originally planning to bring Jax. But I love the thought of walking into the gala with Sterling by my side.

"Don't forget how important this event is," he reminds me before leaving the kitchen.

"I know, dad."

I let out a heavy sigh of relief as I pull into the parking garage of my penthouse apartment. Set in the heart of a small downtown city, the building itself is twenty stories high and my place takes up the entire twentieth floor. The view is beautiful, one side boasts a picturesque view of the mountains while the other side faces the rest of the city.

My phone rings in my pocket, a text message from an unknown number.

Is this Callan?

I roll my eyes because it's probably a booty call, and I don't have time for that shit. Then again, it has been a few months since I've gotten any action. I've been so busy focusing on the company throughout the holidays. Maybe I can make time. The phone pings again, and another message comes through.

I mean Mr. David, sorry. It's Sterling.

Suddenly my blood rushes to my head, and I don't know why.

Yes, what can I do for you Miss Cooper?

I type back. I immediately see that she's typing out a response, three dots motioning to prove it. And then it stops, but no message comes through. I don't normally feel let down when a girl doesn't respond but I was anticipating her next message.

And then, she's typing again.

I have a question about the job.

My fingers tap along the screen, curious what her question could be.

Ask.

I add her contact to my phone while she types out her next message.

It's a stupid question.

Jesus, woman. Just spit it out. I think to myself.

I'll be the judge of that.

The three dots dance again.

What exactly do I need to wear? I see that there's a uniform requirement for employees, but nothing specific to assistants. I just wanted to check in and make sure I'm dressed appropriately.

I think about how to respond. I thought the handbook covered this but then again, the assistant position is new as I've only recently decided to add it after realizing how much paperwork was being neglected amongst other things.

My initial thoughts go immediately to how hot she'd look in a tight dress and heels. Or maybe a pencil skirt. If she can pull off a T-shirt and jeans, she can pull off anything. My cock stirs at the thought of her wearing anything at all. Because it's not what clothes she puts on that make her attractive. It's just *her*. I'm ripped from my daydream when my phone buzzes again in my hand.

Never mind. I'll figure something out.

She sends before I can produce a response. Now I feel like a dick for not answering.

I can't seem to stay focused, rereading her texts and wondering how to reply. But all I can think about are her eyes, the way they looked at me, lost but intriguing. The way she touched her arms, like she felt so out of place. And how her skin felt when I grabbed her wrist. Again, my phone buzzes before I can get a chance to answer her question.

I'll just wear my birthday suit.

What the fuck? I double check to make sure it's the same number, and it is. Did she really just say that?

And now, my phone is ringing. Sterling is calling. I almost don't answer, but at this point I'm curious to hear what else she could possibly have to say.

"Hello?" I try to choke down my surprised tone.

"Oh my God. I'm so, so sorry. I did not send you that last message! I'm babysitting, and Sara, she got into my phone because she saw that I was texting someone and she thought maybe it was someone I met, like a boyfriend, and she told me that she sent the message because I need to flirt more often, because I don't flirt very often and I just, I'm just so, so, so, so, so sorry. It won't happen again." She sounds panicked, quick with her words in hopes of fixing what just happened. I almost laugh, because it's cute how flustered she sounds as she tries to catch her breath.

"WHATEVER, STERLING! YOU SHOULD BE THANKING ME!" I hear a small voice yell from the background.

"SARALEE, SHUT UP!" I hear her whisper-yell under a muffled tone.

"Callan, I mean, Mr. David. I'm so, so sorry." I hear her breathe into the phone, and I should be annoyed. But I'm not. I'm entertained, and honestly, turned on.

"Sterling," I say into the phone, calm and smooth.

"Yes, sir," she responds, and the sound of her voice mixed with the words *yes, sir* makes a certain body part of mine jump. *Jesus*. She just caught me off guard. I feel a tingle in my cock and immediately sit up from the couch to try to ease the hardness.

"Nice jeans and a blouse will work for now. We can talk more about dress code on Monday," I keep my voice as controlled as possible. In reality, I'm anything but controlled right now.

Silence falls over the other line.

"Miss Cooper."

"Yes. Jeans and a blouse. Got it," she replies.

I'm interrupted by another text coming through.

It's from Stephanie. She's one of the many women I've fucked around with. Someone who met me at a business event or something, I honestly don't even remember. She, like all the others, was desperate for my attention. Wanted to go straight to sucking my dick and didn't care if I gave anything back. It's the lifestyle. Women like Stephanie, and Trish, and Salem, and Paula, they all just want to be a part of the show: money, power, and sex. It gave them relevance. I don't do relationships. And most of them are okay with it, others try to have more, none have prevailed. It's a game for them, and I'm just a player. The funny thing about most games though, is that the player always has control.

Hey sexy, are you free tonight?

I'm immediately grossed out by the text. Normally, I'd respond with, *be here in ten.* Then she'd say, *on my way.* I'm a man, and I have needs, and as long as there are no strings attached, I'm all for it. But lately, this game I've been playing feels immature and tiring.

"Hello?" I hear over the speaker. *Shit.* I almost forgot I have Sterling on the phone.

I guess now's as good of a time as any to ask her about the auction gala.

"Miss Cooper, I'm in need of a plus one at a particularly important event we have coming up. As my assistant, I thought it would be best for you to join me. It's this coming weekend, Saturday night. If you already have something planned, I'd like you to clear your schedule to attend."

"Of course, I'll be there," she responds in what I can tell is her best rehearsed professional tone. I hear her breathing through the speaker, and it sends a shock to my dick. God, to hear her breathing like that in my ear while I thrust into her. *Fuck, Callan, you really need to get laid.*

"And before you ask, we can find something for you to wear. It is a very high-end business gala, and the dress code is strict. We can talk more on Monday."

"Thank you, Mr. David. So sorry again about the birthday suit, or ya know, the text message. I hope you have a good night," she tells me before hanging up the phone frantically.

I can't help but feel unsatisfied. It takes me by surprise to find that my dick is still throbbing, and I think maybe I can take care of it myself. I'll be damned if I let any woman have that kind of hold on me.

I could text Stephanie back, let her take care of it. But it's not what I want. So instead, I put away my phone and jump in the shower. Icy water should do the trick. I need to snap out of it.

SEVEN

Sterling

"I can't believe you did that!" I shout at Sara. She's standing on her bed and I'm on the floor chasing her around with a pillow. She jumps up and avoids my swats. *This little brat.*

"Why are you blushing?" she questions, almost excitedly. I can tell she's having fun with this. "Do you have a crush on your boss?" She jumps again as I swat the pillow at her feet, her voice small and playful as she mocks me.

"No, you sicko. That would be against like, so many rules." I jump onto the bed next to her and tackle her down to the sheets. I should be mad; she could have lost me my job. But Callan's response calmed me down a bit. It wasn't angry or upset, he even joked back. Maybe Sara is right, but at the end of the day Callan is my boss.

"It would be hot," she says under laughs as I tickle her armpits.

"What would be hot?" A voice comes from the door frame, Sara and I freeze to see her mom standing there.

"Oh, nothing mom. You wouldn't understand." Sara laughs as she gets up from the bed.

We both laugh at each other and make our way downstairs, into the kitchen.

"Don't do that again," I whisper to Sara, and she chuckles under her breath.

"Thank you so much, again, for coming to hang out with her for a couple of hours." Mrs. Chen sets her purse on the countertop and digs through it for cash. She hands me a couple of twenties and a fifty. It's a lot of money for the short amount of time I've been here today, but I'm grateful to have enough to cover groceries, my electric bill, and maybe even some clothes for my new job.

"No problem. I like watching her." And I do, Sara is the actual closest thing I have to a constant these days. So, I really do love every minute I spend with her even when she irritates my soul.

"I won't need you again for a couple of weeks, Sterling. I hope that's okay. I'll be taking some time off work to stay with Sara over her spring break, while Mr. Chen is on his business trip," she says, but the words *business trip* are layered with a hint of cynicism.

"Oh, sure, that's fine," I respond trying not to sound too disappointed. A few weeks without Sara? That kind of stings.

Obviously, the lack of extra money will suck too, but I'm more bummed to go more than a few days without seeing Sara. She's like a little sister to me, and with the strained relationship I have with my blood family, every minute with her is precious to me. Thankfully, I'll have the job at the dealership to hopefully keep me busy.

"Have any plans for the weekend?" she asks as we walk to the front door.

"Not really, just preparing for my new job."

"A new job?"

"Yeah, I, uh, kinda got fired from the café. Now I'm going to be working as an assistant at a car dealership."

"That sounds nice." She tries to sound excited, but it comes out exhausted. Mrs. Chen seems tired tonight, more than usual. She works a lot and so does her husband, but they're always very well put together. Tonight, she doesn't look so... rich. Maybe she just needs a break.

"I start on Monday, and I already have a business social to plan for next weekend!" I'm excited because this is all something new.

"I'm so happy for you, Sterling, congratulations! I hope it's everything you've ever dreamed of." She walks out of the kitchen, and I collect my things. I give Sara a big hug goodbye before licking my finger and trying to shove it in her ear. When I miss, she chases me out of the house and I laugh so hard, I have to stop and catch my breath before walking down the road to wait for the bus home.

It's Sunday morning and Dakota and I finally have a day off together, so we make plans to go to brunch. She's been working long days at the hospital, and even though we live together, we barely see one another. It doesn't help that she spends a ton of time at her boyfriend's house, too.

"So, tell me about your new job?" I ask her as we take our drinks to a table.

"It's boring nurse shit." She waves off my curiosity.

"I thought it was your dream job," I press.

"You ever think something is going to be the greatest idea ever, then a few weeks later wonder what kind of drugs you were on to think those things? Let's just say it's like that," she jokes as we settle into our seats. "Years of school I'll never get back, but it pays well so there's that. Tell me about your job." She smiles.

"Well, you know I don't start until tomorrow," I say.

"Right, but how did this even happen?" She leans into her cup of coffee, and I tell her the story.

She knew I lost my job and that I tossed the money, I called her right after it happened. But she didn't know that I went back to apply for a job.

When I got home from Sara's last night, there was a hefty hospital bill waiting for me in the mail. It just solidified how badly I need this job and how maybe throwing away that money wasn't the smartest decision I've made, but what's done is done. Hopefully, someone who needs it even more than me finds it and can benefit from it.

"Wait, your boss is Callan David?" she interrupts me mid-story, as if I was supposed to know who he was beforehand.

"Yeah?" I question. "Why?"

"I've heard of him. Some girl I work with told me that they fucked. Said he's like, the biggest dick she's ever had, and it made up for the fact that he's like, a huge player. She was pissed when he never texted her back." Dakota sips on her drink. I don't know why, but I feel kind of disappointed. Of course, other women find him attractive, and at the end of the day, he's my boss and his personal life is none of my business.

"Is he as hot as they all say?" she asks, sitting on the edge of her seat. "I heard he's impressive in bed."

I just shrug my shoulders and change the subject. I no longer want to talk about my new boss and his big dick.

It's already Monday and I'm nervous as hell. I pull on a pair of blue jeans and the nicest shirt I own. It's a blue top with ruffled layers over the front and butterfly sleeves. I slip on a pair of black flats and head to the bathroom to fix my face. I curl my hair in loose waves and swipe on a couple of layers of mascara to accentuate my long, blonde lashes.

I'm not sure why I was disappointed when Dakota told me what she knew. I shouldn't have expected anything less. It's not like we're dating, and I'm sure he doesn't even see me like that, I'm young, dumb, and broke. And he can probably pull any girl he pleases, so why would he want me?

I step outside and walk down to the bus stop. It's nice outside, one of those days where I don't mind walking to get to public transportation. I have to get accustomed to not having a car now that I can't afford one.

I take a seat at the bus bench, listening to the traffic fly by on the highway across the street. I don't live far from the dealership, about twenty minutes away if I'm driving.

Downtown Golden is usually busy but it's still pretty quiet this morning and is a beautiful, small town right off the highway that encompasses the base of the mountains. My childhood home was about two hours outside of the city, but even from that far, we still had a beautiful mountain view. It makes me sad knowing none of my family lives in that house anymore.

Last I heard, my mom and brother have since moved to Utah for a job opportunity my brother received. He always seemed to know exactly what he wanted to do with his life, and he handled the situation with my mom differently than I did. I guess you can say he's a better human than I am.

My phone chimes in my pocket, I pull out my phone to see Dakota has texted.

> I forgot to tell you yesterday. Dress code for my bday is BLACK. Like, eat your soul out, sexy and dark!

I chuckle at her text and I'm glad she sent it because I'd almost forgotten that her birthday party is this Friday. I don't like to complain, but she has to know I have nothing in my closet to fit her party theme, and it's not like I could go shopping for a new outfit. I've got ninety-nine problems and money is literally all of them.

> Shopping later?

I text back, in hopes that I can find something to wear.

I've been sitting on the bench for about ten minutes when a black sedan slowly pulls up across the street. An older gentleman in an all-black suit and flat cap steps out from the driver's door and crosses the street to approach me.

"Miss Cooper?" he asks. *Who the hell is this man and how does he know my name?*

I'm careful to answer.

"Who wants to know?" I grip my keychain a bit harder making sure that he knows I have pepper spray.

"Mr. David has sent me." He walks around to the back door on the driver's side and opens it. He motions me to get inside. *Mr. David?* I think.

He notices that I am confused and corrects himself.

"Forgive me. Callan David. He wanted to ensure you'd be on time for your first day at the dealership." I knew who he was talking about the first time, but I just didn't understand.

I look at the man. I'm a bit anxious to get into his car, I mean, why would Callan send a car for me?

I get up from the bench and proceed to the car. "How do I know you're not going to kidnap me?" I ask him before trusting to get in.

"Because, Mr. David has asked that I see to your safety in getting to the dealership as my top priority today." He shows a slight smirk my way before gesturing to the car door, clearly bemused by my sass.

"He did?" I ask, trying not to sound too eager. Maybe it's a thing he does to seduce women or something. Offer his chivalry before he takes them captive and feeds off them for days. I laugh to myself at the thought. *Stop being ridiculous, he's not some kind of vampire.* Maybe he really is just being a gentleman. But I'm not that easily swayed.

"No thanks," I decline. I don't need him to throw private drivers in my face. I just want to get to work like a normal person.

"Oh. I'm sorry, Miss. But I was asked to bring you to the dealership," the old man says again. And I feel bad, he seems nice. But I don't need to be taken anywhere. I've seen enough horror films to know that this could be my last car ride ever.

"What's your name?" I question him.

"Gerald. My name is Gerald. I'm the family's driver."

Driver? Well, that tells me a lot right there. Callan is a rich boy with family money which means he's probably a huge asshole. *Great.*

"Well, Gerald. With all due respect, you can tell Mr. David that I'd like to take the bus to work. Your services aren't needed." I sit back down on the bench with a proud smile on my face.

I notice Gerald get on his phone; he's talking but I can't hear what he's saying. He hangs up the phone and next thing I know, my phone is ringing.

And what do you know...it's Callan.

I look at Gerald who shrugs his shoulders at me, then gets back into his car to give me privacy as I decide to answer the phone.

"Yes?" I mutter with as much sass as I can muster.

"Miss Cooper. I do not find it amusing that you're making my driver jump through hoops to get you to work," he says, I can tell he's annoyed. I pace up the sidewalk, gathering my thoughts.

"Well, I don't find it *amusing* that you're making your driver come all this way to pick up a very capable woman to fulfill whatever reputation you think you need to uphold," I snap back at him, not realizing that I just insulted my new boss and that I also defended myself so boldly. That's really unlike me.

"My reputation, Miss Cooper, is running a successful business first. Whatever else you think is going on, other than me trying to get my newly hired assistant to her first day on the job safely seeing as she has no car currently, would be incorrect. And I highly recommend you think twice about turning poor old Gerald away. Look at him," he says as my eyes instantly are drawn back to Gerald, stands patiently leaning against his car.

"What has he done to you to deserve your rejection?" Callan's voice is firm, steady, and silky smooth. *Snap out of it.* I nearly forget why I was frustrated in the first place. But I look over at his driver who has a small smile on his face, and suddenly feel guilty. Gerald did nothing wrong, and neither did Callan. Besides, a free ride will save me some money.

Just as I'm about to respond to Callan, another car comes zooming down the street. The car speeds around Gerald's and hits a puddle of water pooling at the corner of the curb right in front of where I'm standing. In the blink of an eye, I'm splashed with dirty, melted, snow water. My outfit is soaked, water dripping from my chin. Poor Gerald looks at me apologetically, like it was all his fault.

Just my luck.

"You're right," I respond with a huff of a shaky breath. "I don't know what I was thinking. Gerald and I will be there soon." I look down at my bra, now on full display beneath my drenched blouse. "But I'm going to be late." I hang up the phone abruptly.

Gerald steps out of the car and re-opens the backseat door for me.

"Mind taking me home, first?" I ask, embarrassed, but he nods at me knowingly.

We arrive at the dealership and Gerald leads me up to the front doors.

"Have a good day, Miss Cooper," he tells me.

"I'm sorry for earlier," I apologize.

"Don't worry about it, Miss Cooper." He simply nods at me and walks away.

The lobby is thriving with clients, most of them in sleek outfits that look like they cost more than my rent. I look back down at what I changed into, a new pair of skinny jeans and white blouse with a black blazer I borrowed from Dakota's closet, but I feel defeated already. My hair is flat, my shoes are uncomfortable and I'm wearing someone else's clothes.

I slowly step inside, not really knowing where to go, then I recognize Cora. She stands at the receptionist's desk holding the phone with her shoulder, while her fingers type furiously on the keyboard. She's like, really pretty. And I immediately wonder if her and Callan have ever...*Ugh, no! What am I thinking? Who cares?* Besides, he said he doesn't date coworkers.

I walk up to the desk and wait for her to notice me. I feel like everyone is staring at me, immediately making me even more nervous. A job like this is so different to me. I've known two things, making lattes and babysitting. I didn't even apply for this job; I have no clue what it could entail. My palms start to sweat, and heat burns in my cheeks.

"Can I help you?" Cora briefly looks up at me, hanging up the phone but continuing to type. I can tell by the look on her face that she recognizes me but really doesn't want to.

"I'm here for my first day and I'm not sure where to go," I offer patiently, but she looks back at me with annoyance.

Without any response, she rolls her eyes and gets on the phone. "Callan, your new hire is here. Yeah. Nope. I don't know. Okay." She hangs up the phone.

"You can head back to the office." She waves behind her.

As I make my way to the offices, I look around at the staff. They all look sophisticated and attractive, like they know what they're doing. I feel completely out of place.

I press my knuckles to the door and knock lightly a few times. I don't know why I'm so nervous. I'm usually open and bubbly, not as much as Dakota but I have a wit about me, and I can usually always produce something to say, but my thoughts are mush right now and I really don't know if this is a promising idea anymore. I'm a mess. Ugh. *What am I doing?*

"Come in." I hear his voice from behind the closed door. I turn the knob apprehensively.

There he is, on the phone. He's wearing a white silk dress shirt, buttoned all the way to the top, with a light pink tie hanging from his neck. He looks up at me from his phone call with a smile and waves his hand, gesturing for me to close the door and have a seat.

I pull the chair out from the desk, and almost get knocked over by the smell of him. Of all the things I could find attractive about him, it's not the expensive watch on his left wrist or his dark hair slicked back, his waves peeking through only a bit. And it's not the way that his arms flex as he grips the phone in his hands or his wicked amber eyes watching me watch him. No. It's the sensual whiskey and tempting oak mix tangling in the air and settling in my core. I've never smelled anything like him. It's all Callan, sexy and mysterious.

"Yes, Jett. I'll have the work done on that mustang by the end of day tomorrow. You got it." He hangs up the phone call, and jots down a couple of notes, giving me a chance to glance over his facial features a bit more. My God, he is wickedly handsome.

"Good morning, Miss Cooper. I see you've made it in safely." He flashes a devilish smile my way, knowing he caught me staring.

"Yeah, I'm sorry for being late."

"No need, Gerald filled me in. I'm sorry that happened to you." He glances at me momentarily before focusing his attention on his computer screen.

"Just my shitty luck," I manage to say under my breath.

"You look great," he says very matter-of-factly, and I can't tell if he's trying to make me feel better or if he hit me with an actual compliment, but either way, my body heats up involuntarily.

He tugs at the sleeves of his shirt as he turns in his chair to look at me and I feel my self-control slowly slipping away. *This is not going to work.*

Think straight, Sterling. You're just nervous.

"So, let's talk dress code." He leans back in his chair a bit and even the way he adjusts himself is hot.

"Snap out of it," I whisper to myself.

"What was that?" he asks.

"Hm? What?" I try to play it cool as I stare at my fidgety hands in my lap, but I'm probably making this even more awkward than it already is. We sit in silence for a few seconds while he finishes typing.

He shifts in his chair again, and his arms flex as he lifts himself up to gain access to his back pocket. He pulls out a brown, tattered wallet – it's just like a man to have all the money in the world and never find it in him to buy a new wallet – and grabs a matte black card from it, sliding it across the desk in my direction.

"What's that?" I question, finally able to look at him.

"Expense it," he says. "You can buy whatever you need for your business wardrobe, just put it on my business card." He waits for me to take the card, but I don't. I don't understand. *What?*

"What do you mean?" I'm clearly confused. Like, what possessed him to pull out his card and offer to pay for whatever I need? *Is this normal?* We haven't said more than a few words to each other, why would he pass me his credit card?

No, it's not normal, Sterling, but he can probably tell by the way that you're dressed that you need an entirely new wardrobe. My thoughts flood my head as I start to feel self-conscious about my appearance.

As if he can read my mind, he stills himself in the chair and he looks at me.

"I didn't mean to assume. But I figured, since noticing your job experience was scarce, that you wouldn't have the attire needed for this job. Buying new clothes for a job is a business expense," he explains. "Take it if you'd like and use it."

"You want me to just take your credit card and swipe it to buy myself clothes?" The question comes out, but I don't give him time to answer, before adding another one. "What if I decide to take off with it and you never see me again?" Again, I beat myself up mentally at my choice of words. Something about being in the same room as this man has my mouth running a conversation of its own without checking with me first.

Callan sits up straight and tilts his head, eyes widening as he makes a mock-serious face.

"Miss Cooper, you'd really do that to me?" He cocks one perfect brow at me, his stoic eyes opening to a bright hazel. A light dusting of freckles runs along his nose and cheeks, just made visible from this angle. Ugh, his perfect face with his perfect jawline.

He brings his elbows to the desk, laces his fingers with each other and rests his chin on his hands.

"You can always pay for your own clothes and bring me the receipts. Whatever is easiest for you. The dress code is business casual, except for important events. Then you'd be required to dress up in formal business attire." He swipes at his brow as he talks to me.

What a joke. He knows he's sexy, he's obviously got money, and thinks he can use that boyish smile to charm me. I want to rattle him. I need to shake this feeling, whatever this feeling is. It's unwanted and inappropriate.

"Mr. David, do you always spend the first day with new employees insulting them by insinuating that they're too broke to buy clothes?" I seek an answer, realizing I'm probably projecting my own insecurities. But how can he not see that this could be somewhat offensive? "Or do you throw your credit card at every woman you meet?" I decide to add.

"Miss Cooper." My name flows from his mouth like smooth whiskey as he pulls himself closer into his desk.

"Yes, Mr. David?" I try to maintain this confidence I've mustered up, but I can't help myself from focusing my eyes on him which leads me to falter.

Suddenly all I can think about is what it would be like, to be that girl from Dakota's story – the coworker who slept with Callan. I don't know why, but I realize that this is going to be the hardest job I've ever had. Spending every day fighting my eyes to look in the other direction is definitely not going to be easy. I snap back to reality when I hear Callan's low, deep voice continue.

"I didn't mean any offense. I thought it might be easiest for you to take the business card to purchase your attire. It's merely a policy that the entire team here at David Dealership expense their work clothes." It seems like a stupid policy. Then again, I worked at a café that never once considered the amount of money I had to pay for uniform shirts.

Giselle required a lot of uniform shirts. Sometimes with different coffee quotes on the back. *Here At Cocoa Café, We Love You a Latte* or *Chill Out with an Iced Cap and Espresso Yourself.* And when we got them stained, even in the slightest, we were required to buy a new one. But not once did she reimburse us. I thought it was just part of the job.

Callan looks at me while I process what he's saying. Again, I'm overthinking his intentions. He's not trying to be an ass; he's just trying to run a top-notch business and by doing so he's providing compensation to his employees for the money they have to spend on clothes. He's literally just doing his job, and I'm over here questioning his every move.

"Well, I appreciate that. Sorry I thought otherwise," I say, as confidently as possible, not knowing whether or not he can see through the façade I'm attempting to put on. I am *anything* but confident right now.

I can tell he's studying me, trying to figure me out. *Good luck, I still can't figure myself out.*

"So, let's talk availability." His full attention is turned to me now. "As my assistant, I do expect you to be here Monday through Friday. I do not come into the office on Saturdays, so I don't expect you to be here either and Sundays we are closed." He stares at me with a slight smile, waiting for me to confirm or reject his scheduling needs.

"I babysit, as you know, mostly Friday nights. I won't be able to work past four on Fridays for that reason but other than that, I'm completely open every day of the week. I mean, I might have to request off some random days here and there, maybe for babysitting or other reasons, but of course I'd give you advanced notice and-" I realize I'm starting to ramble and quickly cut myself off.

A noticeable smirk rises on Callan's lips. I don't know what I said to make him look at me like that, but it sends a chill across my body.

He thinks over everything I just awkwardly spewed at him, looking at his computer, at the calendar, and then back at me. "I don't see why we couldn't make that work," he finally answers.

"Really? Thank you." That was easy. I really need to take a breather and stop overthinking this whole thing. But being alone with him in this office – which seems to have a broken heater – gives me butterflies.

Suddenly I'm reminded that we're not actually alone when the sound of voices cross the hall, and a knock hits the door.

"Come in," Callan calls over.

The door opens and in walks a man. He's blonde, almost as tall as Callan, with blue eyes icier than mine. I see some tattoo ink peeking through from under his sleeves and he's wearing a pair of black plastic frames over his eyes, but I can't tell if they're prescription or if he's just some pretentious hipster wearing them for fashion. He's attractive, nonetheless.

"Can I help you, Jax?" Callan asks him. But he doesn't answer because he's too busy staring at me.

Callan snaps at him. "Hey, do you need something?" Jax breaks out of his trance, my rosy cheeks can't catch a break, and Callan looks frustratingly at him.

"Oh, uh, yeah. Cora needs you. Something about, um, an angry client. She tried calling, but your phone is going to voicemail," he stumbles over his words.

"Seriously?" Callan gets up and heads over to the door, Jax moving out of the way as he passes by. He turns to me before leaving. "I'll be right back, Miss Cooper." Then gives Jax a hint of a death stare before leaving us alone.

"So, you're Sterling?" Jax's voice is low and sexy, while still being upbeat and confident, with a slight southern twang. He walks over to the desk and sits on top of it, his legs dangle right next to me as I stay seated in the chair, looking up at him.

"That's me," I say.

"I've heard so much about you," he quips. *He has? Has Callan been talking about me?* "You're too pretty to be a janitor, I see why he hired you as his assistant instead." He looks at me up and down as he speaks, immediately bringing heat to my cheeks.

"What do you mean?"

"We were hiring for a janitorial position. I'm assuming he got one look at you and decided you'd look better as his assistant, so he gave you the position instead of giving it to Cora. She's actually pretty pissed off to be honest. Won't shut up about it." He sure does like to talk. I didn't even have to ask for this information, but I'm kind of surprised to hear it. It definitely explains why Cora looks like she wants to push me down and shake me for my lunch money every time she sees me.

"But hey," he continues, "I'm not complaining. I'd probably do the same thing. I mean, look at you." He rubs his finger and thumb over his chin, and I hold eye contact. I can tell he's like Callan, smooth with his words and exuding confidence. Though he seems a bit more forthright than Callan who likes to keep his intentions secretive, tucked tight in those dark green-brown eyes of his.

"Not to come off too forward, but you seeing anyone?" he asks, and yeah, it's a forward question but it doesn't startle me in any way; my best friend is Dakota for goodness sakes. I'm pretty used to it.

He sits forward a little more, leaning into me just the slightest. He smells *almost* as good as Callan, but it doesn't have the same effect on me.

"Depends," I say, not wanting to give him as much info as he's given me. Though there's really no info to give. I haven't had a boyfriend, well, ever. I've only had a few one-night stands that never turn into anything more.

"Well, maybe we can go out sometime." he says as his mischievous grin grows. I sit back in my chair, trying to stay relaxed. *What is happening in this place?* I've never been so flustered in my life.

"I thought there was a strict no dating rule within the office?" I point out, trying to remain composed.

"Between you and me, that rule really only pertains to Callan. He's a bit of a heartbreaker, or more, the ladies really love him. Besides, what he doesn't know won't hurt him." Jax licks his lips ever so slightly, and I can smell mint on his breath. He seems like a nice enough guy, but I see right through him. He's one of those guys who loves being a charmer, knows that he's attractive and has decided to flaunt it because, why not? And he seems naturally flirtatious, not in a creepy way. He kind of reminds me of Dakota in that way. And I can tell it works for him, but not on me.

Before Jax can get any closer, we're interrupted by Callan bursting through the door.

"What is going on here?" Jax sits up a little straighter, not scared but enthused. I stay seated in my chair facing forward.

"I was just introducing myself to Sterling," Jax says with confidence, smiling at me the whole time he responds to Callan.

"Get out, Jax," Callan demands but I get up instead, mainly because I want to see the look on Callan's face right now, but also, because I really need to go to the bathroom. As I study him, I'm almost positive I spot a modicum of jealousy, or maybe even anger, flash across his eyes as he looks between Jax and I.

I step out from behind my chair and walk over to the door where Callan is standing. I'm close enough to hear his breathing, slow and calculated, escaping his perfect mouth.

I turn to look back at Jax.

"I'll consider your offer," I say, then turn around to look at Callan who is now fully red in the face with anger, his veins bulging out of his neck.

I'd never go out with Jax. He's not really my type...whatever my type is. But I can't help but notice the way it makes Callan squirm a bit, not really knowing what I'm referring to and wanting to know why he's so irascible to begin with.

"What offer?" he asks as his eyes dart between Jax and I.

"I have to use the restroom," I tell him. "Jax, where are the restrooms?" Jax jumps up off the desk and starts walking toward us when Callan holds his hand out to Jax's chest.

I finally feel like I have the upper hand. Not that I really need it because I've been overthinking this entire interaction with Callan today. But if he's allowed to make me feel nervous and hot, then I'm allowed to irritate him just as much.

"Down the hall and to the left," Callan speaks for Jax; he sounds like he's trying to keep himself from overreacting. I let out a small chuckle under my breath as I turn to walk down the hall, leaving the two of them to deal with whatever weird bro-power-struggle just happened.

What has gotten into me?

EIGHT

Callan

Sterling is not what I expected.

I can't be surprised by Jax's behavior, though. He flirts with every pretty girl he sees. But Sterling? I can't tell if she was trying to get a rise out of me or if she just naturally acts like that.

"We don't date coworkers," I had to remind Jax, who just responded with a chuckle. Sterling walked back in from the bathroom when I said this to him.

"So, asking where the bathroom is, is considered dating to you?" She'd chimed in leaning against the door frame, and she had said it with so much sass it made my dick twitch.

She kind of confuses me, because the proud audaciousness she showcased today was not what I got from her the first time I met her.

I hate how sexy I find her. It's going to make my job that much more difficult.

"Of course not. I just want to make sure you are both aware of our company policies." I was trying to back-pedal and come across as professional as possible. Sterling cut in and assured me she wasn't interested in dating anyone right now. Thankfully, that put an end to the conversation but also made me feel a weird stab of disappointment.

I don't know why it bothered me so much to see her flirt with Jax. Maybe because it's Jax or maybe because it wasn't me. Either way, I have to remind myself that she is just an employee and I have a business to run.

After showing Sterling around the dealership, and going over a few job duties, I realize it's nearing five o'clock, only an hour left till we close for the night.

I get a call from an unknown number as Sterling and I settle back into my office.

It's someone from the moving company. As they talk in my ear, I can't help but watch Sterling. The way she brushes her hair behind her ears, or how she laces her fingers together in front of her while her thumb stokes her wrist softly. The innocence on her face throws me off, probably because I imagine what she looks like when she's doing not so innocent things. But that's the man-in-need thinking. A man who hasn't had actual sex in probably the longest amount of time recorded for me.

The voice on the other end of the phone pulls me back to reality. "We'll just need you to sign these last few invoices, then we'll be out of your hair."

"I'll be there shortly." I end the phone call and direct my attention back to Sterling.

"Miss Cooper, I'll need to take off a bit earlier than usual. Seems my movers forgot to obtain a signature from me the other day. You're free to take off as well, seeing as we've done all we can do today."

"That's fine. I can just tour the dealership a bit more and get to know some of the workers while I wait for my friend to pick me up." She leans over the chair to pick up her bag.

Ever since the situation earlier with Jax, I've been forcing my mind to stay focused and professional. As attractive as this girl is, she is my business partner. And that's all she ever will be.

I scribble a signature on the invoices from the moving company and thank them for waiting on me. Once they leave, I take a massive sigh and slowly pace around the kitchen as I take in the view. The sun sets over the city skyline with the Rocky Mountains in the distance. I can see people starting to fill the streets below and think about how long it's been since I've been out.

I know I don't gain much from going out but being cooped up in here where all I can seem to think about is my new assistant is probably not the best idea for the night. While I did a better job maintaining my thoughts and ideas of her earlier at work, it's different now.

Sterling Cooper. *What is it about this girl?* I'd caught myself in a trance earlier, watching her closely, catching every little quirky thing she does. Her movements and gestures, how her lips move when she talks, the way her eyes drop when she's nervous, how her hips sway when she walks. These are not thoughts a CEO should have about his employee. And a younger woman at that. She has to be at least twenty-five. Young enough to be fun and flirty but old enough to have a maturity about her.

It's been a whole fucking day, for crying out loud.

I need to clear my head, so I opt to go down to the small dive bar tucked around the corner a couple blocks from my building.

On my walk there, I pass by a group of already wasted twenty-something's celebrating their friend's bachelorette party, which is weird considering it's only Monday evening. A few of them turn their attention to me, attempting to flirt but it's not worth my energy, so I keep moving forward.

I turn the corner and head into the bar. It smells good. Like cigars and bourbon. I walk straight to the bar and pull out a stool.

"What can I get you, handsome?" A young brunette stations herself in front of me, pink lips, small perky tits that she obviously is trying to display, and brown eyes.

"Whiskey neat." She turns around to pour my drink.

I take the time to think through some thoughts I have. Mostly about my first big sponsor event coming up and how hard it's going to be to be so close to Sterling without losing my cool. Thankfully, that's still five days away so maybe I can get my shit together before then.

But I can't help but notice how often I seem to be thinking about her. It's annoying really.

The bartender hands me the drink and asks if I'd like to order food. I shake my head and she walks away.

As I bring the glass to my mouth and let the whiskey burn down my throat, a few other things cross my mind. Like the fact that my dad has cancer and not a single person wants to talk about it. How I'm running a multi-billion-dollar car company but I'm not sure what comes after, or if this is even my dream. How comfortable I've gotten living this lifestyle I've grown so accustomed to.

I take another swig from my glass as I hear laughter from behind me. I look over to see a couple of girls walking into the bar from the street. I have to do a double take and almost fucking choke when I see her. Like I conjured her up. Her arm is linked with another girl's as they smile and talk while finding a seat at a nearby booth. *You have got to be fucking kidding me.*

I turn my back to them as quickly as possible, not wanting them to notice me.

I hear her voice; her sultry, soft voice. It reverberates from her table all the way to my ears, and it quickly travels down in vibrations to my dick. *This is not good.*

Her friend breaks the silence with a laugh and I can hear her whisper, "Go say something to him," as she nudges her in the shoulder. I take this moment to quickly close out my tab, toss back the last of my drink and start walking out of the bar.

"Callan?" I hear her voice call out to me as I'm trying to sneak out the door. *Of course, she'd notice you, dumbass.*

I turn around to face her and her red-headed friend. She gets up from her seat and walks my way.

"I'm sorry. Mr. David," she corrects. "What are you doing here?" she asks, seeming pretty uncomfortable, as she gets up from her seat and closes the space between us. I look over her shoulder at her friend who seems to be gawking at us.

She's changed her outfit since work. She's wearing a jean skirt, frayed at the hem, with an oversized sweatshirt that reads Colorado with mountains behind the lettering. She has the sweatshirt tucked up under her bra and a small sliver of her stomach peeks through. My fucking mouth waters. Like I'm a predator hungry for its prey. *I'm fucked.*

"Just grabbing a quick drink," I answer nonchalantly. "But what are *you* doing here?" I question, looking over her head at the table where her friend sits, to see she's still intently eyeing us. That's when I notice that Sterling is about a foot shorter than I am.

"This place has the best pizza," she responds, almost discreetly, like it's a secret that this place serves the best pizza.

"You look too young to be at a bar, Miss Cooper." I purposefully speak a little too loudly and the waitress glances over in our direction out of interest. I thrive in seeing Sterling squirm at the embarrassment in my overreach.

"I'm twenty-two," she defends as she rolls her eyes at me. "I'll be twenty-three in August," she quips.

I do the math. She's younger than I initially thought, which surprises me. That's almost a nine-year difference considering my thirty-first birthday is coming up.

"Anyway...if you're done questioning me-"

"Sorry, what were you saying?"

She laughs, "Nothing, I should get back to my friend." She nods over to her table and walks away like nothing happened. Like she couldn't have been more unbothered but I'm no fool, she was definitely bothered.

Meanwhile, my mind is already spiraling from this sixty second interaction. She's nine years younger than me. And she's my employee. Talk about abuse of power. Or a fucking temptation for that matter. I leave the bar knowing that thoughts of Sterling will not be left behind. But if I don't stop this now, it's not going to end well for either of us.

I go through my nightly routine before bed. I shower, brush my teeth, wash my face, and change into sweatpants. I head to the sink for a glass of water when my phone rings. It's my dad.

"Hey, dad." I try to sound calm, still reeling from the anger I felt towards him last week. Things have been so weird with everything going on, and I never know the right way to act.

"Callan, your mom is getting worried. You haven't called in a few days. Everything okay?" He speaks without even greeting me first.

"Everything's fine," I start, "Just been super busy."

"Well, your mother is insisting on a family dinner next week. Can you make time?" He coughs after he forces out the last words to form his question. I hate hearing him like this, no one deserves the wrath of cancer. Even an old prick like him.

"I'll see what I can do."

"Good, bring that new assistant of yours. I'd like to meet her," he insists.

"I'm not fucking dating her. Why would you need to meet her?" The words fly out of my mouth in defense. But I realize how stupid it sounds considering there's no way he'd think I'm dating her.

"She's helping you run the company your grandfather and I built. I think an introduction would be nice," he snaps sarcastically.

I get where he comes from, though. He still cares about what happens at the dealership, and I do respect that. They've spent decades building this car business to be as grand and flourishing as it's become and have trusted billions and billions of business funds to me to keep it running. But I hate how he feels the need to know every little detail about the business, even after passing it on to me. I hate feeling like he doesn't trust me with this responsibility. Like he still has control over my life.

"I'll have her check her schedule." Before any other words can be exchanged, he hangs up.

I stare at my phone; the time reads eleven-fifteen p.m. Surely, Sterling is already asleep on a Monday night, but something urges me to text her about this sooner than later. I feel like I owe her the courtesy of having plenty of time to prepare for a David family dinner.

You awake?

I wait a few minutes for her response – knowing how casual the text will sound when she reads it – but fifteen minutes later and nothing comes through. She's probably just sleeping. I should probably catch some shut eye myself. I can talk to her about it in the morning.

NINE

Sterling

Walking into my second day of work, I have no idea what to expect. Yesterday, after Dakota was sweet enough to buy me an outfit for her party, we ran into Callan at the bar. And it was like an out of body experience. Like, for some reason, I didn't expect for him to be a regular guy who might enjoy a drink at a bar every so often, and I definitely didn't expect to see him outside of work in general.

Dakota teased me about how hot he is and how lucky I am to get to spend every day in his gorgeous and chiseled presence. Her words, not mine. I'd shut her thoughts down and quickly tried to deny any attraction I might have towards him. But she called my bluff - like she always does.

I make my way to his office, giving a light knock before pushing the door open, surprised it's not locked, but he's not here. I do notice, after turning on the lights, that he's got a pile of paperwork sitting in a tray labeled *file*. I walk over to the pile and see that it just a few invoices that need to be uploaded to the financial database and a couple of inventory papers that need uploaded into their digital files. I remember a little bit of the direction on this yesterday as Callan showed me the ropes after the Jax incident - if you can even call it that. So, while I wait for Callan to make it into the office, I decide to log in to his computer and get to work.

After about an hour of work and still no Callan, I finish up filing the paperwork I scanned in, and log out. I head out to the lobby to look around, but he's still nowhere to be found.

I realize I have two options: I can ask Cora, who is sitting at the receptionist desk scrolling through her phone, or I can ask Jax who is finishing up with a client over at his desk. I think I'll go with the latter. After finding out how Cora feels about me, knowing she thinks I stole her job, I really don't think she'd be willing to entertain me right now.

I approach Jax at his lobby desk just as he finishes closing out a deal with his client.

"Hey there." I wave at him, and he looks up and smiles at me.

"Sterling," he greets me warmly, his blue eyes twinkle in the harsh white lights of the dealership lobby.

"How much?" I ask him in curiosity, tilting my head toward the client that had just walked away.

"He picked up the Rolls-Royce Phantom. He talked me down to four hundred grand for it, but then I talked him back up to four-forty." He smirks in a way that shows that he's proud as he gathers the signed papers. *How does one talk someone up the price they tried to bargain down?*

I never realized how expensive these kinds of cars could be. If I didn't feel out of place before...

"How much does one make from a sale of that caliber?" I decide to question, trying to seem as not-nosey as I possibly can.

"Well, sales reps make anywhere from fifteen to twenty percent of the sale in commission, depending on what level of sales they're in." He types a few things into his computer before continuing. "The dealership gets sixty percent to go back into business and shit. Big boss gets about fifteen percent of that. The remaining usually goes to fees for shit like paperwork filing, title, the business office prep, and whatever fuck else you can think of."

I look at him in shock. If he makes even the bare minimum on the sale he just pushed off, he makes more than most Americans make in a freaking year.

It's not even eleven o'clock yet and homie just casually rakes in over sixty grand?

"You alright there?" he asks – locking up his desk drawers and powering down his desktop – noticing that I'm stuck in stupid surprise, most likely with money bags in my eyes.

"How many cars would you estimate you sell in...say a month?" I press my hands down on his desk, leaning over in anticipation for his answer. There's no way he sells more than one or two.

"About seven or eight on a good month. Maybe three in the slower season. My highest sales month, I sold about fifteen cars. We get people from out of state who want what we got. Callan and his family have built a good rapport with families all over by doing business and doing it right."

"Holy shit." It's meant to be a whisper but it slips out louder than I intend it to.

Jax chuckles at me. "Thinking about changing careers now?" he quips.

"And there's how many sales reps here?" I look around trying to gauge who's doing what.

"There's about twenty total. Ten in shop, and about ten others that work remote and do the online and out of state shit." Jax gets up from his desk and walks around to meet me on the other side.

I notice some of the other reps all have clients at their desks. I wonder what the most expensive car is and if any of them have sold it?

The lump in my throat starts to harden when I realize I am truly out of my element here. Then again, everything is out of my element. I don't belong anywhere really.

"Do you know where Mr. David is?" I swallow hard, wanting to change the subject.

"He's still making you call him Mr. David?" he jokes.

"Formalities," I respond as I shrug my shoulders.

"Callan is in the shop out back, our mechanic called out today, and a client needed work done on his car as soon as possible," Jax explains as he waves toward the general direction of the dealership's shop. "I can take you back if you'd like," he offers.

"No, that's okay. Thanks, though. I want to get to know the lay of the land a bit more today, so I'll find my way over there eventually." I take a moment to think about the interaction we had the day before. Jax being all flirty with me and me purposefully flirting back to stir something up in front of Callan. Looking back, it was immature, but in the moment, I couldn't control myself. It wasn't fair to Jax, though.

"About yesterday," I start, but Jax shakes his head at me.

"No sweat," he says, reassuringly. "Callan is serious about his job and the policies that come along with it. His reputation is the only thing he cares about. Besides, I saw the way you looked at him." He gives a knowing smile as he runs his hands through his golden strands of hair. His ice blue eyes bore into mine, but he's right, it's nothing like looking into Callan's hazel eyes.

"Well, I promise it wasn't my intention to tease you or flirt with you. Call it first-day-on-the-job jitters." I try to avoid the way he basically just called me out for having a thing for Callan. *Is it really that obvious?*

"No worries."

"Right, well I better get moving." I give a little wave before walking past him toward the back of the building.

I find my way outside, past a bunch of used cars. I remember this part of the lot from when I was here the first time. *Geez, I was not my best self that day.* I pick up my pace a little, wanting to get away from that embarrassing memory immediately.

Behind the lot, I can make out what must be the mechanic shop. I hear clanging and whirring coming from inside and I make my way through the garage doors.

That's when I see him.

My boss.

Callan has one arm holding up the hood of a sleek, vintage car, the other hand gripping firmly on a wrench. He moves quickly and with intention as he continues working on the engine, unaware of the fact that he now has an audience. His white button-up is tucked into his back pocket, and his body hangs over the front of the car as sweat drips down his gorgeous chest trailing to his abs. He's solid. I can almost imagine running my fingers over the edges of his stomach right now.

His dark blue slacks stand no chance against the grease stains splattered across them, ruining the pristine look he usually flaunts. Then I notice his belt is half unbuckled. *Headstrong* by Trapt plays in the background which only adds to the sex appeal of this man. The sight of him sends beads of sweat down my back and my thighs suddenly feel tense as I try to control the heat that pools between them. *Holy shit*

It's hard to imagine him this way, all dirtied up, when he's practically a billionaire – knowledge I got thanks to Jax.

He doesn't seem to see me, but he must have heard me.

"You're late," he says, still looking down. The vein in his arm flexes as he tightens the cap to something. He slams the hood of the car down, then takes up a rag and wipes his forehead with it.

"Excuse me?" I manage to finally respond as I swallow down the lust building in my throat as I watch dirty, sweaty Callan work on the car. "I was on time. You're the one who couldn't be found."

"I texted you earlier and told you I'd be back here." He finally makes eye contact with me as he wipes the sweat from the back of his neck. I'm grateful to have a reason to take my eyes off him and reach inside my purse to pull out my phone. Sure enough, an unread text from him was delivered over an hour ago.

"That's the second time you've ignored my text," he mentions. I know he's talking about the one he sent last night. The one that I read but didn't know how to respond. *Is he mad?*

"Sorry, I didn't know I was required to respond to work related messages off the clock." I attempt to joke, trying to make it obvious with a little laugh, but he doesn't think it's funny.

"Sterling, you don't have to be clocked in to have a conversation with your boss. Besides, if you really want to get paid to talk to me, just let me know. I have no problem clocking you in where there's work concerned." Callan walks around the car and checks something by the tires.

"I'm sorry, I didn't mean it like that." I try to defuse the tension from my stupid joke. "Was there something important you needed to talk about last night?"

"Not really, just to ask you to dinner," he says nonchalantly, and my stomach does a little flip. "My parents want to meet you," he adds.

"Wh-why would they want to do that?" I mutter. My words come out sloppy and confused, my heart hammering in my chest.

"Because you're basically helping run a company that they poured their hearts and souls into." *Duh, it's a business dinner, Sterling. Not a personal one. Get a grip.*

"Oh." I'm not sure how to respond. I can't even stand to be in a room with this man for more than ten minutes without being assaulted by nervousness, I can't possibly last in closer proximity with him *and* his family.

Running the company? I think to myself.

"Relax, you're not going," he insists as if he's allowed to make decisions for me. But in this case, I don't mind.

I take a second to try and reset my overtly reddening face.

"Do me a favor?" he asks, and I raise a brow at him. Anything. I'd do anything he asks, especially while he's shirtless. *Geez, Sterling. Stop trying to be a slut for your boss.*

"Can you start the car for me?" He walks back around to the front and pops the hood again. "I need to make sure everything is running properly."

"I didn't know you knew how to work on cars," I say as I walk toward him. Even with all the sweat and grease, he still manages to smell like a rainforest drenched in scotch.

"You really think I'd own a dealership and not know how to tend to my inventory?" His tone is sarcastic but deep. "I started working on cars when I was twelve," he adds.

The image of a younger Callan pops into my head. Cute and curious as he stands at the front of a car, learning and asking questions.

"*Sorry,*" I say as sassy as I can, enunciating each syllable. The car he's working on seems a bit older, but it's gleaming with a glossy, bright purple paint job and two black stripes fall down the middle of the hood.

"What kind of car is this anyway?" I approach the door, but Callan beats me to it, opening the door for me. The gesture makes my chest ache.

"It's a '69 Mustang Boss 429," he states. As I climb into the driver's seat, I sense that he can tell I have no idea what he's talking about. He lifts the hood back up and leans around to meet my eyes.

"Turn the key, will you?" He motions me to start the ignition, and I nervously turn the key. He watches over the engine and the whole car lights up with a loud and deep growl. The vibrations fall all over the car, and I can feel every rumble of the engine deep in my core.

I've never understood the fascination with cars, until now. All I did was turn a key and suddenly, excitement is running through my entire body.

A smile falls on his lips as he watches me from the front of the car over the hood, he can probably see my amusement. He slams the hood again and motions me to kill the ignition.

I pull myself out of the car and close the door. "That felt kind of cool," I awkwardly admit. But really, I feel all kinds of turned on. The rumble of the car, the shirtless man who stands in front of me, the heat from the shop. *I need to get the hell out of here.*

"You're cute," he says almost as quiet as a feather floating down to the ground, as his eyes are focused on cleaning up the tools he was using, and I stop dead in my tracks to try and hear his words again. *What did he just say?*

"So, umm, are you going to actually train me today?" I tease.

He pulls his now-wrinkled white shirt from his back pocket and throws it on. "Oh, I'll train you, Miss Cooper. Patience." He looks up at me through hooded eyes as he weaves each button through their corresponding hole.

I don't know if I'm just reading into things, but I definitely feel like everything he's saying is a double entendre. Waves of need wash over me as his eyes burn into me, the purposeful pursuit they make from my thighs to my chest. *Is he checking me out?*

I don't do relationships. His words keep playing in my head. Yet, I feel like everything else out of his mouth means the opposite.

Then I remember the story Dakota told me. *He's a player.* That explains it. I just have to muster up enough courage to ignore his flirtatious ways and I'll be fine. *He's a player. He's your boss. And he's off limits.*

But my God, is he so damn attractive.

He chuckles as he finishes packing up his tools and closing down the shop. "Let me show you to your new office. We are very behind on the day as it is, due to your inability to be on time." He glances at me, but I can tell he's being playful. "It doesn't help that I'm going to be gone for a few days. And I have some paperwork that is fairly overdue that I'll need you to take care of."

"Did you say you're gonna be gone?" I look at him as we walk side by side. I can tell he's annoyed thinking that's the only thing I heard from everything he said.

But I did hear what he said, all of it. Even the part about me having my own office. Which is nice. But he's leaving? I hate to admit that my heart took a small dive when I heard him say that.

"Yes, Sterling. I have an important business trip, Jax and I are meeting with the owner of the lot for our potential new location in Los Angeles. Now, walk faster please so we can get started on the day."

"So bossy today," I remark with a sassy smirk curled on my lips, though I feel rather disappointed that I won't see him for the rest of the week. "Besides, if you're talking about the stack of papers that was on your desk, it's already taken care of," I add in.

Callan stops dead in his tracks and stares at me.

"You did what?" he asks.

“I took care of the filing. Was that not okay?” Suddenly, I start to worry. Thinking maybe I wasn’t supposed to take on tasks without permission, or maybe, I filed the wrong papers.

“No. I mean, yeah. That’s fine. That’s what you were doing for the past hour?” Callan’s amber eyes melt into me like molasses, hot and sticky. The way he’s eyeing me right now does things to my body that I can’t explain, nor do I want to. It’s too much.

“Yeah. I saw it needed to be taken care of, so I took it upon myself. I am your assistant after all. I don’t need to be asked to do my job, Mr. David.” I turn back around and continue walking, desperately wanting—no, *needing*—to escape the way his eyes make me feel. His footsteps pick up behind me as I lead him back into the dealership.

“How was work?” Dakota is actually home for once as I walk through the door. I look around to see if her boyfriend is also here, but it seems she’s here alone. I hate to admit it but I’m kind of happy about that.

“Work was...interesting.” I smirk to myself not wanting her to sense my amusement.

“Do tell.” She turns from the washing machine and looks my way.

“I just learned a lot more about, I mean from Callan today, and he gave me my own office.” I throw my purse onto the kitchen table and take a seat. Dakota gives me *the eye,* but I choose not to elaborate. Whatever this feeling is, needs to go away, so I might as well shut it down on all fronts before it gets out of hand.

But Dakota sees right past the bullshit. She's always been able to read people easily.

"Are you crushing on your boss, Sterls?" Dakota follows me over to the table and sits across from me.

"How did you extract that from what I just told you?" I roll my eyes and she looks at me like I'm avoiding the question, which I am. She glares at me behind a knowing smile.

"I wouldn't call it a crush." I lie, because it definitely feels like I may have a tiny crush on Callan. "He's just really nice to look at and has this magnetic air about him. I'm sure all of the employees feel charmed by him." And maybe it's been a while since I've flirted, so it's easy for me to get a little giddy in front of someone as hot as Callan, but I don't plan on telling her that.

"Well, I guess there's no harm in getting to know him," she says as she starts the dryer.

"Actually, he's got this strict no dating rule," I counter.

"I said get to know him, not date or fuck him. But there's that too." We both chuckle.

Thankfully, he'll be out of town for the next few days for a business meeting, so I can find time to focus and breathe. I do not need this kind of distraction right now. I need to get my shit together.

"Just be careful with that man. Like I've said, I heard he's a hit and run type of guy and I really don't think you need that in your life right now." She doesn't hesitate to bring out her mom-tone with me. I give her an understanding smile, with as little sarcasm as possible, hoping to move on to another topic.

"You know you've been acting a bit differently these past few weeks." she states.

"You're not wrong. I feel like I don't even know who I am at this point. My whole life got flipped on its axis and then there's Callan and his stupid perfect body. I open my mouth and don't know what's about to come out. It's confusing as heck." My admission surprises me. We both know that there's something off about me.

"Men and their hot bodies." She rolls her eyes.

"The audacity." We laugh, and it feels good. I love having someone I can banter with about shit that may be too irrelevant to even be true, but life can be that way sometimes.

"I'm going to be at Asher's for the rest of the week," She breaks the news to me, dampening the mood. "I hope you'll be okay here by yourself," she adds.

Of course I'll be okay, but she's been gone a lot lately.

"That's fine, Dakota. But are you and Asher going to pick a date soon, or what?" I pester her like a big sister, even though she's older than me by a few months.

"We're not even engaged yet, Sterls." She gets up from her chair to grab her bag. "But I am getting impatient," she admits.

"Well, have you expressed your feelings to him?" I ask. I'm not the most well-versed when it comes to romance or relationships, having had none myself.

"I've dropped a few hints here and there, but you know how guys are. They act helpless and useless when it comes to taking the next step."

I have no idea what else to say. Even though I don't know much about romantic encounters and long-term relationships, I just have this feeling that this isn't right for Dakota. I look at her and give her a small, reassuring smile anyways because that's what friends do, but really...I never liked the guy.

"You got another bill today." She motions her head toward the kitchen counter-top where my eyes meet an envelope. I make a point to ignore it for a bit.

I won't get my first paycheck from the dealership for another two weeks and I've used up nearly all the rest of my money on groceries and other bills. I feel embarrassed that I'm struggling financially. I hate that I feel like I'm not good enough at times.

"I'll see you at my party this Friday, right?" Dakota asks excitedly, before coming over and giving me a hug. I nod my head and she gives me a big smile and before I know it, she's saying goodbye and heading out the door.

I pour myself a glass of wine and raise it. "Cheers to another lonely week," I say to myself, with a little laugh. I throw my hair into a messy bun and change into my favorite AC/DC graphic tee and sweatpants. As I go through my nightly routine, thoughts of the day run through my mind. Callan in the shop, him calling me *cute.* Still wondering if I heard him correctly or if I made that up in my head. But then wondering why I even care. I'm spiraling. I throw back another swig of wine and turn on my favorite nineties rom-com. I could really use the distraction right now.

TEN

Callan

We landed in Los Angeles late last night, and I can't seem to get out of bed this morning. My alarm clock haunts me as it rings across the room. I struggle to get the sheets off, and stumble over to the desk to grab my phone, only to see it's not my alarm, it's Jax calling.

"Jax," I answer sleepily and glance toward the clock. It's nine a.m. I've never slept in this late on a Thursday. Or any day for that matter.

"Still sleeping, boss?" He sounds chipper as he speaks.

"Normal people go to bed after a late flight, Jax, not to the strip club."

"When in Vegas," he replies sarcastically, as the sound of elevator doors ding in the background and I just chuckle.

"Where are you?"

"In the hotel lobby getting breakfast. You may want to hurry. Meeting's in an hour."

"Yeah, I'll be down soon." I end the call.

Even though his behavior may come off as erratic at times, I trust Jax to help run my business. I haven't met many guys who can manage staying up late to enjoy the night life, while still being fully prepared to suit up first thing in the morning and for only being a few years younger than me, he keeps up well. Though I'm starting to wonder if he ever even went to bed last night. Knowing Jax, I'm sure I'll be hearing all about it soon enough.

I hop in the shower hoping it'll give me the boost of energy I'll need to get through the day. I'm already dreading the long, monotonous meetings that await me. Meetings I know have to be done.

As the water falls over me and the steam fills the room, I run shampoo through my hair and close my eyes. Warm suds run down my back, and I can't help but imagine how much more enjoyable this shower would be if I had things my way. A beautiful woman would walk into the steamy bathroom wearing nothing but a silk robe. She'd have wavy blonde hair, and her wide blue eyes would take me in as she looks me up and down. Her pink lips raise at the edges in a sexy smile. As I conjure up the image in my head, I suddenly stop and snap my eyes open. *Fuck. I was definitely just fantasizing about Sterling.*

I can't help that my dick grows hard at the thought of her in the room with me right now, and it's aching harder than ever before. I've never been a man who needed to get himself off, but I cannot, for the life of me, get this girl out of my head.

Without realizing I'm doing so, I grab the base of my cock and stroke forward as I think about her alluringly bright indigo eyes. And her smile, her beautiful, full lips moving in slow motion as she says something snarky to me. The way she can wear anything, and it looks absolutely stunning on her body. The thick curves of her thighs. The thought of her voice is what gets to me the most. The way she says "*Mr. David*" is such a turn on. Before I have time to stop and shake my head back to reality, I realize I am pumping my erection faster now; it doesn't take long before I feel my release rushing through me, my hot cum filling my hand.

I don't allow myself to soak in the euphoria I just experienced, registering how obsessed I am becoming, and I barely even know the girl. *We need to change that.*

After I get myself cleaned up and prepared for my first meeting, I head down to the lobby to meet up with Jax.

"There you are sunshine. If I didn't know any better, I'd think you were the one out all night, not me," he quips.

"I had to take care of something," I respond, trying to hide the smirk on my face when I think about the personal business I had to attend to this morning.

I pour myself a cup of coffee from the breakfast buffet and follow Jax to a table in the corner of the hotel lobby.

"So, tell me about your night." I figure Jax's evening was far more exciting than mine.

"Listen, what happens in Vegas stays in Vegas. But if I'm being honest, I almost went home with one of the strippers. Five minutes before getting into an Uber with her, I decided vodka and bad decisions weren't how I wanted this trip to be remembered. I *am* a professional after all." Jax laughs as he winks and tips his coffee cup at me.

"Sounds like a hell of a night. You made a viable choice considering this is a business trip," I add. "And you do know this isn't Vegas, right?"

"It's just a saying. But what about you, boss?"

"What about me?" I bring my coffee to my lips and blow.

"I know you're not into strip clubs and shit. But any pretty ladies keeping you company these days?" Jax asks, but it seems more like he's baiting me. Like he knows the answer I want to give him; *I'm obsessed with my assistant.* I could never admit to that though, it goes against my own rules and quite frankly, I'm not even sure how I'd be able to explain it.

"I haven't been seeing anyone. You know I don't do relationships." And I'm not lying.

Jax laughs before he gives me a mischievous look.

"What?" I question defensively.

"You know, you may be cool, calm, and collected ninety percent of the time, but I know when a fine piece of ass catches your eye."

I feel my lips twitch when he refers to Sterling as a fine piece of ass, assuming he's caught on to the way I stare at her. Jax doesn't normally talk like that, so I sense that he's trying to get a reaction out of me.

"I don't know what you're talking about, Jaxon." I sip my drink trying to avoid his dagger-like stare while I insult him by using his full name.

"Cal, I've known you a long time. When's the last time you've gotten sucked off? Or laid. Or even had your hand held for that matter?" he asks, and I almost choke on my own saliva. It's not something I expected him to ask.

"I don't know. Why does that matter?"

"You don't know? Well, I do. Would you like to know the answer?" he asks the question as if he's a teacher and I'm the student. I nod for him to continue.

"Enlighten me."

"You haven't had any action since well before you hired that assistant of yours. Which may not seem long in the grand scheme of things but for you, it's a long time. And I saw the way you looked at her when she walked into the dealership that day. Not to mention the way you acted when I asked her out," he chuckles.

"You *did* do that, didn't you?"

"I did, and I know it pissed you off. And I know that you haven't let another woman touch you since she walked in. Am I right?"

I think over his assumption, and I don't want to admit that it's the truth, but he's right. I haven't responded to the usual booty calls or even thought about looking in the direction of another woman. I have been pretty busy on top of that, so Sterling isn't the sole reason I haven't gotten laid.

"You may be correct, but-"

"But nothing, Cal. You, my friend, have an infatuation." He shuffles in his chair and pulls his hands to rest under his chin as he raises a brow at me.

I don't know how to respond to this. He's right, but I don't want him to be.

"Fuck her," he instructs.

"Excuse me?" I lower my cup to the table while I gauge his expression for context.

"Get her out of your system. Fuck her one time and see if she's even worth all the trouble you're going through."

"That's extremely shallow, Jax."

"And nothing you've ever done is shallow, Callan? It's not that big of a deal," he jokes.

"You know that I can't break policy." Not only that but allowing myself to fulfill this fantasy I have of her, I'd hurt her. I really can't have a relationship. And part of me knows that Sterling doesn't want to be the one-and-done kind of girl. She deserves better than that. It would be too much for her.

"Okay. That's one stupid rule that you pretty much made up to convince Cora that y'all couldn't sleep with each other. Though, she still tries." We both let out a small laugh. "You can screw the rule for one night. One night to figure out why this girl is clouding your brain. Listen, I know I might not seem like I have it all together. Trust me, I am getting kind of tired of this lifestyle too. But I don't have an obsession with someone like you do and don't you think you owe it to yourself to figure out why you can't get her out of your head?" He takes one last sip from his cup before getting up and walking away. *Perfect timing Jax, just drop this bomb on me, then walk away.*

My mind is all over the place, I should've spent this morning preparing for our meetings instead of indulging in whatever the fuck just happened here. This trip definitely didn't help distance my obsession with Sterling. If anything, it made it worse.

"So, how were your business meetings yesterday?" Sterling shifts in her chair. Jax and I got back to Colorado early this morning. I immediately texted Sterling and asked her to meet me for lunch and played it off like I needed to go over some work stuff with her, which I do, but really, I also just kind of want to sit down with her. *Look at her.* And figure out why the fuck she's got such a strong hold on me as soon as possible. This shit is perplexing as fuck, but it's also a high I want to keep riding.

She's wearing a red dress that hugs her in all the right places, paired with a black belt around her waist. I love this color on her. *Fuck.* She looks just like a business professional, especially with her hair tied up in a bun. This look of hers definitely doesn't help to settle the ache that continues to grow every time I'm in her presence, but I try to think of something else. Like how proud of her I am of how far she's come from the first day I met her, lost and shy, to now where she has the confidence in her roll at the dealership.

"It went well, but the deal is most likely not going to happen. The owner of the current lot was asking for too much and honestly, it wasn't that great of a lot to begin with," I explain. "Some of the investors were bummed but they seem hopeful with the numbers we're bringing in."

She sits up even straighter in her chair, as a waiter makes his way towards us.

"Anything to drink?" he asks politely, but he's staring straight at Sterling. In fact, straight at her cleavage.

"Yeah, I'll do a whiskey neat, and she'll have a strawberry daiquiri," I interrupt just as Sterling is about to speak.

Suddenly, her facial expression changes and I can tell she's annoyed, but I can't stand this guy staring at her chest. He nods at me and leaves our table.

"Did you just order for me?" She side eyes me.

"I hope that's okay," I offer, but she looks even more uncomfortable.

"Umm, I guess." I think she wants to argue, or say more, but I'm glad she chooses silence. I don't know why I ordered for her.

I didn't really bring Sterling here for business, well maybe not the financial kind. I decided to take Jax's advice and dive deep into why she continues to flood my thoughts from the moment I wake up. But I don't want her to know that I have some kind of extreme infatuation with her. I don't want to scare her away.

"Listen, the truth is, I feel like we should get to know each other better. You're my assistant and I don't think it helps our working relationship if we don't know each other well." Sterling crosses her legs as she listens to what I say. She looks a bit confused. Like she wants to say something again but bites her tongue instead.

"It's a trust thing," I decide to add, but really, it's a me thing. I have myself convinced that maybe if I know more about her, I can drop this fantasy of her I've conjured up in my head.

"Well, you apparently already know my favorite drink, so what else do you need to know? My favorite song or something?" she deadpans. Being sarcastic is one of those things she does that gets my blood pumping because I know that she's not usually like this, but I tell myself that I bring that out in her and it turns me the fuck on.

"If that's what you'd like to share, sure. I think I can guess that your favorite color is red." I look toward her cleavage by default. "But other than that, I don't really know much about you."

I'll take anything really. I'm hoping there's something she could share that would possibly explain the gravitational pull I'm feeling or deter me from this sudden obsession.

A waitress comes back in place of our pervy waiter from before and sets the drinks down in front of us. Sterling looks at her and smiles.

"The first rule of trying to get to know someone, don't just assume their drink order," she remarks, as she reaches over the table and grabs my whiskey, pulls it to her lips and slams the cup back. The liquid pours down her throat in one solid gulp. Every blood-pumping vein in my body goes cold as heat shoots its way to my cock, aching for me to give it what it desires. *That was fucking hot.*

Sterling sets the glass down and glares at me behind long lashes, lips pursed, and legs crossed.

"I hate to admit it, but you were right about one thing, my favorite color is red. My favorite song is *Bring Me To Life* by Evanescence. I like Chinese food, and I'm allergic to cats, I am afraid of heights, and I love reading. Oh, and this strawberry daiquiri is all yours, since you were so dead set on ordering it." She slides the fruity drink across the table. "So, what else would you like to know, Mr. David?"

I look Sterling in her eyes, her skin glowing in the dim lighting from above. She's not even blushing but I can tell she's proud of herself by the rise and fall of her chest. A necklace hangs low into her cleavage and the only thing I can think of in this moment is how fucking nice it would be to rip the chain off of her neck with my teeth before raking my tongue down her chest. But fuck, if I'm not a prick for that thought. *What kind of pretentious asshole just assumes a girl likes to drink daiquiris?* This isn't like me, but this new feeling has me quite confound.

We talk for what feels like hours but has probably only been about forty-five minutes. Opting to order more drinks instead of food, we settle into a conversation that feels natural. I learn a lot more about her. Little stuff, like her favorite movie, which is *The Breakfast Club*. Her favorite place to visit is any small town hidden within the mountains. She's lived in Colorado her entire life and has never been anywhere else. When I ask where she'd like to go if given the chance she mentions states like Maine, New York, Washington, and Georgia. I notice the pattern, she likes the aesthetically pleasing sceneries. She tells me she won first place in a spelling bee one time, and I tell her that I built my first go-cart when I was thirteen.

I love the way she laughs, it's a small chuckle that sometimes turns into a snort and the way her delicate skin bunches over the bridge of her nose makes me feel warm. She tells me more about Sara, the girl she babysits, and I can see how happy she makes her. But when I ask about her family, she freezes up.

"We don't have to talk about that," I offer, and she gives me thankful eyes.

"I actually should get going," she announces, after checking her phone and immediately, I regret bringing up the topic. I was really enjoying this time with her.

"Taking off early for the day?" I joke, knowing damn well I'm not going back to the office after this.

"If that's okay. I didn't realize the time and I have a party to get ready for tonight."

I look at my Rolex as a form of distraction. "A party?" I question playfully. I don't want our time together to end and I hate that she has other plans stealing her away.

This lunch is what I needed. I wanted to get to know Sterling more and she allowed me. But I'll be honest, it didn't go the way I expected. I was hoping there would be something she would say or do to eliminate my feelings for her. If anything, they've only grown stronger. *Again, I'm fucked.*

"Yeah, I told you about it the other day, remember? My best friend's birthday party." I must have been distracted when she told me because I don't remember that conversation.

Sterling reaches for her wallet, but I reach my hand out for hers, resting it gently on top to stop her. She freezes, her eyes slowly reach mine, but I pull away quickly, attempting to avoid the electrifying feeling that just passed between us.

"Miss Cooper, the bill has been taken care of. Business expense," I express as I return my hand to its own vicinity.

"Oh, um, thank you Callan." Her breathing becomes heavy, and I can tell she's suddenly nervous. I can't help but notice that she called me by my first name without retracting and calling me by the formality of my last name.

"Tell you what, I'll have Gerald take you home to get ready for your party. That way you have more time to get ready instead of waiting for a ride." Gerald is already waiting out front, and honestly, I don't like the idea of her getting into a car with a stranger after the amount of drinking we've been doing.

"Thank you, I'd like that." She nods, and suddenly the demure in her eyes returns. She's not so sassy and outgoing anymore. I wonder if it was something I said.

ELEVEN

Sterling

I lower myself into the back of the familiar black car. Still feeling high from the game I played, daring myself to channel my inner Dakota as I slammed back that whiskey. It's something I never would have done but I needed to fight fire with fire.

"Miss Cooper." Gerald nods his head at me as Callan walks around to the other side. He gets in and slides next to me.

My mouth starts to water as his woodsy cologne fills the air inside the car. Mixed with all the whiskey in my system, my head feels dizzy. I didn't realize he'd be joining.

"Are you okay?" Callan asks with a concerned look on his face. And I know he can tell I am, in fact, a bit buzzed.

"Yeah, totally fine. At least now I don't have to pregame before the party," I joke a little too loudly with a slight hiccup mixed with a giggle, and he looks at me sharply.

I settle into the backseat feeling all of the buzz from lunch but also from seeing Callan for the first time in a few days.

Time in the office without him was definitely needed but it also felt empty. If anything, it made me think about him more. And then he texted me asking to meet for lunch and my stomach churned. I thought he'd fire me for some reason. But no, *he wants to get to know me.*

What the hell does that mean?

Callan suddenly interrupts my thought by reaching over my shoulders and pulling my seat belt over my lap, clicking it into place. It feels like he's moving in slow motion, his face so close to my chest that I can smell his hair. He tilts his head up to meet my eyes and licks his lips. My thighs clench together, heat building in my core.

"I can buckle my own seat belt," I say, and he doesn't do anything but stare at me.

Before anything else can happen, Callan clears his throat and returns to his side of the car. A breath that I didn't realize I was holding escapes my lips. Callan pulls his bottom lip in with his teeth as he rubs it with his thumb, staring at the back of Gerald's seat. My stomach flip-flops watching him try to contain himself.

"Did you bring the package?" Callan asks and Gerald reaches towards the passenger seat. He passes back a white box with a gold tulle bow wrapped around it.

"For you." He slides the box in my direction as Gerald pulls the car out of the parking lot and starts heading toward my apartment.

"Me?" I question.

"For tomorrow. The gala." He reaches over for his own seat belt and buckles in. "Strict dress code, remember? Open it."

I untie the bow gently and open the side of the box. Inside is a gold sheet of tissue paper wrapped around a piece of fabric. I pull out the paper and unwrap what it's hiding to find a red silk dress. I stare at it. For a long time. I can feel Callan's eyes burning into me.

He's just my boss. You're not attracted to him. Don't look at his eyes because he will hypnotize you.

I chant to myself before swallowing down the lump in my throat, finding courage to even speak to him right now.

"Why?" I ask, placing the dress gently down in the box before returning eye contact.

"I know there was question about what to wear-" he starts before I cut him off.

"No, why did you get this for me? Doesn't that seem too personal to you?" I put the box back together and place it between us.

Callan looks out the window to his side. I can tell he's thinking carefully about what to say. This is inappropriate, right? I mean, he's my boss and he's buying me gifts? Then again, we just shared like five drinks at a business lunch, which could also be deemed inappropriate.

Callan reaches over to my seat belt and unbuckles it. In one swift movement, he slides the box to the floor, scooches himself to the middle seat, lifts me with ease and slides me over his lap to sit where he was sitting before. He reaches over me to roll down the window and whispers, "Look," into my ear.

My heart is racing, my eyes feel heavy and the wind coming in from the window adds to the buzz. Pleasure forms like tiny tingly needles in between my thighs.

After exhaling the adrenaline Callan's voice sent through my body, I take in the surroundings. I'm facing the mountains where the sun delicately sets behind them. The snow-capped peaks look gorgeous against the warm, water-colored sky. I've seen these mountains my whole life, but something about the whiskey in my system paired with Callan's oaky cologne as the wind blows through my hair, makes it ten times more breathtaking.

"Beautiful, huh?" Callan whispers into my ear from behind me as he leans in closer. I shudder as his hot breath hits the back of my neck.

"The truth is, I fantasized about you on my trip away. I didn't mean to, but I did. After the last meeting, I went out and I saw this dress. I couldn't help but imagine how ravishing you'd look in it. It's what I want to see you wearing when I show up with you on my arm at the most important event of the year. Is that alright with you?" Callan's fingers trail up my arm as he talks into my ear. His touch feels like a thousand lightning bolts as he smooths his calloused hand from my wrist to my shoulder. *Oh my God, take me now.*

"We're here." Gerald's mellow voice makes me jump as he pulls into my apartment parking lot. I almost forgot he was here with us the whole time.

Callan shifts over to the other side of the car and lets out a quiet laugh, mixed with something like an annoyed groan. I can't even look at him, I'm so dizzy. Before Gerald has a chance to open my door for me, I quickly grab my things and jump out of the car while it's practically still in motion.

"Thanks for the ride, Gerald, see ya!" I wave over my shoulder as I speed walk to my apartment building, trying to act normal while completely weak in the knees. *Holy shit.*

My Uber driver pulls up to Asher's townhouse. It's a nice place, not too big, but it's bigger than anything I've ever lived in. I can see why Dakota has been spending most of her time here instead of in our crammed apartment.

My hair is curled in loose dirty-blonde beach waves that go down to my breasts. I didn't have time to do a ton of makeup since my shower took nearly an hour; I was trying to sober up and get Callan out of my head. Every drop of water that hit my skin reminded me of the way his fingers felt, trailing down my arm. And all I could think about was all the other places I'd rather have his fingers.

While I was getting dressed, the white box Callan gave me sat on my bed, haunting me the entire time. I know I'm going to give it back to him now that I'm sobered up. I can't accept it. And honestly, I'm not entirely sure I even remember what happened in that car correctly, and I don't want to give off the wrong signal.

I step out of the car and pull down on my black body-con dress. I layered it with a black leather jacket and combat boots. I nervously smooth my hair, as I approach the front door. Punk rock music is blaring inside, and I notice the door is unlocked, so I let myself in.

Everyone is dressed in all black, Dakota's request. She wanted dark, gothic vibes. She said twenty-three gave her that kind of feeling. I eye the room trying to recognize someone, but everyone here is a stranger to me. These are all Dakota's friends. That's the biggest difference between the two of us, she's popular. I'm not.

"Sterling!" Dakota throws her hands in the air and pushes through the circle of people in front of her to get to me. She pulls me in for a hug. She's wearing a mesh dress that's completely sheer. She's got on a black bra and panty set underneath and chunky-heeled boots that go up mid-calf. Her strawberry blonde hair is curled into little ringlets. Her makeup is dark, and she smells like flowers. She looks like the life of the party, and I would expect nothing less from her, even if this wasn't her party.

"So glad you made it!" She snorts out a laugh as she reaches over to the counter and grabs two shots. She hands me one and takes the other. "Cheers to twenty-three!" She says as she raises her glass towards mine, inviting me to join her in celebration.

I feel like I could puke just looking at the shot, seeing as I just sobered up from my boozy lunch with Callan. But I pull the glass to my lips anyway because it is my best friend's birthday. I have a feeling I might regret this later.

I clink with Dakota and throw the liquid down my throat. It goes down smooth, fiery as hell, but I like it.

Dakota introduces me to a few of Asher's work buddies who insist on taking a shot with the birthday girl. Of course, she insists I take a shot with them too. Followed by another. After only fifteen minutes and three shots, I'm feeling full of life and dizzy all over again. The kitchen starts to crowd with more people, and I find myself having the liquid courage to strike up a conversation with just about anyone in the room. Dakota's tipsy friend, Haylie, shows me a picture of her puppy.

"Isn't he so cute?" she half screams in my ear trying to be louder than the music. "His name is Marlin and ohmygosh I love him so much. Oh, and here's my other pup, Charlie!" She giggles as she tries to zoom in. "Charlie Brown and Marlin Brown! Ahh, I love them!" Her curly brunette hair falls in her face as she drunkenly swipes through her camera roll, suddenly embarrassed when she crosses over an image that was probably meant for her boyfriend's eyes only. "Whoopsie." She pulls the phone to her chest and laughs. Our conversation is cut off when the music abruptly stops, causing everyone to look around in confusion.

The attention is drawn in the direction of Asher who is holding his red plastic cup in the air, like he needs to make an announcement.

"Everyone, I have something I'd like to say," he shouts as he makes his way over to Dakota. Everyone quiets down as they focus in.

"Thank you all for coming to celebrate my boo's birthday. It means a lot to the both of us." He pulls Dakota into him as she lights up with a smile that takes up her whole face. "As you all know, we met about four years ago when she moved to Colorado, but immediately I knew she was my girl." Everyone is staring at Dakota; Dakota is staring at Asher.

"But if anyone knows Dakota, they know how stubborn she can be. Which is why it took her this long to accept my offer to move in with me." Asher keeps going, Dakota looks like she's going to cry, and so do I because I had no idea he asked her to move in. So *that's* why she's been spending most of her time here. *Why didn't she just tell me?*

Dakota is forced away from Asher when he reaches into his pocket for something. She looks at him in confusion and suddenly, he's down on one knee and there's a small black box in his hands. The whole room gasps, and I'm not sure what I'm seeing. *Is he-? Is that-?* How many shots did I really have because...*is he proposing?*

"I knew you were my boo the day that I met you. You're the one I want to love forever. And I know you've been waiting for me to ask you this for a while, so I'm finally getting around to it." He winks to the crowd, some of his frat-bro-friends laughing at his attempt at a joke, but all I can do is roll my eyes. "Dakota Jade Young. Will you marry me?" The question fills the room, it's loud and prominent. Dakota is in shock, her eyes filling with tears. Everyone stares at her with anticipation. She tries to gain her breath and I can tell she's struggling to find words.

Dakota looks straight toward me, and I know she's waiting for the best friend approval. It makes me nervous; it seems too quick to be getting married. Hell, I just found out they're moving in together like ten seconds ago. And I'm drunk off my ass so I can't consciously give her the approval she needs right now. But I know she loves him, and he loves her even though I do have mixed feelings about him sometimes. So, I nod a smile. She turns to Asher and throws herself into him, sealing the deal with a kiss.

He shuffles uncomfortably as he embraces her, waiting for an answer.

"Is that a yes?" he asks.

Dakota looks around the room, with a big smile on her face, but I can see the nervous energy behind her eyes. "Yes, I will. Yes, yes, yes, yes, yes!" She jumps into Asher's arms as he lifts himself up from bended knee to catch her.

My best friend...she's moving out and now she's getting married, too? I know this should be a good thing, but all I can think about is how soon she'll be leaving me. Just like everyone else does. I'm her best friend, and I should be celebrating this moment with her. But instead, I head straight to the kitchen to find anything I can drown myself in. My eyes land on a bottle of whiskey, apparently my drink of choice today. I don't even waste time pouring the liquor in a cup, as I grab the bottle by the handle and put it to my lips, nursing it slowly but eagerly.

It's been an hour or so, I think. But I'm too drunk to really know how much time has passed. I've been wandering around the house by myself, weaving in and out of crowds, seeing Dakota only for a brief second before Asher whisked her away, probably to have newly engaged sex. Must be nice. *Sex*. I accidentally run into a couple of guys in the hallway on the way to the bathroom, making them spill their drinks all over the place.

"So sorry. I can't tell where you're going." I stumble around them and push my way into the bathroom. I pull down my pants and start to pee when I notice two girls and one guy are in the bathroom with me, now staring at me, half ass naked on the toilet.

"Sorry to barge in. Well, I actually didn't know you guys were in here but, I just really, like, could not hold it anymore. Are you guys having so much fun at my bestie's birthday? I can't believe she's having sex before marriage right now!" I snort out a laugh, still peeing and obviously slurring my words.

They all make a weird face at me before leaving. Whatever, they're just mad because I'm having way more fun than them. I pull myself together and head to the sink to wash my hands.

I get interrupted mid hand-wash when two people mid-make-out-session burst through the door. I hurriedly make my way past them; they don't even notice me. But suddenly my body rises with heat for desire. Everyone has hands in places where hands don't belong. Lips are smacking and tongues are clashing. My body goes hot. As I make my way back into the hall, I start to feel a bit dizzy, and I don't know what makes me think of him. *Callan.*

Something tugs at me to pull my phone from my pocket, so I do, and open up a text message to start typing.

is so supr hot in here

I send, not realizing the typos because the alcohol has taken over and I'm too dizzy to notice. Within seconds, I get a text back.

Sterling?

I smile at his immediate response.

NOO ITS GERALD GIVEME A RAISE

I text back, laughing ridiculously at what I said, and realizing my message is now screaming at him in the form of capital letters.

Are you drunk?

Shit, he caught me. I try my best to minimize the accusation.

NOPE. NO DRINKIN 4 ME.

At this point, I have no idea what I'm saying to him. I can't tell if my heart is racing at the thought of texting him or because the half bottle of whiskey is taking over my bloodstream. I'm standing in the middle of the hallway staring at my phone as people are filtering in and out. They obviously don't even notice me, as I keep getting bumped in complete disorder. My phone pings.

Miss. Cooper. I'm going to need you to tell me where you are.

He replies, and before I have a chance to even figure out where I am, another text comes through.

Now.

Damn, he's bossy.

MAKE ME BOSS

I send back, because really...why should I listen to him? It's not like I'm on the clock. Suddenly I feel like I'm going to be sick. I stumble down the hallway until I find a room that isn't locked or occupied by strangers humping each other and trip my way towards the bed.

I lay all the way down on the bed, feeling the alcohol settle deep inside me. The room starts to get hazy, and the dreaded spins start taking over. Thankfully, a breeze coming in from an open window makes me feel a little better. My sudden relief is interrupted when I get another text message.

> Sterling, you should be careful what you wish for.

And then another.

> Start making demands of me and I might just exceed your wildest expectations.

I read Callan's message and almost choke. Did he really just say that? I squint my eyes hard at the message, to make sure I read it right. Blood rushes to my head and heat pulsates through my body, as my phone buzzes once more.

> Location. Now.

I hate how much I'm enjoying bossy Callan. He makes me weak, and I kind of hate him for it. Maybe it's because I've been drinking literally all day, but I kind of like flirting with him, even if I know I shouldn't.

I send him my location and right before I go to reread his messages again, my phone dies. *Great.*

I stare at the ceiling and lay motionless on the bed. I wonder whose room this is. Is it a guest bedroom? Will I ever get an invite to stay over? Will they make it a nursery when they have babies?

I jolt at the sound of the door opening. I can barely move, but I peek up to get a glimpse at whoever is intruding on my drunken daze. A tall, sexy guy who I must not have introduced myself to, stands in the doorway. I try to politely wave at him, knowing my drunk ass probably does more of a flop up and down with my hand. He cracks a smile as he stares at me, eyeing me up and down. I try to get a better look at him, but it feels impossible when I'm seeing double.

I know I'm not seeing things when he closes the door behind him and takes a few steps closer to the bed.

"Oh, sorry. This your room?" I manage to get out. I feel dizzy. Like if I try to move at all, I'll fall into a black hole. *Why did I take so many shots?*

My eyelids are heavy and all I can hear is muffled punk rock bumping outside the bedroom door. Finally, the guy standing in the middle of the room responds to my question.

"Not my room," he says, "But you look like you could be my girl."

Honestly, I should be grossed out. Homie is cringey as hell. But I still have Callan's last text racing through my mind. Paired with my inebriation, I may actually give this guy the time of day. Maybe I need to get this out of my system. Maybe I won't need to keep thinking about jumping my boss' bones if I sleep with this random partygoer. The last time I had sex, if you can call it that, was with Two-Second-Tom. Yeah, that was a mess. But now I have a chance to get this out of my system, hopefully not remember it and completely forget about my boss. Maybe this guy is my soulmate. *Fuck it.*

The thought of sitting up to get a better look at him feels impossible, so I attempt to tilt my head up to meet his eyes. His features are hard to make out in the dark room. I shrug and give him a small nod. Before I can even think about changing my mind, I hear his belt buckle jiggling loose.

TWELVE

Callan

I run almost every red light trying to get to Sterling's location as quickly as possible. From the moment her text came through, I felt the sudden urge to make her my top priority. I expect myself to feel more stressed or overwhelmed, but I honestly don't mind the adrenaline rush. It's just how I feel when I'm around Sterling. *Alive.*

I practically fly up to the house. The street is jam-packed with cars, and I can easily identify which house she must be at, as partygoers crowd the front lawn. I whip into the empty driveway, honking to break up the sea of people standing in my way.

I get through the front door and almost hit three people with the door on my way in. It's packed. Sterling can't possibly feel comfortable here, she never struck me as a party girl.

I weave my way through the crowds of people when I hear my name. It's not the voice I was hoping to hear, but it's a familiar one. I turn to look when my name is called again.

"Callan, wait!"

I can't seem to place the voice until I see her face, it's Stephanie. She texted me for a booty call the other night, but I blew her off. I roll my eyes and turn back the other way, heading towards the kitchen.

"Callan!" She's following me now and if it weren't for the sweaty couple basically dry humping in the narrow pathway of people I'm trying to push through, I'd make an escape. Before I know it, Stephanie's hand gropes my ass.

"Why are you running from me?" she cries, her yellowing bleach hair falling into her eyes as she pouts her fake lips at me.

"I'm looking for someone," I explain, knowing damn well I don't need to explain anything to her.

"Well, I'm right here, daddy." She teases as she drags her fingers down my chest and toward my crotch. *That word.* I can't stand that word. I smack her hand away and try to move past her, but she blocks me.

I let Stephanie suck my dick once, like a year ago. Once! That's it. I let her have a little, but it's never enough. I hate being chased down by women, yet here I am chasing Sterling around in the same way Stephanie is trying to chase me. The irony.

"I'm not interested, Stephanie."

"But you need this as much as I do." She pouts at me again, pulls herself up to my neck and blows hot breath against my ear. I couldn't be turned off more.

"I don't need anything from you." I attempt to move away, but I'm trapped between Stephanie, the fridge and the couple making out next to it.

A group of stumbling girls shove past me and launch me forward, Stephanie's lips landing on mine. I push my hands against her shoulders to get her the fuck off me, but she bites down on my lip. Hard. Without consciously thinking, I shove her off me and onto the ground. A few people stop what they're doing to look at us, as Stephanie cries out.

"What the fuck, Callan?" she shouts.

"Don't ever do that again." I rub my finger against my lip to see there's blood. *Bitch.*

"I just wanted to take care of you." She lifts herself up from the ground and dusts off her pants.

"I don't need you to take care of me. Ever. Now get out of my way. I'm here for someone else." I push past her but before I get too far, I turn back to finish things. "And lose my number." I continue to look for the only person on my mind right now. Sterling.

I walked quickly through the hallway, eyes darting back and forth hoping to catch Sterling. She's nowhere to be found. I try a few doors, but they're all locked. I reach the last room at the end of the hallway expecting it to be locked too, but when I turn the knob, it opens. There's a man, a boy rather, with his back toward me. He must not notice me because he doesn't look back, he just continues standing ominously at the edge of the bed. When I hear his belt hit the floor, a pang of anger runs through my chest. I approach him from behind quietly. And there she is, on the bed looking very out-of-it and extremely uncomfortable. I take a step further into the room. Her jacket is on the floor and her dress is pulled up past her thighs. Rage floods me instantaneously.

"What the fuck is going on here?" I announce in question, making him jump before turning to face me.

He looks at me up and down and laughs. "You her dad?" he asks mockingly, then turns back to face Sterling. "Close the door on your way out. I have business to take care of," he whispers as he waves his hand behind him, motioning me gone.

"You have no business being in here, especially with *her,*" I demand, trying desperately to keep my cool, but this jackass better be careful with what he says next.

"Dude, what the fuck is your problem? Can't you see I'm busy?" He rolls his eyes as he turns back around to face me.

"Busy with what? Thought you'd take advantage of a very pretty, and also, very drunk girl?" I take another step forward, this time putting about four inches between his face and mine.

"No, I-" He puts his hands up at me and practically whimpers. "Is she your girlfriend? I was just... it was a mistake," he stutters, reaching down to pick up his belt.

"If I ever catch you near her again, you'll be very fucking sorry. Now get the fuck out of here before I beat the actual shit out of you." He doesn't waste a second, tripping over himself all the way to the door. I follow behind him to shut and lock the door.

Immediately, my attention is turned to Sterling who lays semi-unconsciously on the bed, still fully clothed, thank God.

"Sterling?" I shake her, trying to get her to wake up. "Are you okay?" I struggle to stay calm as I'm panicking inside.

"Oh, hey big boy," she finally responds, slurring with sleepy eyes. Even at a time like this, my cock still nudges at her alluring voice.

"Did he do anything to you?" I have to ask, though I'm fairly sure I stopped whatever was going to happen. Her eye makeup is smeared, and I can smell the alcohol on her breath. I try to help her pull her dress down but she swats at my hand and adjusts it herself.

"Did you make him shit his pants?" She's laughing now but I don't find this funny. She made me drive out of my way to find her just so she could laugh in my face?

"Sterling, I don't have time for jokes. Get up!" I demand. And she suddenly jolts up to sitting position.

"Yes, sir." She gestures a salute over her heavy eyelids, the blue in them looking like a romantic midnight sky.

"Did he hurt you?" I ask again, this time with more solemnity to my tone.

"No, no. I thought about just letting him have his way with me though. I'm sure I look pretty hot tonight." She's still slurring her words.

"Did you want him to have sex with you?"

"No, obviously not. I just didn't really care if it was going to happen," she fades off.

"Sterling, why the fuck did you let yourself get like this?" I'm enraged at this point.

"You sound kind of bossy," she giggles as she sits up next to me, our thighs touching as she crosses her legs.

She rubs her eyes, smearing her makeup even more. I hand her a box of tissues and she wipes her face lazily which makes me laugh.

"You're my hero," she whispers, her eyes rolling back to her head as she reaches her hand out to my chest. I feel bad for wanting her, I don't know why I do. I can't think of a single time I've ever actually *wanted* a woman for anything other than a release. That makes me feel like such an asshole, honestly.

The sound of the music pulsates around us. I almost forgot we were at someone's house party. I reach one hand behind her back, using my other hand to grab hers, as I help her to her feet.

"You make me feel all tingly." The words tumble out of her mouth. I need to maintain my etiquette here. The alcohol is probably speaking for her. But, God, this girl is fucking beautiful. Even with her mascara smeared and her hair in a tangled, curly mess.

"Thanks for getting here so fast." She wraps her arm around my waist as we head out of the bedroom.

"You're drunk, and I wanted to make sure you got home safely," I respond, matter-of-factly.

"Dakota says you're a player." She goes for a chuckle, but it comes out as a hiccup.

I ignore her comment. How does her friend even know who I am? But to her defense, she's not wrong. Or maybe now she is...oh, who the fuck knows.

I try to hurry us out of the house, avoiding anyone and everyone, ideally. A pair of eyes land on me, belonging to the girl with fiery orange hair, the same one I saw with Sterling at the bar. She scowls at me, but I don't know why. She should be thanking me for getting her friend out of this mess.

I drive around for about thirty minutes before I realize that I don't even know where Sterling lives and she's no help asleep in the passenger seat. I could call Gerald, but it's nearing midnight and I can't wake the old man. I should have been paying attention when we dropped her off earlier, but I was too focused on her.

I can't drive around forever, so I may have to make a somewhat questionable decision.

I pull into the parking garage of my place and lightly tap her thigh, trying to wake her up. She turns in her seat a bit but doesn't fully come to.

"Sterling?" I lay my hand on her shoulder. Still nothing.

I'm wracked with the sudden feeling of...protection. Like it's my job to keep her safe, because it's obvious no one else is stepping up to the plate.

I get out, walk around to the passenger side and open the door. "Sterling?" I call out a little louder this time, and finally, she budges. She pulls herself awake and I reach over her to help unbuckle her seat belt. My nostrils fill with her perfume, a mix of vanilla and spice. The thought of getting closer to her scent makes me unstable in all senses, but I focus on the task at hand.

"Easy now," I offer as I help her out of the car.

"My head is pounding," she complains.

"Yeah, you're definitely gonna be hungover," I warn her with a little laugh as I walk her to the elevator.

As the elevator doors glide open to the foyer of my penthouse, she's already tugging at her clothes.

"I need to get this off of me." She tries to yank the bottom of the dress away from her skin. "It's too hot."

"Just wait, Miss Cooper. I can give you clothes to change into inside." I turn the lights on as I lead her inside. I realize how fucked up this looks. I need to tread carefully here.

"I like when you call me that. But I'd like it better if you just called me by my first name," she demands as she throws herself on the couch.

I don't bother to answer, knowing that she's mildly inebriated. I head to my room and find her something to change into. Of course, my dirty mind goes straight to undressing her myself. *Why can't I keep my shit together?*

"Any day now!" I hear her shout from the living room. I chuckle as I hurry to grab her a pair of my gym shorts and a T-shirt. I know the shorts will be a bit big, but they have a drawstring.

I walk back into the living room to find Sterling standing by the windows.

I've now seen so many different sides to the woman standing in my house, watching the same view I watch daily. I've seen her shy, secret-kept side. I've seen her get sassy and even throw a little bit of unprofessional shade. I've seen her laugh and smile. I've seen her dressed down and dressed up. I've seen her be flirtatious then act annoyed all in the same day.

It's not a bad thing. I like to think of it as a sense of comfortability; when one can show you who they really are without really even knowing it. She's a breathtaking woman.

"Wow, this is really beautiful," she exhales. I can't help but notice her reflection through the window, the moon shining bright above. All I want to do is grab her by the hips and press her skin against the cold glass.

"Do you really live here?" Her voice drifts off as she glides over to the kitchen and runs her fingers over the marble kitchen counters, while looking over her shoulder at me.

"Yeah." I can't help but smile at her. She looks cute when she's curious.

She throws her hands up in the air carelessly as she does a little twirl in my dining room. Her hair falls messily back over her shoulders when she stills. She laughs a little, then reaches to balance herself against the table.

"Oh, man. Booze and ballet do not go hand in hand." She stifles a laugh as I approach her, and I can't help myself from reaching out to push her hair behind her ear, just like I've watched her do over and over again. My hand barely touches her skin, and I gauge her reaction. It's just like mine.

Entranced.

"Here are some clothes, Sterling." I meet my gaze with hers as I place the clothes on the tabletop and take a few steps back. "There's a bathroom in my bedroom, you can change in there." I gesture over to my room. She turns around, takes the clothes, and starts toward the bathroom.

I head to the kitchen to fill a glass of water, grab a couple of ibuprofen and put them out on the counter for her. I grab a blanket and pillow from my linen closet and lay them out for myself on the couch. Sterling appears at the door frame of my room moments later, and when my eyes meet her, my whole body feels like it's catching on fire.

She looks adorable in my oversized black T-shirt, as it falls to the middle of her thighs. My blue basketball shorts go past her knees, and she's managed to throw her hair up into a sexy messy bun. She also must have washed off her makeup, as I gaze at her beautiful bare face. My body aches for her. Sterling, standing here in front of me, in all her natural beauty. And seeing her in my clothes, it's more than a want or lust. No, it's something different. And I can't for the fucking life of me explain it or figure out why.

The sight of her makes my heart race a million miles a minute and all I can think about is pulling her in for a kiss, a hard but passionate kiss. *I need to get her out of my head.*

"You okay?" she asks, interrupting my daydream.

"Yeah, everything's fine." I try to contain my thoughts, rubbing the back of my neck. "I got you water and some medicine for that headache of yours. I'm gonna take the couch and you can take the bed." I move over to the sectional and start laying my makeshift bedding down. She walks over to the counter and pops the pills into her mouth before chasing them with water.

"Why didn't you just take me home?

"I didn't know where you lived," I admit.

"Callan, why did you come for me?" Her tone is calm, and her words more well-formed, which makes me believe she's becoming more aware of her surroundings now; not as drunk as she was when I found her.

"You weren't making sense to me. You obviously drunk texted me. I wanted to make sure you were okay." We're standing on opposite sides of the room, and in an instant, the nervous tension between us feels tangible.

"I'm not your problem," she replies, shifting on her feet. She seems embarrassed and on edge, I can see it all over her. None of what happened tonight was truly normal for her, I gathered that. It wasn't normal for me either.

"I didn't mind."

"That's not the point," she says, sounding almost irritated. "I'm just your assistant. You're just my boss. I am not your responsibility." Sterling stands motionless, and the space between us seems to have gotten bigger, the tension growing with it. But I don't know how to diffuse it. The words, *you're just my boss*, are stuck on repeat in my head.

"Don't you think I fucking know that?" It's all I can say because I'm starting to get frustrated with the situation. And I don't mean to come off aggressively. Can't she just be grateful that anyone cared enough to help her out? Because she's right. I shouldn't be doing any of this, feeling any of this. I shouldn't have gone out of my way to pick her up. I should have just ignored her text and gone to bed.

"I'm sorry," I offer more calmly now. "I didn't mean to overstep. I was just trying to be helpful."

I let my words linger, hoping she'll see this for what it is – just someone trying to be there for her and ensure her safety.

But I can't even convince myself of that. The war between what's right and what's wrong rages on inside of me. What I want to do, versus what I need to do. But in moments like this, they seem like the same thing. As if my want is a need.

"You don't have to sleep on the couch," she breaks the silence and takes a few steps closer to me.

"I can't make you sleep on the couch, Sterling." I'm tired and I can tell she is too.

"I don't mean that. I mean, your couch barely looks big enough to fit one person. Can't we just sleep on different sides of the bed?" She cocks her head slightly at me.

Wait. *What?* She went from practically telling me that this was all too much, to offering to share my bed with me? *What the fuck? Is she playing with me?* If I wasn't so exhausted, I'd question it a bit further. But I grab my shit and head to the room, Sterling following behind me. I wait for her to pick a side and I hop in on the other. It's awkward, I can tell. And I'm confused as fuck. If I wasn't already questioning my intentions, well, I am now.

This girl is insufferable. But I kind of like it.

THIRTEEN

Sterling

I want him to touch me. Roll over and wrap his arm around me. I wish I could ask. *Hold me*, I'd say. Of course, I can't, but it'd sure be nice.

He saved me, is all I can seem to think. But it causes a tornado of need and confusion to twirl around in my head as I think about why he did it. It's forbidden, he's got rules. But I don't know many other people who get drunk at a party and their bosses are the ones to pick them up.

The room is pitch black with the only source of light coming from the digital clock on Callan's nightstand. My mind can't seem to quiet, meanwhile he seems to be sleeping peacefully. I hear his deep yet quiet breathing coming from what feels like miles away but is really just the other side of the bed. I wonder how much this bed cost. I wonder how much everything in this penthouse costs. I guess I should just be grateful to get one night of sleep in luxury before going back to my lonely ass apartment.

I finally feel my pounding headache start to dissipate thanks to the magic of H2o and ibuprofen. My eyelids feel heavy, and my thoughts become floaty. Laying in this giant bed is like floating away on a cloud to heaven. I make a mental note to ask Callan for mattress recommendations first thing in the morning as sleep overcomes me.

The flames are bright and hot. I feel them burning on my skin even as the snow falls from the smoky sky. I can't seem to get out. I'm stuck.

My head lifts from the steering wheel as the horn blares and my headache turns into severe pulses as I open my eyes. The flames engulf me, there's no way out. I'm going to die here.

"Sterling." I hear softly but there's no one around.

I'm desperate to break free from the car. This time, I pull so hard on my seat belt that the edge of the rough material cuts into my palm and blood drips from my skin. I let out a scream from the pain and before I know it, the fire swallows me up; every inch of my skin burning.

"Sterling."

I jolt awake, looking around frantically. I'm sweating. I was dreaming. A nightmare, maybe? But a dream. *The accident.*

I stare at the ceiling. Not my ceiling though, and suddenly I'm frozen when I remember where I am. Then, I hear him, his breathing. I look over and see him staring at me with distressed eyes.

"Are you okay?" he asks, a look of concern on his face.

"Oh, umm..." I trail off sleepily. Waking up to Callan's face directly above mine has my heart on a rollercoaster. From a terrifying dream to a dreamy reality. "I'm fine, just a nightmare." I give a slight smile and his face softens from concerned to content.

Callan opens his mouth to say something when suddenly, I smell smoke.

"Is something burning?" I ask as I pull the covers off of me.

"Shit!" Callan runs out of the room, and I lazily follow him, trying to wipe the sleep from my eyes and the embarrassment from my face.

I follow Callan into the kitchen to see him throwing a pan into the sink, turning the water on over it. Smoke emanates from the pan and the fire alarm starts going off. He grabs a hand towel and waves it in the air aimlessly.

"Open that door!" he shouts as he nods to the sliding glass door. I run over and open it and eventually the smoke calms and the blaring of the alarm stops.

I give him a confused look as he pulls his hands through his hair. I glance into the sink, and there the culprit lies. *Bacon*. He burned bacon. I stifle a giggle and Callan turns his attention to me, looking a little annoyed. But I can't help it. It's kind of funny.

And then his laughter, small but husky, breaks the silence and we both look at each other wildly as we laugh together. My giggle turns to cracked chuckles which then turns to cries. Manically, tears start falling from my eyes and Callan's laugh disappears as he walks in my direction.

He takes me in his arms, the pressure feeling comforting, safe, unjudged, as he squeezes me tight in his hold.

It's new to feel his touch like this, in an intimate embrace. It creates more of an emotional tide within me that I can't seem to control.

"You're okay," he says calmly. His hand strokes my back up and down and my tears start to relent. I pull myself out of his reach knowing I only want to dig myself deeper into him.

"I'm so sorry," I breathe out. He pulls his fingers up to my cheeks and wipes the tears away.

"Don't be sorry," he stresses to me gently.

"I'm a mess." I try to hold back more tears, not wanting to feel vulnerable in front of Callan but after everything that's been going on, crying feels like the only way to release my feelings.

"Hey, we're allowed to be a mess from time to time." His words are soft and sincere and it's nothing I've ever heard him say before. He's different, not as hard or rough around the edges. Not firm or bossy. "I'm here if you want to talk about it. Or anything really." His hand is still warm on my back, and he uses the other to push hair out of my face, his fingers brushing the skin on my cheeks bringing even more heat to them. The gesture seems intimate, and the assault of butterflies in my belly takes over.

"I think I'd rather talk about how unsafe it is to leave bacon unattended for too long." I try to joke, and I receive a quiet giggle from Callan's throat.

He pulls his hand away from my face and studies me. I do the same with him. The sunlight coming in from behind me highlights his golden skin and five o'clock shadow. His hazel eyes are the most affected by the glow of the sunrise. They shine gold and green as he gazes at me. *Do you see me the same way I see you?*

Callan lowers his face to mine, my breathing suddenly quickening. I can feel my heartbeat in my chest and goosebumps rushing down my skin. He brings his hand back up to my face as he lets his thumb caress my chin gently. His touch ignites something in me. A flame. It's warm and wicked.

This is it. He's going to kiss me. And then finally, maybe, I can't figure out why I have this intense want to defy his rules and be the girl he breaks them for.

I look up to him, our eyes so close and our noses are touching. I wiggle slightly in his touch, giving him the silent permission he may be waiting for, to make the next move. *Kiss me.*

But as quickly as the flame ignites, it's extinguished. Callan's hand is no longer on my skin and the warmth of his body against mine goes icy cold as he steps away from me. Disappointment pours over me.

"You should get home." Callan takes another step back and leans against the wall next to us, throwing his head back gently until he's looking up at the ceiling. His chest flexes as he puts his arms behind his back. I can't help but stare at him. I wish I could read his mind. Is he mad? Is he annoyed? Is he going to pretend like none of this happened? There's no way he didn't feel that.

But he's right. This is stupid and wrong and as much as I can't deny my attraction to him, it's just that. There's no way a man like Callan wants anything to do with a girl like me.

Without arguing, I gather my things. My dress is folded on his side table with the rest of my things neatly placed together in his entryway. He must have cleaned up after me last night. As if I couldn't feel any more embarrassed right now. To top it off, I'm still in his oversized clothes from last night and will resemble the walk of shame back home in them.

I turn and start walking toward the elevator door, but I feel a tug at my wrist before I make it too far. I'm turned around with force as my eyes meet Callan's bare chest, his body so close to mine again. I try to breathe, almost choking on air when I draw my eyes up to meet his, fierce and fiery.

"You were going to let that boy fuck you last night," he says sharply, almost angrily, as he stands in front of me. I don't know where to look. His eyes, his chest, his growing erection in his taut, gray sweatpants. No matter where my eyes roam, I feel weak.

I think back to what he's talking about. I was. I was going to let that guy from the party do whatever he wanted. I thought I needed to get the thoughts of Callan out of my head. Besides, I was pretty tipsy.

"I just, I was drunk. I don't really remember much." I lie. I was drunk, but I definitely remember wanting someone to fuck Callan out of my system.

His hand releases my wrist and makes its way up my arm, his fingers treading lightly along my skin leaving goosebumps in their wake.

"What are you doing?" I muster out. God, his touch feels like fire on my skin.

I watch his hand trail up my arm from my wrist to my shoulder, slowly. He takes his finger, tucks it inside the collar of his oversized shirt I've got on, and traces the hem over my collarbone, over my chest and to my other shoulder. I hear him suck in a deep breath, his eyes also watching his hand. This feels wrong. Or at least that's what I'm telling myself, because it *should* feel wrong. But it really doesn't. Want grows inside of me and my core starts to ache. I'm so wet, But before I can let the feeling settle deep enough, he removes his touch and turns me back around. He grabs my hips firmly. My back is now flush to his chest, my ass pressing against his cock. He lowers his mouth to my ear.

"I'll pick you up tonight at seven sharp. Don't keep me waiting. And I want you in the dress I picked out for you," he whispers warmly, and it takes everything in me not to buckle my knees. I almost forgot about the auction gala tonight but I'm grateful for an excuse to see him again later.

He reaches over my shoulder to press the button that summons the elevator, then breaks the space between us. I step inside the elevator when the doors open and only turn around once they've closed. I let out a shaky breath. I need to get home and take a cold shower. Callan David is my new favorite high.

FOURTEEN

Callan

It's been two hours since she left, and I still can't get her out of my head. I tried slamming weights at the gym, went for a three-mile run and I even smoked a cigar. I tried to relax by watching some TV but as I was flipping through the channels *The Breakfast Club* was airing – her favorite movie. So, it's safe to say that thoughts of Sterling prevail.

"Fuck her." Jax's words echoed in my head when I lowered my face to hers this morning. I wanted more than anything to *taste* her. After seeing her in my bed, everything felt heightened. The only thing I could think about was, if I crossed into that territory, I would ruin her. *I would love to ruin her.* It was such a bad idea to bring her back to my place.

She smelled like warm vanilla with a hint of cinnamon liquor when I picked her up last night. That scent still lingers on my sheets, and I can't help myself from breathing it in deeply as I make the bed. I spend ten minutes cleaning the burnt bacon pan and finally feel a sense of ease looking around at a clean home.

I take a quick shower before getting ready for the gala tonight. There are still a few hours left before I have to leave to pick up Sterling, which is motivation enough to look my sharpest. I make it fast, wanting not to repeat the actions of the shower I took in LA. Once I'm clean, I jump out and wrap a towel around my waist. Before I can even get dressed, my phone rings.

"Hello, son," my dad answers as soon as I pick up, as if I was the one who called him.

"Hello, Father." I roll my eyes.

"I'm calling a family meeting," he says behind a tired tone.

"Is this about the dinner Mom wanted us to have? Sterling is unavailable." I remember that my parents wanted to have dinner and had invited Sterling. I knew I wasn't going to go through with it because there was absolutely no reason to, but I sort of forgot to touch base with them.

"No, this is different."

"Then what is this about?" I groan out of annoyance. The last thing I want to do today is have a stupid, pointless, family meeting.

"Can you be here in an hour?" He avoids my question by asking his own.

"Umm, I suppose. But I have the gala tonight, and I need to pick up my assistant beforehand," I explain as I head into my closet and pick out the suit I'll be wearing tonight. I land on a light gray suit with a red silk tie. It'll humbly match Sterling's dress but confidently announce that I'm the boss.

"I start chemo soon and it's important we discuss what's next. When I die, I want to ensure your mom and Virginia aren't left to pick up the pieces." My dad's words slice like a knife. *When I die.*

I wasn't expecting him to say those words, ever. Even though it's inevitable. And he makes it seem like it's a birthday party.

"Yeah, I think I can make it," I respond, and the line clicks dead. Typical.

I finish getting ready, slick my hair back and brush my teeth. I wasn't planning to show up to a family meeting about cancer and death in a suit and tie, but here we are.

I pull into the David estate a few minutes before five. I'm already worried I'm going to be late picking up Sterling.

My family home is fairly big. And I say *fairly* lightly. It sits on about forty acres of land and is fully landscaped with twin fountains in the front, beautifully stone-paved driveway. Bushes shaped into different, ridiculous things. There's a tennis court and pool in the back. A separate sunroom and guest house. It's three stories high and houses about eight bedrooms.

Now, who needs a house this big, right? Well, that's the logic that's missing when it comes to my father. The bigger, the better. It's a luxury he has the means to carry out and it's my family home regardless. But the memories inside are what really matter, the people even. And not every memory is a happy one.

I step inside and hear everyone chatting ominously in the family great room. I smooth my suit jacket down, trying to calm my nerves, and take a deep breath before joining.

"Nice of you to join us, Callan," my dad announces as I turn the corner. He acts like I wasn't going to come, when I literally just told him I would be here.

I walk to my mom first, and lean down to kiss her on the forehead, before I take my seat across from Ginny, whose hands are laced nervously in her lap. Everyone is quiet. The air is thick with tension. I scoot my chair in and pray that this will end peacefully.

"I hate to rush things, but as you all know, tonight is the annual auction gala, and the first I will be attending as the owner of the dealership. So, let's get right into it." I feel a twinge of guilt, being so stone-cold about the situation, but someone has to take charge here.

"Callan, your father and I have been laying out plans for you and your sister for...what comes next," my mother starts, clearly doing everything to avoid the word 'death' altogether. "Obviously, your dad is sick, and the cancer is only getting worse."

Virginia bows her head a tad trying to hide the tears rolling down her cheeks. Of course, she's sad, she's always been close with our dad. I, however, have not.

It's like the dad who raised Ginny was a completely different man than the one who raised me. With her, he's always been involved, compassionate and sometimes even seemed desperate for her approval. If someone would've used those words to describe him during my adolescence, I would've laughed in their face. With me, it was all tough love and critical analysis of my every move, usually to his disapproval. I can't blame her for being sad, but I also can't blame myself for feeling numb at the thought of him being gone.

As I study my dad, I notice that he's a lot thinner than the last time I saw him; his hair is starting to thin out, too. He looks hollow, which is fitting to his personality. The dim lights that hang from the kitchen ceiling only make it worse, like the life is being sucked out of him.

"Callan, seeing as you already got the company, I'm going to be leaving the house in Virginia's name with you as beneficiary seeing as she's still a minor. Obviously, she'll get access to her trust fund when she's eighteen and you will help oversee her assets until then." I look at Virginia who doesn't seem surprised by this news. My first thought is, *why isn't mom getting the house? The place she made a home and raised two children in.* Because *that's* how big of a piece of shit my dad is, to not leave your wife the home you've shared for decades?

"Callan, here is the info for my lawyer, Charles. He'll be the first person you'll need to contact once my death is announced. He's handling my affairs and estate accounts, all of which you will have sole control of once this disease takes over," he continues, and again there's no mention of my mom. I look over to see a look of sadness blanketing her face.

"Virginia, you get forty percent of the shares in all my stocks and your brother gets the remaining sixty percent. This is also outlined in my will." He pats his hands down on a pile of paperwork sitting in front of him on the counter.

I'm trying to keep my cool, but I am about to blow up on this asshole. Does he really hate his own wife enough to leave her out of his plans like this? Is he really going to leave her high and dry when the inevitable happens?

"And lastly, Cait, I will make one final transfer of fifty thousand dollars into your personal savings account by next Friday." My dad struggles to get out his words as he chokes on air, he shakes as he reaches for water before continuing. "As per our understanding and agreement."

Okay, I've fucking had it.

"What the fuck is wrong with you?" I slam my hand on the counter, Virginia jumps, and a small yelp escapes my mom's mouth. "You really are a piece of shit, you know that? What the fuck has Mom ever done for you to treat her with so much hate and disrespect, huh?" My tone is heated when the words fly out of my mouth. My body feels red with anger and my blood boils under my skin.

"Callan, please sit down before you embarrass yourself," my dad threatens gently.

"Fuck that!" I challenge. "Fifty thousand dollars? That's laughable. You just handed over a three million dollar home and over seven hundred and fifty thousand dollars in stocks to a fifteen-year-old! And your agreement with Mom is a measly fifty grand?" My anger strengthens when I see my mom on the verge of tears.

"Callan, please stop," Virginia sobs, pleading.

"Ginny, this wasn't meant to offend you. But this needs to be said. I've watched this bastard belittle our mother for too long. Belittle *us*. And I can't stand that he would treat her like this. He needs to know his fucking place." My mom's sobs get louder as I stand and turn to my dad.

"How would you feel if some asshole treated your daughter the way you're treating our mom?" I slam my fist into the counter.

"Callan," my mom whispers in between tears.

"You know what, fuck your stocks and fuck your trust funds. Fuck you!" I throw my chair back and it hits the floor behind me.

"Callan, please don't do this," Ginny begs behind watery eyes. My dad looks like he's enjoying this which pisses me off even more.

"Virginia, I'm sorry. I didn't mean to scare you. But our father needs to hear this." I lower my tone to speak to her, tears springing from the corners of her eyes.

"*Your* father," she whispers.

"What?" I must have misheard her.

"Callan, your mother and I have an agreement in place. This is what she agreed to. This is what the plan is. We talked about this before the cancer came. If you or Virginia decide to share or split any of your inheritance with your mom, that's your choice. But that's our agreement." My dad straightens the paperwork and slides it my way, across the counter. "Disloyalty gets you nowhere," he adds quietly and insidiously.

"Why, mom?" I look in her direction. Her eyes refuse to meet mine. "Why let him get away with this?" I genuinely don't understand. Why would anyone subject themselves to this kind of disrespect? My mom deserves the world. It's my dad who doesn't deserve shit.

"Mom?" I plead, confusion washing over my face.

"Callan." Her voice is low and crackly.

I see something cross her eyes. Fear. Or maybe anger. Possibly a mix of both. But I can tell that whatever she's feeling, there's a secret attached to it. She wants to tell me something. Something she's not ready to tell me.

"Mom, what is it?" I settle my anger, try to approach her with a calmer tone. What could possibly explain why she's getting so fucked in this deal? After everything she's done for this family, all the shit she's had to put up with. Me included. God knows how unruly and wayward I was as a kid, even worse as a teenager. You can thank my bastard of a dad for that, but nonetheless, she stayed. She put up with everything and more. What could she possibly be hiding from me?

"Callan." She gulps a sob. "There's something you need to know."

FIFTEEN

Sterling

I've never felt more out of place in my life. The auction gala venue sparkles around us. It's lit up with crystal chandeliers, purple and blue mood lights reflecting off them. There's violin music in the background and people gather around with drinks and laughter. It's classy, but it's definitely still a party.

I look up at Callan as we walk in, hoping the upbeat vibe of the gala can turn his mood around. He barely spoke the whole car ride here, and I could tell he was frustrated, by the way he was gripping the steering wheel. I didn't attempt to break the silence, but I couldn't help but worry that he was mad at me for being a drunk idiot last night.

As I look up at him now, I'm relieved to see a slight smile on his face as we pass by a few of the gala-goers. He looks so sexy in his gray suit, his hazel eyes illuminating in the lighting of the venue. Even angry, he's hot. I felt it in the car, my want for him. Ever since I left his house earlier today, I've been dreaming of all the things I want his hands to do to me. I think back to when his hands were on my skin earlier, how close we were. But I tell myself it's just the lust speaking. He's rude and confusing and I know from the grapevine that he's a player. But he's also shown that he's caring and thoughtful and takes pride in his hard work and success. I can't for the life of me figure out why I can't stop this need inside of me.

My daydream is cut short when I hear Callan introduce me as his assistant to another business owner.

"Nice to meet you." She reaches out her hand to shake mine. "I'm Celeste, I own Fantasy Travel International. I hope you're taking great care of Callan." She winks as she releases my hand, but I hang on to her words. *What the hell does that mean?*

"She is." Callan places his hand on the small of my back and leads me away from the conversation. I look back and see her professional smile drop as her face contorts to what looks like jealousy.

Callan's hand is still touching the bare skin on my back, where my dress dips into a low V. It really is a beautiful dress he picked out for me. I was hesitant to wear it, but as I was getting ready earlier, I realized I didn't have much else that would be fitting enough to wear to an event this formal. Besides, he pretty much demanded I wear it tonight. I wouldn't be an exceptionally good assistant if I denied the instruction of my boss now, would I?

The red silk is flattering against my pale skin tone. There are slits on both sides that come up to the tops of my thighs, leaving very little to the imagination. One wrong move and the whole venue gets a show. The straps of the dress are haltered behind my neck, which gave me no choice but to go braless. My hair is in tousled curls flowing freely down my back. I really regret not bringing a jacket of some sort because I am getting a bit chilly, and the goosebumps only worsen as Callan's hand presses against my skin. I feel my nipples harden at the thought of his touch, I hope and pray that the material of this dress can stop them from showing through.

"She seems nice." I attempt to break the awkwardness. "Very pretty," I add, trying to get him to respond. But he doesn't even look at me. Instead, he removes his hand from my back and suddenly I'm pissed at myself for opening my big mouth.

I know there's something wrong. He's not himself, but I don't have time to ask him why, as an announcement begins from the speakers overhead.

"The auction will begin in about fifteen minutes. Please make your way to your seats, we will begin shortly," the voice declares cheerfully.

"I guess we should go sit down." I look up to Callan as we stand at the back of the room. Black chairs lined up in rows fill the space in front of us leading to a big stage at the other side of the room. People start making their way past us, all dressed in fancy clothes, dripped in luxury jewelry and smelling like top shelf perfumes and colognes. A great reminder that this event is way out of my league.

Callan doesn't respond to my question and I'm starting to feel at a loss here. *What did I do?*

Next thing I know, another business owner greets Callan, and he emerges into full conversation with him. *So, he does talk. Just not to me.*

I'm not going to stand around and look even more out of place than I already am. Without giving notice to Callan, I walk toward the front of the stage to find my seat.

I make my way to the third row, where our seats are located. Everyone is assigned a seat and it doesn't take long to realize that someone is sitting in mine, the second seat in from the aisle.

"Excuse me," I start, trying to do my best impression of a polite rich person – don't ask why. "I think you may be in my seat. Any chance you could move down one?"

The man looks up at me and I'm almost caught off guard. His light green eyes glow back at me as the light in the rooms dims down lower, kind of like a movie theater when the previews are ending. He's attractive. He doesn't hold a candle to Callan, but at the same time, he isn't my boss.

"I'm sorry," he whispers up at me. "I'm technically seat four but the person in seat five wouldn't stop chatting my ear off. I pretended I had the wrong seat and needed to move over." He shoots me a crooked smile. I give him a knowing nod and try to hide my amusement.

"I'm Leo Dale, by the way, of Dale's Jewelers. What's your name?" He stands as he offers me the seat he was just sitting in and moves over to seat three.

"Sterling," I share as I take my seat. "I'm the assistant to the CEO of David Dealership." I place my sparkly clutch on the floor, trying to figure out how to properly sit in this dress.

I look behind me, my eyes searching for Callan, but I can't seem to spot him even as the crowd lessens. I'm annoyed. He made a big deal about this thing, even told me what to wear and he just ditches me?

"You don't mind if I stay seated here, do you, Sterling? I really don't want to be stuck next to Chatty-Chad all night." He glances over at the person two seats down who waves excitedly at us, and I let out a small giggle.

"I don't think that's a problem. My business partner is in seat one," I clarify.

"Good." He breathes quietly as the last few guests take their seats and the music comes to a stop. The auction is about to begin. Leo leans a little bit closer to me, lowering his voice so only I can hear. "I'd rather be talking to you all night anyways." He winks before leaning away from me and turning his attention to the stage.

I feel nervousness wash over me as Leo's whispers stain my skin. All it really does is remind me of Callan whispering in my ear and trailing his fingers over my skin earlier today. My nervousness turns to frustration when I hear the announcer speaking to indicate the start of the main event and Callan is still nowhere to be found.

The announcer starts going over the rules. He explains how the auction works, which is helpful because I've never done one of these before, and then he goes over some of the items up for bid.

"Every dollar raised tonight goes towards a charity of each donor's choice," He explains.

"What did David Dealership bring to the table?" Leo asks me, scooting a bit closer to me so that I can hear him over the speaker.

"I actually don't know," I admit.

"A McLaren Elva," a familiar voice speaks above me, and I look over to my shoulder to see Callan, as he takes his seat next to me. Simultaneously, I notice that the girl from earlier, Celeste, is also just finding her seat across the aisle from us.

"Nice of you to join us," I tease, but it doesn't seem like his mood has improved.

"Who are you?" Callan says looking over at Leo.

"Oh, this is Leo Dale. He's the CEO of-" I start, but I'm so rudely interrupted.

"I don't give a fuck where's he from, he's in my seat." Callan's arm rests on the back of my chair as he stares straight ahead, not looking at me or Leo as he whispers sharply to me. But his whisper isn't quiet enough because not only does Leo hear him, so do the people in front of us who look back with a questionable glare.

I lean a little closer to Callan as Leo shifts awkwardly in his seat. "Callan, *you* are in your seat. Besides, I told him it wasn't a big deal. No one else is sitting there anyway."

"It's a big deal to me when I paid for that chair," Callan says quietly as he turns to look at me. The eye contact makes my heart drop because it's the first time he's put his attention on me since we got here. I can't help but give in to the butterflies in my stomach when he looks at me with his dreamy honey green eyes.

Leo shoots me a confused look.

"You bought three chairs? Is someone else joining us?" I talk quietly over the auctioneer who has already started the bidding war for the first item.

"No," Callan says, but his answer only confuses me more. What is the point of paying for three seats if we only need two?

"Callan, what's wrong with you? Why are you so hot and cold all of a sudden?" I dare to ask and I regret it, instantly.

"I want this random dude out of the seat that I paid for. He's too fucking close to you." His voice is raised a bit and a few of the guests look over at us again. Embarrassment washes over me, but Leo must have gotten the hint as he moves back over the fourth seat. Immediately, chatty Chad starts whispering to him. I feel bad, he's a nice guy who wasn't doing anything wrong.

"What the hell, Callan? No one is sitting there, what's the problem?" I glare at him while he stays facing forward, pretending like he's paying attention.

"Going once. Going twice. Sold! For two hundred thousand to Kerri Bills!" The auctioneer announces as a voice makes a small cheering sound from the back.

Callan turns to me as the crowd gets restless in between auctions, laughter and chatter start to fill the auditorium. He removes his hand from the back of my chair and places it firmly on my thigh.

His hand.

My bare skin.

Touching.

Then squeezing.

My stomach flips at the feeling of him applying pressure to my thigh, his rough hand seemingly staking claim.

"I bought that seat because I couldn't stand the idea of some pig sitting too close to you. Is that what you want to hear, Sterling? Now be a good girl and pay attention." Callan's sharp whisper trails over the lobe of my ear then tingles over the rest of my body. Without warning, I'm wet, having no choice but to clench my thighs together. What the hell happened to this man? Callan removes his hand and drags his thumb over the bottom of his lip seductively, showing that he knows what he just did to me as he stares where my legs are crossed.

This man is all kinds of confusing. He's scorching-hot, then freezing-cold. He talks to me, then ignores me. He tells me he doesn't flirt with coworkers, then he bosses me around in an obviously flirtatious way.

The rest of the auction is uncomfortable. I'm in a dress that I don't know how to sit in, the slits almost showing the string to the thong I'm wearing. I'm still hot between my legs, making any kind of movement unbearable; desire growing heavily inside of me.

Callan's donated car sells for a whopping two million dollars, which makes my head spin just thinking about it. The auctioneer then announces that the final item is up for bid. The crowd begins whispering amongst themselves trying to guess what it could be.

"Our final auction item of the night is an all-inclusive three-night, four-day stay at the most luxurious hotel Venice has to offer. All airfare, amenities, and excursions paid for." The crowd grows louder with excitement. "You'll enjoy compensated meals for the entirety of the trip along with a complimentary private boat and captain to use throughout the stay of your trip. This dreamy vacation for two totals out to be a little over four hundred thousand dollars in value and is donated by Celeste, of Fantasy Travels. Who wants to start off the bidding? Do I hear one hundred thousand?" The auctioneer starts the bidding war.

People are raising their hands left and right, he can't speak fast enough. The price rises quickly, it's now at three hundred thousand.

"Do I hear three fifty?"

"Me!" A woman screams from behind. My head feels dizzy from glancing back and forth between people raising their paddles.

"Four hundred thousand?? Three fifty going once-"

"Here!" A man shouts back.

"Four hundred thousand over there going once. Do I hear five? Going twice."

I look over at Callan, I can't tell what he's thinking. He hasn't said two words to me since he basically told me to shut up and pay attention. He's acting cool, calm, and collected sitting in his chair. That's when I notice Celeste is turned to the side with her eyes glued on Callan. This vacation is her item up for auction. Shouldn't she be focused on that and not on my boss? It makes me extremely uncomfortable. I'm sure he was with her earlier when they both got to their seats late. *Did they hook up?* Do I expect anything less from Callan, given everything I've heard about him? No, I don't.

"Five over here, five over here." It sounds like it's coming to an end soon. "Do I hear five fifty? Going once."

"Here!" The woman from before throws her hand up.

Finally, the auctioneer slows down the bids for this vacation, which is already extremely overpriced if you ask me.

"Do I have six?" The crowd silences for a few moments, Celeste glancing between Callan and the stage. Just as the auctioneer is about to pound his gavel, I jump when I hear the voice next to me pipe up.

"Here," Callan shouts calmly from beside me, nonchalantly holding up his bid paddle. I look at him in shock. He hasn't bid on anything all night. I'm sure he can afford a trip of this magnitude times ten, so why bid? But then I remember that this event is about appearances and charity. He wants to show the community that he can be available for philanthropy among his busy business ventures.

"Going once. Going twice. Sold for six hundred thousand dollars to Callan David of David Dealership!" Everyone applauds and Celeste glances our way one more time to wink at him. *Bitch.*

SIXTEEN

Callan

I chase after Sterling, who stormed off toward the parking lot after the auctioneer released us from the auditorium.

"Sterling, what the fuck?" I shout as I finally reach her, as she's already waiting at my car.

"Take me home." She's on the verge crying and I feel like an ass.

"What's wrong?" I reach for her arm, but she swings away.

"Leave me alone." She turns her back to me.

"Sterling, talk to me." She faces the passenger door, pulling on the locked handle. I know I showed my anger today. But the anger was with my family. I didn't realize it would affect her.

She turns back to face me, and I see a look of frustration on her face. Her blue eyes deepen as she stares at me but all I see when I look at her is how beautiful she looks in the moonlight. Just looking at her earlier made me hard, which is what led me to the bathroom before the auction began. Had I continued to stare at her, I would have taken her in front of everyone.

Celeste approached me when I left the bathroom. She told me she heard about my dad and asked how everyone was doing. She's been my family's travel agent for years. I asked her if she'd throw in a few extra days for the trip if I bid high enough, and once I told her why, she agreed.

"Do you like her?" Sterling's sharp tone cuts my thoughts like a knife.

"Who? Celeste?" I scoff. Then I remembered the look of jealousy Sterling expressed earlier when she noticed Celeste eyeing me from across the aisle. "Even if I did, why would it matter to you?" The question comes out before I have time to reevaluate it.

"I don't think this is funny. And you know what, I don't care. But what was the point of bringing me here just to ignore me?" She breathes heavily, trying to keep her voice down as other gala-goers make their way to their cars around us. "Remember what you said to me in the car yesterday? And what happened between us this morning? You're a really confusing man, Callan. Not to mention your hand on my thigh. What was that?"

"Nothing happened between us," I respond, clearly lying to myself. And I can tell this hurts her a bit, but she can't possibly understand why I'm doing this.

This night was not supposed to go this way but once again my dad had to make everything about himself and I let my family shit affect my emotions. Sterling doesn't deserve this. But maybe it's good she's mad at me, maybe it'll deter the attraction between us.

"I hope you have fun on your stupid little trip to Venice. Sounds wonderful. Maybe you'll meet someone and move far away from me, so I never have to see you again," she adds, and I can tell she's just trying to make me mad.

"You don't mean that," I say as I move closer to her. More people are filtering out into the parking lot now. I hate that I've created such a confusing war inside of her.

"I do. Now take me home, Callan. I want to take this stupid, uncomfortable dress off!" she shouts, loud enough to grab the attention of a few people walking by.

"You're being really immature, Sterling." And as soon as the words leave my mouth, I fully regret them.

Without warning, she reaches in my pants pocket, sending lightning straight to my cock. She yanks out the car keys and clicks the unlock button. She pulls on the handle, but before she can open it any further, I reach around her, closing the door shut.

"What the hell?" she shouts again, putting emphasis on each word.

"The trip is for my mom, Sterling. It's a long story. Do you really think so little of me that I'd bid on a trip to impress another woman? The only woman I wanted to impress tonight was you," I defend myself and hope to ease her mind at the same time. Maybe it's time Sterling knows, in words, what she does to me. Maybe we're both sending mixed signals. Maybe we just need to give in to whatever this is. "And I obviously failed."

I've never felt the need to impress anyone before. Ever.

I see the war in her eyes. She feels guilty for acting out of jealousy, but she's also hurt because she's right, I did ignore her all night. But it's only because I had other things on my mind, it was not intentional.

"I don't know how to explain this, but-"

"Just take me home," Sterling interrupts, before I can explain any further. I want to share this part of my life with her. I want to tell her about the situation with my family and how I wanted to give my mom something special, to prove that she's still worthy in my eyes, even after her betrayal. I want to talk about everything with her. But now isn't the right time, and honestly, I'm not sure there ever will be a right time because I'm no good for her.

I speed up on the ramp to the highway and slide over into the express lane. Everyone drives too slow on the highway, in my opinion. I look over at Sterling and she still looks upset and rightfully so. I was a dick to her. And I know that I gave her mixed signals after this morning.

"Am I going too fast?" I ask, looking over at her, hoping she'll meet my eyes. Honestly, I just want her to say something to me, anything.

But she doesn't answer. Her cheeks are rosy, but not from makeup. I'm starting to notice that she always wears her nervousness on her cheeks.

Her skin looks soft, like velvet. As she breathes, her chest rises and falls inside of her dress. I can't help but admire her, even though she's mad at me.

I put my focus back on the road, but I catch her turning to look at me, out of the corner of my eye.

"I didn't mean to get so mad at you back there." Her small, seductive voice breaks the silence in apology. "I'm sorry if I caused a scene. I guess I was just upset."

"Upset?" I question, wanting her to explain. "If that was upset then I'd better prepare."

"Yeah, maybe more than upset," she tries to explain. "I thought you were flirting with – you know, it doesn't matter. I shouldn't care what or *who* you do in your free time. But I do think you owe me an apology for completely ignoring me back there. If anything it was super unprofessional. I'm already out of my comfort zone here and it was truly humiliating." Sterling doesn't look at me while she talks.

I feel like an ass. And even more so because I don't know what to say.

The highway is basically empty as we make our way back into town. I crack the windows slightly and the cool air breezes through, making strands of her hair fly around ever so gently.

I see what she means about her dress, the fabric in between the side slits rests between her legs. Crossing them exposes everything and just one glance makes my cock stir. *Now is not the time, Callan.*

"I'm sorry to make you feel that way." It's all I know to say. I'm not sure there's anything I can say to make it right. "But I'm not hooking up with Celeste," I add. "Actually, I'm not hooking up with anyone. Let's just get that out of the way."

"You're not?"

"No." I stifle a laugh, noticing how relieved she seems after that admission.

I think back to the whole reason my night was ruined. That stupid family meeting. The anger builds in me again, and I speed up a little more, now hitting ninety miles an hour. I don't do it on purpose, but my foot gets heavy.

"You didn't do anything, Sterling. It was some family stuff." I try to reassure her.

"I can understand that, but it doesn't excuse the way you ignored and humiliated me." She looks at me briefly before turning to look out the window.

"I really am sorry; I know I fucked up your night. If I could, I would turn around and start over. You deserved the perfect night and I promise I'll give that to you next time." I don't know how else to respond, realizing that I just promised her some kind of redo. And I really do wish I could go back in time, say no to the family meeting, and go directly to pick Sterling up for the gala. She didn't deserve the shitty night I gave her.

I catch a hint of a smile cross her face when I glance over. I hope my apology came across to her as genuinely as I meant it. I can feel the tension in the air fizzle as she takes a relaxed sigh. She runs her hand across the sleek dashboard before leaning back more comfortably in her seat.

I'm driving my Drako GTE tonight. It's classic, apple red, almost the exact shade as her dress with an all matte black interior. I push my foot on the pedal and accelerate in a matter of seconds. Ninety-five. Ninety-eight. One hundred and two. One hundred and seven. I look over at Sterling. She's wiggling in her seat. I can't tell if she's uncomfortable or enjoying herself. But the speed of the car will be a good distraction for her.

I roll the windows all the way down, the cool air now blasting through the car. She looks at me annoyed but she's too stubborn to speak up. She's going to have to use her words if she wants something.

Her expression softens as we continue coasting for a few moments. Before long, she looks like she's enjoying the ride.

She looks over at me for a brief second, adrenaline coursing through my veins as I see the ocean in her eyes.

"Faster," she says, a devious smirk curling on her lips.

Yes, ma'am.

She throws herself back into her seat as I pick up the speed and her eyes close softly. I push harder on the gas, almost to the floor. We're at one hundred-ten now.

"What are you thinking, Sterling?" I ask, both hands gripping firmly on the wheel. I know that the moment I allow myself to remove a hand, it's going straight to her legs. The rush I felt when I gripped her thigh at the gala was a feeling I'd kill to experience again.

"What makes you think I'm thinking anything right now, Callan?" she shouts over the wind. "Maybe I just want to enjoy the rest of this shitty night."

"I can see on your face that something is bothering you."

"I might have been a tad jealous earlier," she admits without hesitation, and I look over at her, our eyes locking for a brief moment, before I look back at the road.

"Why?"

"Because she looked interested in you. You looked interested in her. And it upset me because I'm interested in you. I mean- *shit!*" she stammers, realizing that she just admitted the forbidden.

"I'm your boss, Sterling," I state the obvious. But I need to make sure she's aware of what comes next if she admits that she doesn't care; that she wants to cross that line as much as I do.

"I'm fully aware of that. But it hasn't stopped you from overstepping your own rules. I'm not stupid." Sterling takes a nervous, deep breath. She's right. I'm the one with an obsession that I can't get under control, and until right now, I had no idea that she knew.

She leans back in her seat and spreads her legs a little, the fabric of her dress between the two slits falling perfectly between her knees.

One hundred-fifteen.

I look between her and the road. Her eyes are shut. She seems deep in thought. Without a second thought, I reach over her and unbuckle her seat belt.

"What the hell?" she shouts as she sits up straight.

"Show me," I tell her. She looks at me behind heavy lids and a confused look.

"Show you what, Callan?" She purses her lips.

"Show me how jealous I made you tonight." I grip the wheel. "Touch yourself."

One twenty.

Her face is now almost as red as her dress. Her lashes dance across her cheeks as she blinks lustfully at me. Her breath quickens and the wind continues to blow around us.

"Callan," she breathes, my name sounds fucking sinful coming out her mouth. "That's an absurd request." Her eyes turn away from me as she shuts them and pushes back deeper in her seat. I can tell she's feeling the tension I'm feeling.

"*Fuck*. Just do it, Sterling. I promise it'll feel good."

The vibrations of the speed fall over her as she takes her hand and gently traces her thighs with her fingers until they're under her dress.

"Good girl." I praise her, wanting her to show me how she feels. Show me how jealous I made her. And it turns me on just thinking about it.

One twenty-five.

"Callan, I don't think I want-" Sterling moves her hand out from under her dress and looks straight ahead as she trails off.

"Use your words."

"I'd rather you touch me," she admits and my dick twitches in my pants, creating friction against my zipper.

"I can't do that right now, and I know you have tension you want relieved." Her breath hitches as I focus on the road.

I look at her, then back to the road. "Touch yourself, sweetheart. I want you to feel yourself one last time. One last time before I take what's mine."

Her hand moves back under her dress without argument, and I can tell the exact moment she feels herself. She sighs, her body slowly rocking with her hand and the speed of the car. She lets out a small moan as her eyes flutter shut. She's so fucking hot. My pretty little assistant. Teasing and touching herself.

One thirty.

One thirty-five.

"Look at me," I demand. Her hair falls over her face as her fingers explore her pussy. She's fingering herself so beautifully as she turns her attention to me.

"Do you like that?" I ask her lustfully. I see a side of her I've only fantasized of seeing, adding to the ways I've seen my pretty little rose. Opening up for me, blooming right in front of me.

"Yes, Callan. You made me so jealous tonight." She's moaning so softly and she looks so heavenly, pleasuring herself. I can practically smell her arousal and I do everything I can not to pull this car over.

I notice her glance out the window and retract a little when she sees us pass a few cars on the highway.

"Callan." Her tone is low and sultry, but nervous.

"No one can see you, sweetheart. We're going too fast." She continues to pleasure herself, relaxing into a motion that I can see creates euphoria within her.

"I want you to go faster, Callan. Please," she begs and I wish it was me she was saying it to instead of referring to the speed of the car, but I do what she asks.

One forty-five.

I hardly take my eyes off her, darting back and forth between the highway and Sterling. The want to touch her is growing heavy inside of me as she plays with herself, grinding against her hand. She throws her head back, eyes now closing as she sinks into her orgasm.

She cries out with beautiful whimpers and moans. "Oh, God." She hits her peak and lets out one last breathy groan right as I hit one fifty.

She slides her fingers out of her pussy as she lays back into the seat; I slow the car back down to a comfortable speed. Her breathing is heavy, so is mine. That was so fucking hot. I've never seen a woman take herself like that.

I feel her gaze at me through those mesmerizing, dazed blue eyes of hers.

"Did you like that?" I ask her, grabbing the two fingers she just used to get herself off and swipe my tongue across them as I keep my eyes straight ahead. She tastes as sweet as she looks. She nods as she lets out a heavy sigh.

"Take me to your place," she whispers as she buckles her seat belt back over her lap.

"That was always the plan."

SEVENTEEN

Sterling

I can't remember the last time I felt this good. The adrenaline rush I just had in Callan's car is something I've never experienced in my life. And I've never touched myself like that, especially not in front of someone. But I just let my boss watch me as I fingered myself in the passenger seat of his car and I've never been more turned on in my life.

We pull into the parking garage and once we're parked, we walk over to the elevator. I can't keep it together; I need to be touched by Callan.

He looks calm, his suit tighter on his body than should be allowed. It shows everything. We wait patiently in the elevator as it climbs up the building, the anticipation rising with each floor we pass.

We finally reach his floor, the elevator doors opening slowly. He walks out confidently; he loosens his tie as we walk into his foyer, which only makes the ache in my core stronger. I follow behind in silence. I can't tell what he's thinking. I wish I could read his mind right now.

Next thing I know, he's headed straight to his bedroom. He doesn't make eye contact, doesn't even say a word but I follow him anyway.

Before I can even say anything, the door to the bathroom closes behind him and the shower starts running. I knock on the door, but he doesn't answer. *Did I do something wrong?* Maybe I misread the signals. Maybe he's waiting for me to join him? I jiggle the handle, but it's locked. *What kind of game is he playing?*

I try to distract myself as I glance around Callan's bedroom. There isn't much to see, simply perfect beige walls with perfect black and white cityscapes framed along them. I twiddle my thumbs as I sit at the edge of the bed, adjusting and readjusting my increasingly uncomfortable dress. I expected this dress to already be on the floor by now.

I hear the shower stop running and feel a twinge of nervousness and excitement all at once. But the minutes continue to pass, and I continue to sit in silence, awkward and alone.

I'd prefer to be passing the time on my phone, but it's almost dead. I don't feel comfortable rummaging through Callan's apartment to find a charger, and I'm getting increasingly annoyed by the minute. The time is nearing midnight and the last bus stops running in about thirty minutes. I guess if I miss it, I can walk.

"Callan," I shout through the door, tired of waiting another second. "Is everything okay?" I wait for a moment but all I get is silence. I knock at the door. "Hey, I think I'm gonna head out now so I can catch the last bus," I try to hide the disappointment in my voice. But he still doesn't answer.

I wait for a minute, letting out a frustrated sigh in realization that I am way in over my head here. Confusion runs through my mind like a plague, wondering what I possibly could have done wrong.

"I guess I'll text you when I get home." I relay before turning on my heel to head toward the front door. I don't know the protocol for this type of thing...being taken to a guy's house but then being stood up immediately? I stop myself from hitting the elevator button, hoping if I give it one more minute, he'll be on his way out to stop me. Maybe he couldn't hear me, maybe he just wanted a shower before we did anything. I don't know why I get my hopes up though, so I press the button in defeat.

I step into the elevator, barefoot and holding my high heels in one hand, my dead cellphone in the other. As the doors are about to close, a hand reaches in abruptly to stop them. I look up to see Callan in sweats and a t-shirt, hair still dripping with water. I blink in anticipation, hoping all of this was a misunderstanding. I'm embarrassed to admit it to myself, but beyond my frustration, I'm still aching for him. And him standing in front of me fresh out the shower *really* doesn't help.

"We can't do this," he says, motioning me back inside. Part of me wants to stay in the elevator and press the button to force-close the doors. But the other part of me is weaker and pulls me back into the dimly lit entryway. People always talk about it in the movies, but I've never been so torn between my head and my heart.

He senses my confusion, as he lets out a husky sigh. "Say something," he encourages, but I don't know what he wants me to say. "I'm not a good man, Sterling. I would destroy your life if I let this go as far as I'd want it. I just-" He cuts himself off as he walks deeper into his living room, running his hands through his hair.

"Destroy my life? That's an irrationally strange thing to say." I start. "Then why did you bring me here?" I feel sick, I kinda want to cry but I don't.

I can tell Callan is thinking hard about what he's going to say to me before he opens his mouth, dragging his hand down his face. My body feels tight when he steps closer to me.

"Because, when you're around me, all I can think about is you. Hell, even when you're not around." He takes a deep, gravelly breath. "And seeing you pleasure yourself in my car, I didn't care if I was going to hurt you. All I could think about was bringing you here and fucking you hard, giving you a night of sinful pleasure that you would never forget." He takes another step closer to me, his voice rough and deep. My skin is burning with desire. "I can't get you out of my fucking head, Sterling. And I was so close to giving in. But I can't because you deserve better than what I'd be willing to give you. Which is just one night, one night that would ruin the rest of your life because I can't give you anything more."

My breathing is ragged, heated both in anger and in lust from the things he's saying. I can feel my pulse down to my toes as my center aches.

"You practically demanded I touch myself in your car. What was the point of that?" I challenge him, braving to take a step closer.

"I'm sorry if I made you uncomfortable-"

"I'm not," I start. "Yeah, it was out of my comfort zone but I'm not sorry it happened. I wanted it as much as you. But if you're playing at some kind of game here, Callan..."

We're both silent for a beat, but we refuse to break eye contact.

"So, you're telling me that you have been flirty, and sweet, and caring this whole time for nothing? Or more, for a pathetic one-night stand?" I question, trying to control the shakiness in my voice.

"I'm not sweet, Sterling."

"I'm calling bullshit, Cal."

"Don't," he demands, stepping back as I step forward once more.

"No. Because if you're as bad as you claim to be, why go through all of this? Why go through all the hot and cold with me, the push and pull? Why the fancy ass auction gala for crying out loud, Callan. What was all that for?"

"The auction gala was a business event, Sterling." His tone bites sharply. "You work for me, remember?"

"Real professional of you, Callan. You tell me that you fantasized about me on your trip. You tell me that I drive you crazy and that I need to touch myself one last time before you take what's yours. Does any of that ring a bell, Callan?" My tone bites back just as harsh.

"I don't have the answers you're looking for," he answers with a shaky breath, his hands in his pockets as I take another step toward him. "I just know that I'd hurt you."

"You know, you're starting to be a real pain in my ass. You're like a sour patch kid. Do you know what a sour patch kid is, Callan? Well, they're sour then they're sweet. And they smell like shit in vomit form." I realize I'm rage-rambling, so mad I don't even know what I'm saying. I can see him smirk. I roll my eyes at him, but pain spreads through my chest. Being around him makes me feel so alive and even though he's pushing me away, all I can feel is the gravitational pull my body has toward him.

"Don't act like you don't like the attention, Sterling," he snaps back at me, obviously pissed by what I said. His voice vibrates in my chest.

"Are you serious? You think I'm here for the attention? I didn't ask for any of this." My hands are balled into fists, my nails digging crescent shapes into my palms.

He pulls his hands out of his pockets and walks toward me. I nearly stumble backwards on my feet as I try to move away, but that only lands me flush against the wall of his living room. Callan pins me between the wall and his body, placing both hands on either side of my head. I gulp hard trying not to look him in his eyes. But staring at his chest doesn't help. So, I cave and make eye contact.

"If you don't back up, Mr. David. I'll be forced to pull that silver spoon out of your mouth." I force myself to say, realizing that I also am a sour patch kid. Just not as rude or cruel as he's been. I just get so confused when I'm around him, and all these different sides of me are coming out. Sides I didn't know I was capable of showing.

He looks angry. *Pissed.* But all I can think about is pressing his lips to mine and kissing him, hard. I almost flinch when I feel his dick harden where it touches my stomach, but I don't dare look.

"Sterling." His tone is demanding and deep and I know he notices the effect it has on me when I clench my thighs. "We can both run around in circles playing the blame game," he whispers heavily into my ear as he leans down.

My knees almost give out at the smell of him, his sage body wash and minty toothpaste make me want him even more. God, I really hate myself right now.

"One thing you need to learn about playing games, is that you have to be a really good player to win." He removes one of his hands from the wall and uses his fingers to brush my hair behind my ear. I stare into his hazel eyes as I unwillingly let a small moan escape my mouth. Without notice, Callan crashes his mouth down to mine.

His lips are hot and rough against mine, claiming me while he kisses me hard. His tongue traces my bottom lip before parting them open, tangling in a wet dance with mine. I grab his hips with my hands to pull him closer, but he growls into my mouth as he takes both of my arms in one hand and pins them above my head.

Another breathy moan leaves my lips as he takes my bottom lip in between his teeth and lets it go with a *pop*. When he doesn't come back for more, I squirm under his possession. He drags his eyes from my lips to my chest and back up to my eyes. A small smirk forms on his lips before he opens them to speak.

"This is just a hint of what a night with me would feel like, Sterling. A moment of lust, followed by disappointment. Because once the rose petals fall from their perfectly bloomed bud," he traces his finger along the underside of my chin, "you no longer have a beautiful flower. You're just left with a tainted mess." He keeps his hold on my hands, still pinned above my head. "I told you that this was a mistake. It won't feel good. Now, be a good girl and let Gerald take you home. He's already waiting for you downstairs, my *little rose*." He finally releases my hands and pulls me away from the wall. Trying to keep my composure, I walk towards the elevator. My breathing is shaky, and my head is spinning. I can't tell if I'm feeling pleasure or pain right now.

I straighten my dress as I walk deeper into the elevator. But before it closes, I take my chance.

"There's one other thing you need to learn about playing games, Mr. David."

"And what's that?"

"It's usually better with two players."

The elevator doors close at the perfect time, not giving Callan a chance to respond. I cross my arms, feeling proud of myself, while still trying to rid the ache between my thighs. When I reach the lobby, I peek at a clock on the wall and realize that I've already missed the bus. And of course, it's snowing.

I really don't want to give Callan the satisfaction of taking a ride from his driver, but I hear poor Gerald shouting my name from the parking lot. He's waiting with the car door open for me in his perfectly tailored suit and signature flat cap. On top of everything, I'm pissed at Callan for making this sweet old man come out past midnight in shitty weather. My guilt takes over as I slide into the back seat and give Gerald a nod of appreciation.

As we drive down the empty city streets, tears silently slide down my cheeks. I don't even think I'm sad, just humiliated, and angry. I can't believe I really thought I had a chance with my boss.

EIGHTEEN

Callan

God, I'm such a fucking idiot. Why did I think that any of this was a good idea. I should have just taken Jax to the goddamn gala, or even Cora for that matter. This whole night could have been prevented.

But classic Callan, I have to go a do the one thing I said I would never do and that's fuck around with one of my employees. But she's got me in a trance that I can't seem to break.

I saw the look in her eyes when I denied her. It was the feeling of being unwanted and that fucking stung. Still, even sleeping it off and waking up, the sun shining in all its beautiful Sunday glory, I still feel the frustration of my actions. Leading her on and turning her down, but the fucking teaser of a show I gave her before she left my presence was the real frosting on the cake.

I can't control the fact that I want to fuck that girl from behind so fucking hard, it'll make me hurt. I can't help that I want to kiss her sweet lips, touch her soft breasts, claim her body and soul as mine. But I also know that I can't actually do that because it's not what I really want. I don't want long term. I *can't* do long term. I wouldn't even know how to manage that. How to fit that in. And after everything I've learned about my own family, it's not fair. It's not fair for me to assume that any woman would betray me the way my own mother has my father. Nor should any woman feel untrusted in their relationship. But also, I've never been in an actual relationship, so there's that. And let's not forget the fact that I told her I'd practically ruin her for no real reason other than to protect her from me.

It's just not fair to Sterling. To fuck her once and throw her away like some kind of broken toy, or a wilted rose.

My little rose.

How I would love to wrap my hand around her throat and hear her gargled words begging me to take her or whisper into her ear how beautiful she is as she takes me into her mouth.

It's almost too much. The confusion going back and forth in my head. It's like I'm losing control of what's real and what's a fantasy and it's driving me fucking insane. Sterling is driving me insane.

But as I sit on this couch and look around at everything I have, I realize it's nothing more than a bunch of junk if I have no one to share any of it with.

God, that sounds fucking crazy coming from me. But it's a thought that feels right taking up space in my head. It feels like my truth. I need someone to share this life with.

Could that someone be Sterling? I really don't have a clue. But I know that sitting here and denying myself all while being a complete ass to her isn't going to help. So I have to do the one thing my dad actually taught me to do...man up.

NINETEEN

Sterling

"What's wrong?" Dakota asks behind sleepy eyes, walking into our living room noticing that I'm already awake, which is not normal for me on a Sunday morning. "I heard you come in super late last night, is everything okay?" Her sarcastic tone is almost annoying to me even though I know she means well.

"You were right," I pause the show that I'm watching, "Callan is an ass and I am such a loser." I realize how stupid that sounds, because I'm not in a relationship with anybody and I certainly didn't get any clear signals from Callan. He was supposed to just be my boss. It wasn't supposed to play out like this. And even though I knew it would never work, I didn't think it would end like this...me being rejected of something that wasn't even there.

Dakota looks up at me, confused. "Callan?" She questions and I run my fingers under my eyes to dry the tears.

"Yeah, impressive in bed. Big dick, even bigger player...my boss." I snap, mimicking some of her words from what she's told me about him.

"What happened?" She sits down next to me on the leather couch.

"What happened is that my life isn't as perfect as yours is, Dakota. I'll never have the perfect job, a beautiful engagement, a boyfriend who loves me, and a family who cares. My life sucks, that's what happened. And I played into this idea, this fantasy, of something more with my stupid asshole of a boss." I let out harshly in as few breaths as possible.

I don't mean to take my anger out on my best friend. But I do. Because maybe I'm jealous that she's got it all and I'll have to keep combating bad luck after bad luck.

"Whoa, don't get sharp with me, Sterls," Dakota demands as she stands up from her position. "You came in here like all hell broke loose at one in the morning, nearly waking me up. I should be the one who's angry, but I'm trying to be here for you right now." Dakota looks offended, but I'm so angry that I don't really think to check myself before I speak.

"Sorry if I woke you last night, but you can't possibly know what I'm going through, Dakota. Because your life is so perfect. You have tons of friends, a supportive family, and a boyfriend, oh wait, *a fiancé,* who loves you. Must be so hard to have it all." My words come out like lava before I can even process what I'm saying.

"What's that supposed to mean?" She crosses her arms as she looks down at me, an unreadable expression on her face.

"Nothing," I say as I stand up from the couch and brush past her on the way to my room.

"No way, you don't get to take your anger out on me because you're mad at some boy." She follows me to my room, feet heavy behind me.

"Like you even care what I do. You're so far up Asher's ass to even notice your so-called best friend is in pain." Again, I don't seem to have any control over my words and *pain* is a pretty strong one. *Am I really in pain from what Callan did?* If so, I really do have some serious problems to work on "You didn't even tell me that he asked you to move in with him," I add.

"No, I didn't. Because I hadn't made any decisions on what I wanted to do. I wanted to ask you for your opinion but as usual, we always end up talking about you and your drama and your life. Which is fine, because I'm your best friend and I want to talk about these things with you. But I don't deserve this, Sterling and you're acting very immature. I think you need to look at the bigger picture here, not everything is about you." Dakota is standing in the doorway while I rustle through my closet pretending not to listen, but really, her words cut like a knife. Before I get the chance to respond, Dakota is already storming off to her room.

She's right. She has been supportive of my weird situation-ship with Callan, even though she already knew he was a total ass who would end up hurting me. She was right the entire time. She's the last person I should be taking my anger out on.

I take a deep breath ready to walk out of my room and over to Dakota's to apologize but before I make it across the hallway, the front door is slamming shut. I hear the lock turn and I realize that she's left, probably headed for Asher's. I've created such a mess tonight.

I wake up from my nap feeling like shit. Sundays are usually the perfect day for me to unwind and prepare for the upcoming week but today feels like a train wreck and I literally just opened my eyes. I was a mess last night. *Everything is a mess.*

I wander over to Dakota's room and it's still empty. I know she's probably still mad at me, but I need to fix this.

Dakota, I know I was a jerk earlier. I was angry and took it out on you. Can we talk?

I hit send, then immediately face my phone down. I know staring at the screen and waiting for her response would only increase my anxiety. I hop into the shower hoping to distract myself for a while.

My mind drifts from Dakota to Callan. It's hard to decipher where things went wrong last night. And I'm the asshole who let it bleed into my morning.

Why was I even mad? The entire night was basically an emotional whiplash on a loop. I don't know why I was so surprised by his behavior; I knew he was trouble. I knew not to get involved. And here I am being a big baby about my boss turning me down.

Why should I care so much? We are nothing but coworkers so this shouldn't be an issue in the first place. But the way he makes me feel, intentional or not, is unreal.

And that kiss.

There was something different about it. I felt it to my core, and I know he felt it too. And sure, he kissed me to be an asshole, to warn me that we can't proceed, to tell me I'd be disappointed and then fed me some bullshit about roses. But I can't get the feel of his lips removed from mine no matter how hard I scrub. His touch and scent linger on me even after lathering up with my own floral body wash. Am I drawn to the gray parts of him, of his actions? Maybe, but I can't for the life of me figure out why. Don't most women spend a majority of their time running from these kinds of things? And here I am overlooking it all because he's the only one who's making me feel...seen.

After my long shower, I throw on a pair of leggings and a hoodie. I start combing my hair when I hear my phone vibrate on the counter. I rush to it, hoping Dakota has texted back. I open the message notification on my phone, but it's not from who I was expecting.

> Last night did not go the way either of us planned. But I really think we should talk. Can we meet?

I take a beat to reread the message. But before I can decide if I want to respond, my phone is ringing in my hand, almost as if he could read my thoughts.

I quickly slide the red decline button across the screen. But just as quick, another text comes through.

> You don't need to be immature about this, Sterling. I really would like to talk.

I type out a response, then delete it. I'm not sure what to say.

Immature? That's the second time someone has called me that and both from people I care about.

Care about...can I really say that about Callan?

I really would like to talk to him, and maybe figure that out. I've never really had a *fight* with a man before, I don't usually talk to one long enough to get that chance. And the war in my heart has to mean something, right?

Another message buzzes in.

Please.

Is Callan begging? I love how good that feels but I also hate how quickly I respond, my fingers type faster than my brain has time to catch up.

Pick me up in twenty.

I attempt to do something with my wavy hair, opting for a messy top knot and throw on a dusting of blush, realizing I looked a little pale. I take one final deep breath before heading out the door.

I don't make it far before something catches my eye. An envelope is taped to my front door. I lock up before pulling it from the door and opening it. I wonder how long it's been sitting here, if Dakota didn't notice it when she left this morning. As I start reading, my eyes fill with tears and knots form in my stomach.

EVICTION NOTICE

IT HAS COME TO OUR ATTENTION THAT HALF OF YOUR RENT HAS NOT BEEN PAID FOR THE MONTH OF MARCH. THIS NOTICE IS TO INFORM YOU THAT AFTER SEVERAL

FAILED ATTEMPTS TO COLLECT PAYMENT, YOU ONLY HAVE 48 HOURS TO PAY THE TOTAL AMOUNT DUE INCLUDING LATE FEES, OR YOU WILL BE INSTRUCTED TO VACATE THE UNIT.

PLEASE CALL US WITH ANY QUESTIONS.

BEST,

GOLDEN GATE APARTMENTS

.

Fucking fantastic.

I make my way down to Callan's car. I send Dakota another text on my way down.

We really need to talk...

The car ride is silent. I don't even know where we're going, I just know Callan has been driving for a while and we're at least thirty minutes outside of the small city by now. The words from the eviction notice play on a loop in my mind. I hold the folded piece of paper in my hand but can't bring myself to open it up again. My anxiety builds as time passes, and Dakota still hasn't responded.

"Everything okay?" Callan breaks the silence.

"Yup. All good." I crumple up the paper and shove it in my purse.

"What is that?" he asks, keeping his hands on the wheel and his eyes on the road.

"An eviction notice," I admit, feeling the slight ping of embarrassment from my confession.

"Wait, what?" He sounds genuinely shocked.

"It's nothing, Callan."

It's none of his business, and for him to sound shocked by the fact that people have real lives and real problems, makes my blood boil even more. How can I be so attracted and caring towards a person who makes me want to rip their head off?

He pulls over into a parking lot of a shopping center. As soon as the car stops, I can feel him eyeing me. I don't need his pity and I don't need to feel embarrassed either.

"Sterling. What's going on?" He unbuckles his seat belt and leans over, placing his hand on my shoulder. His touch is comforting, but it doesn't make me forget the words we shared last night.

"I'd rather not talk to you about it." I swipe the sudden tears from my cheeks and take off my safety belt to get out of the car. "I'd really rather be alone right now. This was a bad idea." I step out and close the door behind me, leaning against the car. Callan immediately joins me outside of the car.

"It's okay to let someone in." Callan walks around to meet me where I stand with my arms crossed.

"Says the man who just banished me from his home after I so willingly allowed myself to be vulnerable in front of him. Way to make a girl feel special." I seethe, but in a more sarcastic tone than an angry one.

"Please talk to me," he whispers.

I fight back the water pooling in my eyes as I look up at him. His dark chocolate-colored hair falls in a perfect mess of curls, like he didn't take the time to gel it back today the way he normally does.

We both stand in silence for a few moments before he finally takes a breath and speaks.

"Sterling," he says, stepping even closer to me now.

"You're like, really fucking stupid you know that?" I begin, feeling all of the emotions from the last two days. The confusing mess of poetic lines he's been spitting at me mixed with his carnal flirtations and gentlemanly gestures.

"I know. I know. I just-"

"You just, what, Callan? You like picking people up and then breaking them apart?" I don't want him to see that he's affected me too much, but unfortunately for me, I have a mouth with a mind of its own whenever he's concerned.

"You said you were going to take the silver spoon out of my mouth." Callan's tone is lower and much calmer than it was yesterday. Yesterday, he seemed possessive and eager to show off his manpower. He shoves his hands in his front pockets.

"Well, I'm sorry." I hold my hands up in front of me, thankful that the parking lot is empty and no one will have to watch us act like idiots. "But that was after you said something about me only being around you for the attention and something about destroying my life. You're not that entitled that you get to throw around stupid stuff like that Callan."

"You don't have to apologize." Callan tries to step closer, but I put my hands up in the space between us to stop him.

"No, please. Let me talk." I suck in a deep breath before continuing.

"I didn't mean to belittle you. I had no right to call you out like that." He drops his head as I continue my unplanned monologue. "It did hurt, feeling like you led me on. Maybe I read into things the wrong way, but I didn't deserve to be humiliated like that. To let you see a vulnerability of mine just for you to push me away. I know that you and I messing around together is forbidden, and I know it's wrong, I know that," I breathe shakily before continuing, "But I'm grown enough to know what I want and it's not fair for you to make that decision for me because you have some kind of misconception about how you'd ruin my life." I finally uncross my arms as I stare up at him, gesturing quotations around those last three words.

"It's safe to say we both reacted immaturely. I just, I don't want you to think I'm intentionally trying to hurt you."

"Well you leading me on just to kick me out while calling me a nickname seems pretty intentional and honestly, confusing." It's clear he's got a fight going on in his head just as I do. But why? Why does this have to be hard? Who cares if we work together. But I guess I'm just trying to understand why this is the way it is between us.

"I don't know what else you want me to say, Sterling." Callan tucks his hand into his pockets. "I'm sorry for making you feel embarrassed," he adds.

"Maybe there is nothing to say. Maybe this is just some stupid infatuation that just needs to be forgotten," I presume. "Maybe we just need to get it out of our systems. Maybe we're just two people who are attracted to each other, but we're trying not to be attracted to each other."

Callan has his hands at his sides, fingers balled into fists. I can see the vein popping out of his neck. I know he feels something more, people don't react this way over nothing. But I can't keep doing this back-and-forth thing with him. We either do or we don't but I won't be able to move on until this temptation is either satisfied or removed all together.

TWENTY

Callan

I know I fucked up last night, I knew it the second she left my house. I don't know why I overreacted the way I did but seeing her pleasure herself in my car did things to me. Sinful, nefarious things. I didn't care if I was gonna hurt her, break her until there was nothing left. I'm a man who prefers no strings attached and she's a woman who deserves the fucking world, from what I've seen. A world I know I *can* give her if I just allowed myself to feel.

But maybe this can work, if we can both agree that there will be no strings attached. Fuck, I can't believe I'm even trying to rationalize this right now.

"Sterling, I live life in the gray areas. I don't step out into the light much. I've done things that no one should be proud of..." I trail off, thinking of all the things I've done that make for a shitty excuse of a man.

"I've been a selfish lover, using women for my own personal pleasure," I continue. Not once have I felt bad for it, until now. Until the debate in my head where Sterling is concerned. And there's that unspoken thing I did not long ago. The part of my life I've chosen to block out that no one knows about it. But I do. And I'd be lying if I said it didn't eat at me every now and then. And there's my fucked up family. And my need for power is more than my need to feel.

"I'm just not a good man," I admit, finishing my statement. Even if we didn't work together, this would never pan out pleasantly for her.

She watches me with her mysterious eyes, usually she's pretty readable. But as we stand her in this stupid parking lot, I can tell she's annoyed, confused, hurt even.

"Elaborate," she says.

"I don't know-"

"No, start with the selfish lover thing." Her eyes are shaded with something intense but swirled with a hint of sadness.

"What?" Why would she want me to elaborate something like that? Is it not self-explanatory?

"You heard me."

"Well, one-night stands, mostly, always on my terms. But mostly, I just don't find interest in attachment, or something more. Sex is just sex." My confession holds heat on my tongue as I watch, trying to gauge her reaction. I'd never really been ashamed of that lifestyle, until I spoke it out loud in front of a girl I could maybe see more with. But her sweet blue eyes only hold mine more intensely.

"Why is that such a bad thing?" she asks, stumbling over her words.

I shift in my position, the air feeling sticky around me. But I know it's only because my want is growing deep. And her question pisses me off because it feels as if she's asking for permission, like she's curious as to whether or not I'd grant her that luxury.

And I would.

So fucking fast.

But she deserves better than that. Imagine me giving in only having to fire her because I can't give her what she wants and I'd have to live with that every day by looking at her.

"What's wrong?" she asks, obviously seeing a look of uncertainty on my face.

God, could she be any more oblivious? If she wasn't standing there, looking so fucking sweet with her doe eyes staring up at me, cheeks red with desire, hair wrapped up so perfectly, waiting to be let down and pulled, I'd leave her here. Because if it were anyone else, it wouldn't be worth my time.

"I can't give you what you want. I just can't."

"How do you know what I want?" She pulls in her bottom lip with teeth. I hate that she has a hold on me. "Tell me what's so wrong with fulfilling each other's wants, Callan?"

Honestly, despite everything I'm telling her, I want this. I want her. I want to claim her, I want her to claim me. But I'm scared of the feeling that will probably conjure up from even a one night stand with her, because I feel them in the way I look at her. When I'm around her, I *feel* things. Good things. I think my confusion and war comes from me not knowing how to manage those feelings. Who knew being so damn attracted to a woman could be such a hard thing. Who knew that when she found herself in my dealership that day, that we'd end up here, fighting over what is right and what is wrong. Acting like immature idiots instead of consenting adults who can manage taking care of each other's sexual frustrations.

"God dammit, Sterling!" I rake my hands through my hair frustratingly, knowing I'm going to take this further than I expected.

"You want to know what's wrong? It's you! *You* are what's wrong with this whole thing!" Her facial expression contorts from almost seeming scared, to confused, to the soft demure I'm used to seeing. "I've tried time and time again to push you out of my mind," I continue, "To push you away. But despite my best efforts, you keep evading my mind with those fucking blue eyes and your sweet fucking smile and the way you put me in my place with your sassy remarks. Do you have any idea how much fucking power you hold over me?" I suck in a deep breath trying to preserve any restraint I may have left.

"I'm trying to warn you, give you a head start to run and never look back. Why aren't you running from the obvious red flags?" I lean in and hold her face in my hands, something I've been dying to do again. I can't keep being an asshole to her just because. I'm such an idiot and this needs to stop. But I need to hear her answer, anything that tells me that I have permission to do what I want to do next. Because I have to have her.

She takes a deep breath, closing her eyes, her lashes feathering lightly on the tops of her cheeks. Then she whispers, "Red is my favorite color, remember?"

"Get in the car," I demand feverishly. Every ounce of emotion I was feeling before is replaced with a heavy lust and the need to fuck this woman into oblivion, but she doesn't move. She doesn't listen.

I pull my hand up to my mouth and rub my bottom lip with my thumb, looking back at her darkly.

"Now!" I command, as I open the door for her, and she doesn't waste another second.

TWENTY-ONE

Sterling

"This is it, Sterling. If we go here, there's no going back. I am going to break my rules for you, but we can only do this once." His voice hits low in my belly as the elevator doors close behind me.

To think that I was just here less than twenty-four hours ago fleeing from the embarrassment and pain he'd caused, practically telling me that he'd ruin me. But what he didn't seem to grasp is that I didn't care. My heart is erratic and I'm not sure if I should be nervous or excited, but I know for damn sure the thrill turns me on.

And I want this. Oh, how I want this. He said he's a selfish lover, and sure he's confusing as hell, but I just want to feel something again. Something other than what I've been feeling...unwanted and alone.

We walk further into his penthouse, the fiery sunset gleams through the floor-to-ceiling windows illuminating the room in rays of pink and yellow. I try to steady myself, needing to catch my breath, but my whole body lights up with a fire that needs to be tamed.

He steps in behind me, grabs me by the waist and spins me around. I stare up at him, his eyes trail up and down my body burning holes through my chest. I can't control my breathing.

"Do you understand what you're getting yourself into?" He takes a step back from me and swipes his thumb across his bottom lip. *Only once.* I think I can manage only once.

"Yes, sir," I say with a shaky voice, and something changes in his eyes. The browns darken the greens, and his amber eyes fill with desire. I feel it in my cheeks, the heat from the arousal that spreads within me.

In one fell swoop, Callan pulls me in and up. Grabbing me by my ass, his fingers holding on tightly as he throws me over his shoulder and turns to his bedroom. He gently lays me down on the edge of his bed and closes the door behind us.

He walks over to his window and opens the curtains, making the late-afternoon sun fall over us, creating an ethereal effect. He runs a hand through his hair as he seductively saunters back over to the bed, and I feel like my heart is going to explode out of my chest with anticipation as he gets closer.

He leans over the bed, one arm on each side of me. His lips are so close to mine as he lowers his body down onto me. I can smell him; every perfect inch of his sculpted body exudes bourbon and wood. I feel myself tensing, wanting him closer and wanting his lips to find their home on mine. His dark curls fall effortlessly over his eyes and all I want to do is run my fingers through them, but my arms are pinned underneath him. Heat pulses from my cheeks and runs all the way down to my core.

"I have a confession," he starts as he tugs gently on my leggings and slowly pulls them down until he gets them off. Goosebumps rise on my thighs, but heat is still radiating between them.

"Would you like to know what it is, Sterling?" he asks. The look in his eyes is carnal. Like I'm about to get devoured whether I like it or not.

I can't get out a word, so a soft mumble escapes my mouth as I pull my bottom lip between my teeth.

"I have an obsession with wanting to fuck you," he admits as he pulls his shirt over his head. I see every hard line of his abs trace down into his pants and the obvious outline of his cock becomes even more apparent as his length hardens. "And you've made it awfully hard to resist. You're like the beautiful, bright Heaven to my deep, dark Hell, Sterling. I crave to dip into the purest parts of you and take you to the dark side with me."

My breath is ragged hearing his words. "I think...I think I want that too," I dare say as my voice is shaky and ragged. The ache between my thighs tightens with greed. Suddenly, all of the confidence I had mustered up before we came here is pretty much out the window. I know I want this, after all the teasing and arguing and not knowing what the hell either of us wants, this is it. *Just once.* But I won't lie, I am nervous. Nervous it won't be good, nervous it will be too good.

"You with me?" he asks, and I give him the most reassuring nod I can manage.

"You have no idea what you do to me." He runs his hand up my bare thigh, his fingers catching every goosebump. My legs quiver at his touch as his grip tightens. "I think we've established that you drive me crazy. No matter what I do, all I think about is you and all I want to do is tie you up and fuck you for making me feel this way." He moves his body in, his lips closer to mine.

The air in the room turns hot and I can hardly see straight. I've never felt so weak before. Everything in my body is shutting down and all I want to do is drown in Callan. Maybe he's right, maybe this is a mistake. But all I can think as he traces circles on my stomach under my sweatshirt with his fingers is *take me under.*

"Do it." It's a whispered threat from my lips.

"What did you just say?" He quickly leans back, leaving me lying on the bed as he towers over me.

"Tie me up." I make sure to give him my most confident eye contact, staring at him as he watches me.

"I need to be sure you want this." Callan's tone is rushed and laced with heat as he stares down at me.

"I want this," I respond without hesitation. "Please."

He leans back down, positioning his knees on either side of my thighs, then closes the proximity as he buries his face into my neck. His hardness presses into me making me squirm as he grabs me by the wrists and yanks my arms above my head. He reaches to the hem of my hoodie and pulls it over, the cold air creating pebbles against my skin.

He looks over my bare stomach and as his eyes trace up to the lacy white bra I'm wearing, his irises darken.

"Are you ready to be a good girl for me, Sterling?" He bites down into my neck, the pain stinging up to my eyes as water pools in the corners, but then, it turns soft. He kisses my neck gently as he glides his fingers from my wrists up to my shoulders.

"Stay right here." He gets up from the bed and the cool air invades the warmth of my arousal. My hands are still placed above my head as he disappears into his closet, then comes back out with one of his ties. The pink one.

My hips thrust a little, out of my control, when he moves back onto the bed and this earns me a kiss. A kiss so hard and deep, my soul feels its imprint and shatters into a million tiny pieces. The kiss is fierce and intense. Like this very well may be the last time. But I fully welcome his tongue as it dances with mine, our lips molding into each other's. I try to push myself closer to him but there's nowhere further to go and before I know it, my hands are tied above my head with his tie, the silk fabric creating a delightful sensation on my skin, the tightness of the constraint creates pain. But I welcome it.

"If anything gets to be too much, just tell me and I'll stop. That understood?"

"Understood," I repeat back to him, trying to catch my breath as I get comfortable with my hands above my head, and he spreads my legs with his knees while giving me one last, rough kiss. I want every part of it. Every part of *him.*

I look at him in unfairness because I desperately want to get his pants off. He catches my drift because he gives me a small nod as his lips curl up into a smirk and he wastes no time giving me what I want. I watch my very own strip tease take place, I lay helplessly on his bed. His movements are slow and effortless. Once he's undressed fully, my mouth waters for him. His length is...impressive. I don't even know how to form tangible thoughts right now. *God, this better be worth it because he's right...he looks like he could destroy me.*

He leans into my neck, tangling his hand in my hair and tugging lightly to allow him better access to the sensitive skin on my throat.

"Miss Cooper," he whispers, sending a shiver down my neck. "The first day you walked into my office, you were wearing the sexiest red blouse, already dressing the part as my perfect little assistant." He moves his mouth down to my chest, leaving light kisses along the way, "I remember you listed 'flexible' and 'enthusiastic' on your resume. I'm looking forward to seeing your skills tonight." He trails his tongue from my earlobe to my collar bone. I'm so wet, soaked with lust and desire.

I feel how hard he is against me, every nerve in my body is screaming for this man. He's taking his time to prepare me for that unforgiveable night of pleasure he promised he wouldn't give me, but here we are and I crave every ounce of it.

He grips my hair a little harder and gently lays my head back to rest on his plush pillows, maintaining eye contact the entire time.

"Are we going to have sex without a condom?" I ask, feeling really silly for potentially ruining the moment, realizing I asked the most immature question a woman could ask, but it just slipped out of my stupid mouth. But I don't let the embarrassment wash over me entirely as I realize that I liked teasing him with the idea of him pushing inside of me bare.

"I'll be really fucking honest here, Sterling." He takes his index finger to trace the silhouette of my body from the top of my shoulder down to the curve of my ass. "The idea of fucking you with no barrier sounds dangerous as fuck. But it is what I would like to do. I won't do anything you don't feel comfortable with. I'm clean, but whatever you say goes." He trails off as he reaches behind my back, I arch for him so he has better access while his fingers linger over the clasp of my bra. The electricity that courses through my body at his touch sparks a flame deep inside me. "I have a condom if you want me to use one."

His dick is pressing against my thigh. I look between us and see every hard line and vein, he rubs it once against my thigh and I can't help but whimper.

He lowers his head and our noses are practically touching now. I look into his eyes and take a deep breath to calm my nerves.

"How many times have you done that?" I ask.

"Without protection? Never," he states. And I don't have to ask further to know he's telling the truth, and to see that he wants this as badly as I do. I know I'm on birth control still, and the idea of it sends sparks all over my body causing even more liquid pooling at my core.

"It's what I want," I answer. Knowing damn well that if this is going to be my first and only chance to be with a man of this magnitude, to be with Callan, then I want to feel every part of him inside of me.

Our bodies create so much heat, it feels like we could catch on fire at any moment. The way his skin feels on mine ignites the spark even more. He puts his lips to my neck, soft and sweet. I'm starting to think he really likes it there, but I won't complain. I've never had the chance to explore sensations, what feels good to me, where I like being kissed the most. And honestly, it probably doesn't matter much because everywhere Callan puts his lips is like a hidden treasure of kinks I never knew I had.

He trails small kisses from the bottom of my chin to my earlobe before he whispers, "I am going to ruin you for any other man, Sterling. Anything you want, and everything you need. This is about you." I nod, my face buried in his neck as his lips graze my ear and I don't miss the opportunity to sucks on the side of his throat. He hums in my ear and all my worries disappear.

"I'm yours," I whisper into his skin as butterflies flutter deep in my belly.

"Holy fuck, say it again," he growls as he sits up slightly and wraps his fingers around my throat, his other hand grips his dick, applying the tiniest amount of pressure to both. I can tell I've hit a cord, something that turns him on even more.

"I'm yours," I whimper.

At almost the same time, he snaps my bra off and pulls it out from under me, exposing my breasts, while pulling my bottom lip in between his teeth. He nibbles gently on my lip while his finger grazes my nipple making everything feel, somehow, even more heightened.

Everywhere.

I am on fire everywhere.

I need him inside of me.

I thrust my hips, my wet core hitting against his hard cock. He removes his lips from mine and watches me with hungry eyes.

"I've got you." He acknowledges my actions, knowing I need him.

Then he wastes no time bringing his head down in between my legs. He tugs on my lace thong with his teeth, then uses his hands to assist in pulling it off completely. He breathes deeply and heavily into my center; his warm breath sends sparks flying all around the room, like the whole sky could come crashing down at any moment and I'd be safe right where I'm at.

He swipes his tongue from my entrance to my clit, his tongue lapping at my heat. My whole body shakes as I moan out, rocking my hips as his mouth takes me in. He grips my hips, his fingers digging deep into my skin. Everything feels light around me, like I'm floating away on the waves he creates inside me. I pull my tied wrists down to his head, twist my fingers into his hair trying to pull him closer and though it's harder than I thought with bound wrists, he understands my want. He pulls me into him, both hands gripping even harder into my skin and the pain is almost too much but then his tongue finds my bundle of nerves again, and I squeeze my thighs around his head with every motion his tongue makes.

He gives my clit one gentle, sensitive kiss before he comes up for air but not before replacing his tongue with his fingers.

He pumps two digits inside me, hating this damn tie from allowing me to grip onto something while he finger fucks me. I feel his eyes burn over my skin as I shake under his touch.

"Oh, Callan. That feels so good!" I murmur as I move my hips with his pumps.

"My pretty fucking girl," he breathes out with a gentle smile. His words linger in the air like clouds, pillowy and soft. And so beautiful. I've never been complimented during sex. It heightens everything.

He leans back down, and presses kisses to my clit, then sucks gently. I feel like I'm about to explode. I've never been eaten out so intensely and carefully. Everything he is doing is with precision. My whole body is shaking.

He pushes faster, sucks harder. I feel like I'm coming undone. This is the best I've ever felt. I'm about to let go, fall over the edge but I'm not sure I can take the feeling that's overcoming me.

Like Heaven and Earth are colliding.

No.

That's not right.

Like Hell and Earth are colliding.

Everything in this moment feels like a perfect sin.

He pumps faster and harder and everything in me tenses. Another moan escapes my lips and I surprise myself with what comes out of my mouth next.

"Stop!"

Callan pulls away from me immediately.

"What's wrong? Did I hurt you?" He wipes his mouth with the back of hand and searches my eyes for any sign of hurt or pain. But he won't find it.

"No. That felt amazing," I pant breathlessly.

"Then what's wrong? Why'd you stop me?" He's clearly confused.

"I, um-" I start but I don't know how to say what I want to say.

"What is it, Sterling?" Callan leans into the bed and reaches over to untie my hands.

"This is going to sound really pathetic but..."

I look at Callan's eyes, hunger flaring inside them, I don't want to ruin the moment but my entire body is buzzing and I know what I want next.

"I've never had an orgasm before. At least not one that wasn't at my own hands if you can even count that. I was almost there, just now. But I want my first orgasm to be with you inside of me," I admit, feeling a little out of my comfort zone. But I know this will only work if I use my words, just like he had asked.

"Are you fucking serious?" His expression contorts from confusion to anger to more confusion. I'm not sure what he's thinking. *Is he mad at me?*

"Did I do something wrong?" I'm suddenly pulling at the covers trying to hide my body.

"What? God no, Sterling. Absolutely not. I just can't believe that whatever assholes were lucky enough to be with you never made you come."

Callan reaches his hand out for mine and pulls me up to sitting position. His features are stunning. His chest is bare and smooth, his stomach is etched like a god's. His eyes are drinking me up as they roam all over my body. One of his hands smooths my hair down my back as the other is placed sensually against my neck, his thumb brushing the front of my throat.

Even though he said that this was only for one night, I feel a future in his words as they brush over my lips and seep down my skin and into my core creating electricity that buzzes through my body.

I give him a wanting nod.

"Use your fucking words, Sterling," he growls. "What do you want?"

He brings his lips down to my breast and pulls in a nipple. My skin pebbles all over as he sucks gently on the hardened bud; I throw my head back to give him more access.

"I want you to fuck me," I moan out. "I want you to make me come. And I want the tie around my neck."

And in no time, Callan has me flat on my stomach. He unties the restraint from my wrists gently then wraps the tie around my throat and ties it so it's secure but comfortable. He yanks the tie a bit, forcing my head back and I relieve the pressure by propping myself up on my hands and knees.

"That's my girl," he purrs.

TWENTY-TWO

Callan

She's so fucking tight, like she was made for me. I take my time with her because she deserves it. I want to be rough, but something tells me to slow down with her. And I can't get enough. But having this tie around her throat is making it really hard for me to be anything but rough.

She's never had an orgasm before.

This girl?

Sterling?

How?

She should be worshiped.

Good thing I plan on doing just that.

I can tell I'm hurting her, at least at first. I can tell she feels the pressure, but she doesn't tap out as I slide deeper into her. She bites down on her lip instead and digs her nails into my pillow as I slowly thrust into her, not quite to the hilt because I know I'll wreck her. I've never felt so good inside of a woman before. I feel every part of her inside and out opening up for me. Just like my little rose.

"How does that feel, sweetheart?" I ask her, even though I can tell she's in pain.

"It feels so good, Callan. You're just really big," she says behind small breaths, gargled as the tie pulls against her neck.

When we got out of the car earlier, I was thinking of all the reasons why we shouldn't do this. After listening to her defend herself and put me in my place, I was done denying my want for her. My *need* for her.

Carnal.

That's how she makes me feel.

A forgiven sinner at best.

I keep pushing myself in and out. She's so wet. And all I can think about is making her mine. No other man will ever be able to touch her after I'm done with her. Because I'll never be done with her.

"Oh, Callan." She's past the pain now, feeling the pleasure. Her hips rock back into my pelvis a bit more. The heat between us is unbearable and I can already feel my release coming close, but I try to hold out. I will not finish before her.

"You're doing so good, Sterling," I whisper to her, leaning over to her ear. The praise she's highly deserving of.

"You can go faster now," she moans out. I grip the inside of the delicious curl of her hip as I pull her faster into me, my other hand is wrapped around the tie controlling her movements.

I thrust my cock into her sweet pussy faster, making the bed shake. She's breathing heavier, digging her nails deeper into the bed.

I fuck her like she deserves.

"Fuck, sweetheart. You feel so fucking good." I grab her ass and push myself even deeper inside of her. "And you look so beautiful taking my dick."

I decide to flip her over, the tie still wrapped around her throat and the sight of it along with the way her tits bounce as she lands on her back sends even more need coursing through my veins.

I bring my mouth down to her breasts and take in one of her nipples as I tug on the constraint. The little bud fits so delicately into my mouth as my tongue plays with it. We keep rocking together. The sound of her moans make me harder than I thought possible but every time she lets out the lusty sound, I fill her up even more.

"Callan." *Thrust.* "I love it when you say things like that to me." Her words feather over my shoulder in a sigh of appreciation, like a thank you note laced with the need for more. She drags her nails down to my ass and the feeling of her grip intensifies everything. I pick up pace, slamming relentlessly into her.

Her moans come hard and deconstructed as she tries to hold on to me.

"You hangin' on baby?" I kiss her neck as I wait for her to answer.

"Ye-Yes," her breathing is ragged. "Harder, please"

I attempt to go even harder, even deeper. I'm a selfish prick. I can't help my hunger for her. The face she makes as she takes all of me. The rhythm our bodies create as I fuck her harder than she can probably take.

I lean down and remove the tie from around her neck, the obvious hitch of her breath releases as I toss it to the ground. But then I place my hand over her throat, rubbing over the marks it left behind, but also applying more pressure. Pressure she needs to help her feel her orgasm in the most euphoric oblivion.

"Can I...fuck...can I..." She tries to breathe through my grip so I let up a little bit.

"Can I get on top?" She's finally able to get out.

I don't want to stop, this is where I like her. But I know I'm going to give her what she wants.

"I've... I've never..." I thrust into her harder as she tries to get out her words.

"I've never been on top before." She reaches up and runs her hands through my hair.

"Seriously?" I feel myself asking again. I feel so much pleasure knowing that I'm taking some of her firsts.

I take no time maneuvering us into the new position, letting go of her throat entirely and moving to grip her hips as I flip to my back and help her over me. She looks down between us and moans before closing the space as she wraps her pussy around my cock.

The new position gives me a different sensation. One of utter pleasure. I can't believe how unreal she feels on me. Her hips rock slowly at first, her hands placed gently on my chest as I hold onto her, my hands still possessing her hips.

"Fuck," I growl, and her hips move faster. I sit up with her making our bodies closer than ever. I release my grip from her hip to push her sweaty hair out of her face. I use my other hand to help her grind on me harder and faster.

"Oh, God. Cal, I'm...I'm so close," she cries, and I give her a little boost by pushing my hips up as she rocks. Her cries come in waves as her orgasm takes over.

"Callan!" She muffles her screams into my neck as she leans in and shakes on top of me, her whole body tensing over me. I hold her tight, moving one hand to the back of her neck, to make sure she feels every ounce of pleasure possible, pushing her down over my aching cock.

"Good girl, baby. That feel good?" I unconsciously tighten my grip on the back of her neck.

"Mm, hmm," she purrs, her body now slowing down and resting on top of mine as I lay back down. I run my fingers down her spine and she giggles seductively into my ear.

"That was amazing, Cal." She brushes her fingers on the nape of my neck. "Did you come?" she asks.

"No, not yet. I wanted you to finish first," I assure her.

"I want you to come," she tells me and I give her the slightest smirk before bringing her in for a kiss. She licks my bottom lip, then fully takes my mouth with hers. She's like a lioness awakened.

Sexy and smitten.

Like she's been hiding away this whole time

Another part of her opening up to me.

I reach up for her breast as the kiss deepens, her tongue claiming mine. I run my thumb over the sensitive part of her tit, and she reacts by thrusting her hips slightly creating friction against my throbbing dick that still sits hard inside of her.

"I want you to come," she repeats with a pleading tone. I gently roll her onto her back, stand up near the end of the bed, already missing her warmth.

"How are you so fucking sweet for me, my little rose?" Her eyes swirl with blues and grays that exude desire. I could stare into them forever. "Turn back over," I demand.

She gives me a soft peck on my check then flips over immediately and steadies herself on her hands and knees. I climb onto the bed behind her and grip the inside of her hips to pull her in closer.

"You're so fucking pretty, Sterling. Are you ready to take me again, baby?" I ask her as I grip her hips from behind, my thumbs press into the curve of her ass.

She looks back at me, her eyes heavy and her lips curved into a devilish smirk.

"Yes, sir."

That's.

It.

I slam my dick into her, guiding her ass all the way back, thrusting in and out, taking her from behind. Her lithe body fitting so perfectly over mine.

"Oh my God," she whines out. Her breathing turns scarce, all I hear are mangled noises mixed with the sounds of our bodies clapping together in rough, sweet, thrusts.

I place both of my hands on her shoulders, guiding her upright just a tad and squeezing a little to anchor myself while I fuck her roughly from behind. We keep a steady pace together; both of our bodies are wet and hot. I'm about to break loose inside of her, but I'm going to make her come again.

I reach my hand under to her breast keeping us steady with my other hand wrapped around her shoulder. I grind her ass against me, playing with her tits before I make my way down past her stomach.

She purrs as she arches her back deep enough to bury her face into the sheets, the angle she's giving me is almost unbearable. "Callan!" My name spills from her mouth, muffled.

"Sterling." I growl out her name as I quicken my tempo on her clit still thrusting into her, hard enough to break her.

"Please," she pleads, and before I have time to say anything else, she screams out my name. "Callan, you're going to make me...oh, God." She arches her back further, her fingers digging into the bed as she folds into her orgasm.

I'm right there with her, her pussy tightening around my dick as she whimpers and cries. I don't hide my pleasure either, both of our moans filling the air.

My cum jets inside her, and I've never felt so released before. She falls on her stomach still panting, and I watch our mixed arousal seep out of her and onto the bed. *Fuck.*

I pull away from the bed and stand for a moment, staring at the beautiful woman blessing my space.

I lean down to the back of her neck and give her a lingering peck before going to get a towel. When I come back, she's flipped over onto her back and before I know what I'm doing, I swipe at our cum and spread it around her swollen pussy watching her squirm and moan as we watch my gesture together. *She's so fucking perfect.*

I gently clean up the mess I've left all over her legs as she lies on the bed, breathless with her eyes closed.

I lean down and kiss her forehead until her breathing slows to a normal pace, then head to the bathroom to start the shower for us, because she will be joining me.

I stand at the mirror looking back at a man who has the world at his feet, never wanting for anything. A man who feels nothing, living life with rules and regulations. A man who was taught love doesn't exist and life is nothing but a game, the finish line easily obtained if I stay focused.

But I'd give it all up to be able to give her everything she deserves.

I have to go back on what I told her. *This can only happen once.*

I'm so completely fucked. Not a chance in hell that I'll back down now. Sterling is mine. *Mine.*

All this time, I thought I'd be the one to ruin her. But I was wrong. *I'm the one who's ruined.*

TWENTY-THREE

Sterling

I missed three text messages from Dakota. Her first message was agreeing to meet up with me, the second an apology, which she definitely didn't owe me. I'm the one who took my anger out on her when all she's ever done is support me. The third was a ***HELLO*** followed by three question marks. I didn't hesitate to call her immediately and she agreed to meet up with me so that we can talk.

After Callan and I had cleaned up and put our clothes back on, I asked if he wouldn't mind giving me a ride. He insisted that Gerald drive me instead; said he had business to take care of. I have this feeling that he wasn't being honest. Who has work to do at eight p.m. on a Sunday night? But despite my suspicions, I didn't press the matter because really, it isn't my business. So agreed to have Gerald drive me.

We pull into the parking lot of the bistro Dakota suggested we meet at. It's a cute little spot that serves late night coffee and cocktails, one of the first places she and I hung out at when we became friends. It gives me hope, her asking to meet up at a place where we've made some of our best memories.

The fight that we had was pointless. I took my anger out on my best friend because I'm an idiot, to put it simply. I've already lost so many people in my life, probably of my own doing now that I think about it, but I can't lose my best friend over some silly argument about boys.

"We've arrived, Miss Cooper," Gerald speaks softly as he looks at me through the rear-view mirror, probably noticing I was in deep thought.

"Gerald, can I ask you a question?"

"Of course, Miss Cooper. How can I help?"

"Did Callan really have business to attend to? Is that why you took me instead of him?" I don't want to insinuate that I don't trust Callan because again, it is none of my business. But he barely spoke to me after his shower, which is leaving me a little uneasy.

"I don't think I'm inclined to speak on behalf of Mr. David. But I would expect that he's busy, if he says he is," Gerald responds in his kind and professional way. He steps out of the car to open my door for me.

"I'm sorry for asking, that wasn't fair of me." How silly of me to assume he'd tell me anything. He works for Callan, not me.

"Don't worry, Miss Cooper. I know uncertainty when I see it. Callan is...what is it the cool kids say these days? Into you." I let out a small laugh as he closes the door behind me, and we give each other a smile and wave goodbye as I head inside. I feel stupid for questioning Callan. He made it very clear that we would only be together once, and I agreed to his conditions. I'm probably just overthinking things as usual.

As soon as I walk in, my eyes dart to the far left corner of the bistro. Surely enough, Dakota is sitting in our usual spot, a small booth just big enough for two. We've spent so many late nights here, laughing our asses off over the stupidest things. I desperately miss those nights.

"Hey," Dakota greets me softly as I approach.

"Hey," I offer quietly. I hate the way we left things last night, and to be met with the eviction notice this morning was just the gasoline on top of the dumpster fire. The thought of telling her makes my stomach tighten with nervousness, but she's my best friend and I know we can get through anything together.

I sit at the table and we both stare at each other before breaking the silence.

"I'm sorry," we say at the same time, which immediately breaks the tension as we both smile at each other.

Dakota's green eyes look exhausted. She has her hair thrown up in a messy ponytail and is still wearing her scrubs which tells me she probably just got off from a twelve-hour shift at the hospital.

"Me first," I insist, and she nods. "Listen, Dakota. I'm sorry for being selfish. You were right and I needed to hear everything you said. I was feeling sorry for myself, and I took that out on you." I take a sip of the iced latte she ordered me. "You are my best friend, my only friend. And I don't want to lose you over something that shouldn't have even gotten in the way to begin with. I had never felt so confused and when I came home, I don't know. I guess I just let my feelings spill out all over you without considering your own feelings. I really am so sorry." I stop talking to let her take in my words.

"I love you, Sterls. And I'm sorry for the things I said and the way I left. I know I could have sat down and talked to you about Asher and me, but the timing never felt right, and everything seemed to be moving so quickly. And honestly, I have a lot of going on in my life right now as well," she chokes out behind foggy eyes. "Ever since your car accident, I feel like things have been off between us."

"I agree, I've been acting immature and I guess I was just caught up in the tension between Callan and I and you've been busy so I took it as you ignoring me. I guess we both just need to slow down and make more intentional time for each other." I smile back at her, loving that we can come to this understanding together.

"Well, that's the other thing," Dakota starts. And I perk up in my chair.

"What?" I ask.

"I, um-" She takes in a breath. "I'm moving." She looks down into her lap.

"I know Dakota, I wasn't *that* drunk at your birthday party. You're moving in with Asher."

"No Sterls, I have to go back home. I have to go to Charlotte." She finally meets my eyes with hers and I can tell she's pained; she doesn't want to do this.

"Is everything okay?" I ask.

"Not really. My mom isn't doing well. Her health is going downhill. And she needs me," she explains.

"Your mom? What's going on?"

"Well, she's sick. And there's no one there to take care of her." She shifts uncomfortably in her seat, I can see the fear in her eyes. Gosh, I'm such a bitch. I had no idea and I just tore into her this morning because of guy issues.

"Is Asher going to move with you?"

"Well, we kind of got into a fight about it. Right before you came home last night. Which is probably another reason why I was so on edge. He doesn't want me to go. He has to stay and finish school and we obviously just got engaged and were starting to plan our lives together. So, understandably, he's upset."

"I'm so sorry, Dakota," I whisper as I reach my hand across the table to hold hers. Tears drop silently from her eyes.

"When do you have to go?" I struggle to ask. The idea of her leaving is so hard to think about.

"Next week." Her answer stings. But there's nothing I can do about it.

Dakota pulls her buzzing phone from her purse and takes a heavy sigh.

"Ugh, Sterls, I'm so sorry, I'm on call this weekend. The hospital must need me back for the night shift." She lifts herself up from her chair and I match her gesture.

She pulls me into a hug, and it feels like it'll be one of our last. I want to soak in this moment, but I need to ask her about the eviction notice.

"Did you know we got an eviction notice?" I pull away from her and meet her eyes. No need to dance around the questions.

"About that, I got an email this morning." She holds my hands as she speaks. "What happened?" she questions.

"I guess it slipped my mind after the accident. I didn't even put it together. And all this time, I just totally freakin' spaced it. I'm so sorry. I'm gonna fix this," I try to reassure her, but really, I'm the one who needs reassurance. I know she paid her portion on time, there's no excuse for what I missed it. I got my paycheck and it's more than enough to cover my bills and more now.

"Well, I called them in the car on the way over here, offering to pay your half but they said it was already paid and the eviction notice was lifted." It takes me a moment to register what she's saying.

"It was paid?" I ask behind blinking eyes.

"That's what they said. Did you not pay it?" She drops my hands at my side as her phone rings. "It's work again, I better take this." I give her an understanding nod as she steps away to answer the call.

I definitely didn't pay it, but if Dakota didn't pay it, and I didn't pay it, then who did?

TWENTY-FOUR

Callan

I've ignored several calls from both of my parents. The way they've been hiding this massive secret for years and just expected me to be okay with it, doesn't sit right with me. If I'm honest, the only person I want to talk to about it is Sterling, but I'm still trying to process it myself.

For my entire life, I've always sympathized with my mom. Especially in the last decade and a half, she's had to deal with my dad's asshole tendencies and still continued to raise two children with a smile on her face. I never understood my dad's anger until my mom finally confessed the truth the other night, between sobs and apologies.

My dad isn't Virginia's dad.

My mom cheated and got pregnant with another man. And now I understand why the arrangements that were agreed upon have been put into place and why my sister has been acting the way she has. But it doesn't explain why my father treated me as if this whole time I wasn't his kid, instead of the other way around.

In a way, it makes me think a little differently of him. He had a reason to be angry the whole time. He wasn't required to stay with my mom or to raise Virginia as his own child, but he chose to take care of them both.

I don't let myself think about it too much. I throw my shit down on my office desk and close the door behind me. I know Sterling is already in, the light peeking from under her office door down the hall confirmed so. But I intend to stay in my office as long as it takes to shake my head into place.

My head is still reeling after our phenomenal night together. If I'm being honest, it's the best sex I've ever had and that scares the living shit out of me. I don't want to keep my distance, but I know I should because I don't know what comes next.

Suddenly, there's a knock at the door. My pulse quickens. I don't know if I can handle seeing Sterling right now. I know I wouldn't be able to keep my hands off her. Before I can respond to the knock, the door creaks open, but it's not who I was secretly hoping it would be.

"Mr. David." Cora sticks her head through the door and smiles at me with her big buggy eyes. The same eyes she's used time and time again, in an attempt to seduce me. But as I watch her slide into my office, all I can think about is Sterling bent over in my bed with *her* beautiful bedroom eyes as she calls me by the formality that Cora just used.

My dick nudges awake in my slacks just thinking about Sterling. It doesn't last long when Cora's shrill voice cuts in.

"You looked super stressed coming in today," she whines, "wanted to see if everything's okay?" I'm instantly annoyed. First of all, it's none of her business. Second, do I really look that bothered? I've never been the type of man to be readable. I keep my facial expressions in check.

"Cora, shouldn't you be working on something?" I snap, sounding more bitter than I intended, but I have so much pent-up frustration between my unexpected feelings for Sterling, and this breaking family news, stacked on top of all the work I need to get done. I feel like I'm losing control.

Cora doesn't respond. She simply backs up into the hallway, disappointment spread across her face. Her expression turns to disgust as she looks to her right. It's not until I see Sterling appear in the doorway that I understand what Cora is looking at.

"Can I come in?" Sterling gently moves past Cora and makes her way into the door frame as she knocks lightly on the door.

"Of course. Close the door please." I shift in my chair because even though my plan was to avoid her, I can't help the way my body reacts when I finally get to see her, and I've been thinking about her nonstop since she left my house yesterday.

She looks stunning in her outfit today. She's wearing a skintight black dress, probably not long enough to pass the dress code but I'm too mesmerized to even care. Her cleavage leaves just enough to the imagination. Her hair is in a high, sleek ponytail, straightened today instead of in its wavy allure. I can think of one way to put that ponytail to good use.

"Everything okay?" I ask, assuming there's something wrong from the expression on her face.

"I think so." Her tone is soft and unassured.

"What is it?"

"What happened after I left yesterday?" she asks as she pulls the chair out from the opposite side of me and sits, her dress sliding up her thighs.

I think to answer, but I can't control my thoughts. The truth is, she's all I can think about. Which is why I needed space. I originally told her we could only do this one time, but I can't think of a reason why we wouldn't continue this arrangement. She wants it, and so do I. *Bad.*

The truth is it scared the hell out of me. I tried to avoid the aftermath, which I'll admit, was pretty tyrannical of me. It's what I normally do after sex with other women. Of course, Sterling is not like other women, and I knew that from the beginning. I've always been able to move on quickly; not a single woman has ever had this kind of hold on me. I can't seem to focus on anything but how perfect she is and thoughts of what's hiding under that dress of hers. Even though she was on full display for me yesterday, every delicious inch of her body spread wide for me, waiting to be taken, it wasn't enough. I need more of her.

All of her.

In and out of the bedroom.

Instead of answering her question, I share a concern of my own hoping for a change in topic.

"Sterling, that dress is entirely too inappropriate for work."

She moves uncomfortably in her chair as her cheeks redden.

"I'm sorry, I thought I looked good in it." She pulls her bottom lip into her teeth and bites gently. She seems more confident today than I've seen her.

"Don't do that," I counter.

"Do what?" she asks. I can't tell if she knows what she's doing or if she's genuinely clueless.

"You know what," I challenge, rubbing my bottom lip with my finger. What has gotten into her, *into me?*

Sterling gets up from her chair and walks toward the door. She leans herself back into the door and crosses her arms behind her while she stares into my eyes.

"You didn't answer my question, Callan."

"You're right, I didn't."

"Well, why not?"

"I feel like your disregard for our professional dress code needs to be addressed first. It's a distraction." I try to remain as lowkey and steady as I can, knowing that everything inside of me is coming to life.

"A distraction to who?"

A few seconds pass, and I still don't respond.

"What was that you said to me the other night?" she sarcastically ponders. "Oh yeah. Use. Your. Words." she pronounces each word like a syllable as her lips curl into a flirty smirk.

"Sterling. I need you to head home and change out of that dress immediately. I can practically see your ass." I'm trying not to lose my cool but she's making it impossible not to. I can't tell if she's pissing me off by defying me or if I'm pissing myself off by denying what I really want.

"You cannot see my ass." She rolls her eyes.

"I can if you bend over."

"Well, good thing I'm not bent over then, Mr. David." The words slide off her tongue nefariously and it's the way that her top teeth meet her bottom lip as she says the V in my last name that sends me over the edge.

I stand up from my desk abruptly, wasting no time getting to her. She tenses when I reach her, as I place my hands against the door on either side of her head, a position we now know well.

Her breathing quickens.

"Are you trying to tempt me, Miss Cooper?" I plant my words like a heavy whisper over her lips as I stare into her eyes.

She leans into my embrace, reaching up until her lips are almost touching mine. "Why? Do you find me tempting?" Her question lingers on my lips but only for a second, as I pull her into me and kiss her deeply.

I need to taste her.

Her tongue takes no time to meet mine, her fingers finding their way into my hair. This kiss is angry, wet, and rough. Like we both have things we need to get off our chests, but we use each other instead.

"Hands on the desk. Now." I break away and step aside. Her breathing is sporadic as she walks over to the desk.

She looks at me with patient eyes.

"Turn around." I walk over to the desk and stand behind her as she faces the front of my desk and leans over it. I pull her flush against my body; my erection digs into her ass as she stifles a moan.

Sterling grinds her ass into my stomach, begging for friction and leaving her wanting as I lean down and suck on the delicate skin of her neck.

"Don't move," I command. I dip down and lightly run my fingers from her knee up to the hem of her dress. "You can't wear this here again."

I trace my hands along her collarbone, and she shivers under my touch. I lean over her, seeing her nipples harden beneath the fabric of her dress.

"No bra in the workplace?" I ask in a mock-scolding tone and she wiggles a little under my touch. "If my hand finds it way underneath your dress, what am I going to find, Sterling?" I tease, tracing my hand from the top to the bottom, reaching just to where it stops, a few inches above her knee.

"Guess you'll have to find out," she whispers.

Fuck.

What am I doing?

What is she doing to me?

But I can't stop. I don't want to. I want to take her right here and show her what she does to me.

I flip her over so that she now faces me. She leans back a little, arching over my desk. I grip her by the ass and flawlessly sit her on the desk. I pull the bottom of her dress up and bunch it up past her thighs, allowing it to pool at her waist.

I take my hands to the inside of her knees and spread her legs open, a moan escapes her lips as she watches me carefully and I'm shocked to see that she is wearing absolutely nothing under this dress.

"Sterling," I growl. I'm so turned on but at the same time, displeased with her. A sense of protection washes over me. It's a careless move. What if someone else accidentally got a peek?

What if we were in a meeting and she uncrossed her legs and someone else got to look at what's *mine*?

"Part of my job as your assistant is to make things easier for you. I was only trying to help," she deadpans but it's sexy as fuck.

I waste no time unbuckling my belt and pulling my pants down, setting my aching erection free. I take my length in my hands and drag it against her thigh, leaving traces of my precum glistening against her skin.

I lift her off the desk and flip her back around, making her gasp. I ensure her dress stays put as I trace my cock against the sweet flesh of her ass, pressing it against that tight, puckered, bud, teasing her there before lowering back down to her entrance.

"What are you doing to me, Sterling?" I wrap my hand around her ponytail and pull her head back as I lean in to graze my lips against her ear. "All I want to do is show you how obsessed I am with you. I want to worship every part of you, inside and out. So be a good girl, my little rose, and keep your hands on the desk. Don't move until I'm done." I use my tongue to trace the outside of her ear, and she writhes under my heat.

"Yes, sir," she pants heavily as she presses her ass against me. I push her forward, pressing her stomach against the desk as I position myself behind her. I place my tip against her entrance and push slightly.

Sterling's moans fill the room and I yank her ponytail up so I can cover her mouth with my hand.

"You're going to have to be really quiet, sweetheart. Wouldn't want anyone to hear their boss fucking his assistant in his office, now, would we?" Sterling shakes her head in my hand.

I use the other hand to grip her hip and pull her onto me, as she groans into my hand, her muffled cries still seem so loud. But it only makes me thrust harder, faster. She's gripping the table as she bounces against me, each thrust going deeper than the last.

It doesn't take long before her orgasm reaches her, and I release my grip to help push her over the edge; my finger finding her clit and circling it relentlessly.

"Jesus, Sterling," I whisper in her ear. Her breathy moans are still covered by my hand. I unload inside of her and her tight pussy squeezes around me as I come. I find myself growling into her neck as the last of my cum spills into her.

"You're so goddamn unreal." My words barely make their way out as we both try to catch our breath. She clamps her teeth into the skin of my hand, biting me hard as she finishes riding out her orgasm. And fuck if that doesn't make me want to take her again.

But suddenly, there's a knock at my door making both of us jump at the same time. I pull up my pants and try to straighten my hair. I hear the doorknob jiggle but to my surprise the door is locked. Sterling must have locked it behind her when she backed up against it earlier. *Clever girl.*

"Just a moment," I holler as I help Sterling's dress back down.

"Callan." My name escapes in a breathless pant. I lower my lips onto hers and give her a sincere kiss before I answer.

"Yes?"

"Your cum is dripping down my leg," she whispers.

I turn her around to face me, I pull my finger under her dress and find the wetness she's referring to. I swipe the liquid off her thigh and put my finger up to her lips. She willingly opens her mouth for me and sucks my pleasure off of my finger. Her eyes are wide and wanting and the sexiest moan escapes her lips as I slide my finger out.

"That's what you get for not wearing any panties, Miss Cooper. Don't let it happen again," I tease before walking over to the door and unlocking it.

"I'll debrief with you after lunch," I say to Sterling as a cover, as she looks past me and walks into the hallway. Jax is waiting on the other side with a knowing look.

"What's up, Jax?" Annoyed, I let him in.

"Dude, please tell me you didn't..." he assumes, but I don't confirm or deny. "Okay, none of my business." He put his hands up in front of him as I situate myself back at my desk.

"Listen, I wanted to talk to you about some future plans here. Specifically, my future." I see the look on Jax's face and it's a serious one. So, I motion for him to sit.

"Talk to me."

"Well, honestly man, I'm not sure I see a future here. I think my time is up." Jax is usually insouciant and jaunty. So, it throws me off guard when he speaks earnestly. I try to focus on what he's saying but I'm interrupted by a text from Sterling.

> I forgot to ask you something... you don't happen to know who paid off my lease, do you?

TWENTY-FIVE

Sterling

There's a confidence in my step that I've conjured up since meeting Callan. Or more so since we've given in to the temptation of us.

I like the way he makes me feel. And even though he promised only once, I'm pleased that he's decided that we can still have fun and be professional at the same time.

The last three days have been just that, sometimes we debrief for meetings, sometimes we have sex on his desk. But I haven't seen him since Thursday night; I asked for Friday off and my weekend has been filled with helping Dakota pack for her big move back home. I'm trying to spend as much time as I possibly can with her. Callan offered to help but I politely declined, knowing I wanted to spend every second possible with Dakota without distractions. Because let's be honest...Callan is a distraction.

"I can't believe he did that for you," she explains breathlessly as she tries to load a box into the back of the truck.

"I know. I just don't know how I feel about it," I admit. Buying me a fancy dress to wear to a mandatory business event was one thing, business expense and all. But straight up paying my rent?

"Honestly, I'm surprised he hasn't bought you a car yet."

I load the last box into the back of the moving truck as Dakota comes from behind me to close the gate. There's a look in her eye that I haven't seen before. One of sadness but also excitement. I can tell she's nervous to make this move, but I know it'll be good for her.

"That would be something, wouldn't it?" We share a little laugh.

"So what's the big deal about tomorrow night?"

"Not a big deal, but it's his birthday and we're going to some fancy restaurant. I feel like everything I do with this man is out of my comfort zone." I admit. "And honestly, he went from telling me we can only dip our toes into this whole "one night of pleasure thing" thing, but he's definitely not sticking to his own rules. I'm glad he stopped being an asshole about it, but I'm also a bit nervous."

"Why?" She blows a strand of her hair out of her sweaty face.

"I don't know. You know me, always overthinking. I just don't want to disappoint him and catch feelings."

"That's got to be refreshing though, no?" Dakota slides me a smirk as she sends a quick text message, presumably to Asher.

"It is, it's just different." I shrug my shoulders.

"Well, have you ever considered that maybe he's already caught feelings?" She licks her lips, lowering another box.

"That's crazy," I reply. But really...it's not. But I think that's what makes me nervous. I'm not sure I'd know how to handle that.

"Besides, just because we fuck sometimes doesn't mean we still really know each other," I add.

"That's what this dinner is for."

"No, this dinner is because his family couldn't make it, and I offered to take their place." I pick up another box, trying to not trip off the sidewalk.

"To get to know him better." Her sarcastic tone makes me laugh, she's relentless.

The silence sits between us for only a few moments as we come to the realization that this is goodbye.

"I can't believe this is happening," she tells me, leaning down for her water bottle.

"You'll call me every day?" I ask, looking into the sunset lowering behind the mountains, hues of purples and oranges layering the barely-there clouds.

"We'll never lose touch. I promise. I just hope I'm doing the right thing."

We sit down next to each other on the curb of the sidewalk just out front of our apartment complex. I look to my left and can barely see Callan's building in the distance touching the sky in all its luxurious glory. I wonder if he's there now.

Dakota leans over and rests her head onto my shoulder.

"I have to be honest; I'm pretty pissed off at Asher." I know it's a tough topic for her, but I can't seem to understand how someone's fiancé couldn't even spare a couple of hours to help pack.

"It is what it is." She picks her head back up. "He'll at least drive me to the airport." She waves off nonchalantly. "But while we're on the subject of being pissed off at men, I need to tell you something about Callan. And I know this might not be the best timing, but it never is these days."

"Uh, oh." I turn to face her on the sidewalk.

"Remember the night of my party? Well, I know Callan swooped in and rescued you, when you were pretty drunk. I saw him taking you out of Asher's house." Dakota takes a deep breath, but I'm not sure why she's telling me this, when I was there to experience it.

"Okay?" I reach over and push strands of her fiery hair behind her ear, trying to busy myself from worrying.

"Well, just a few moments before that...I saw him in the kitchen." I'm not sure why, but my eyes start to prick with tears. I can tell this isn't going down the road I want it to go down, the one with rainbows and sunshine and daisy-lined dirt drives.

"One minute he was alone, walking through the kitchen. The next thing I know, he's up against the fridge with another girl's lips on his. I didn't recognize the girl and I wasn't sure how long they'd been that way because I was bumped by Asher's friend and when I regained balance, he was gone, and she was on the floor crying." Dakota sucks in a shaky breath as she squeezes my hand. The lone tear falls before I have time to comprehend what I'm being told.

"What are you saying, Dakota?"

"Well, I know for sure I saw them kiss. After that, I'm not sure. But someone told me that after they kissed, they got into an argument, and he hit her."

I feel like the sidewalk is being pulled apart right out from under me, taking me down with it. The cracks getting bigger until I slip right in between. My whole body goes numb. He wouldn't do that...would he?

But then again, we weren't together. We *still* aren't together. But that doesn't make this hurt any less.

"Listen, babe. I didn't mean to spring this on you. I wanted to tell you earlier but then we got into that fight. Who knows if that's how it really went down, but I know what I saw and needed to let you know, regardless." I can tell Dakota is just trying to do the right thing as my best friend, with no ill-intention. She's just looking out for me.

"Thank you, Dakota. I'll, um...I don't really know what to say. I'll keep my eyes open."

She doesn't know that Callan and I have already crossed the line, further than either of us anticipated. Multiple times. I'm not sure how to handle this news, but I'm going to hold it close for now.

"I just have to make sure you're being treated right. I don't know much about Callan other than what I've heard, and I know that right now he makes you happy. I know you'll make the decision that's right for you, Sterls."

I lean on her shoulder now, grateful to have such a supportive friend.

"Okay, before I go, there is one more thing I need to ask you." She drags out the words in a singsong as she pushes up off the sidewalk and pulls me up with her.

"What is it?" I ask, wiping the tears from my eyes.

Dakota turns around and walks over to the cab of the truck. She opens the door and pulls out a shiny gold gift bag with navy blue ribbons hanging from the straps.

She walks back over and holds it out to me.

"What's this?" I question as I take the bag from her hands.

She grabs onto one of my hands and smiles the biggest smile I've maybe ever seen.

"Well, it's probably way in the future and who knows if it'll even still happen, and just know that I wanted to ask you a different way, but..." she rambles on for a few seconds before I stop her.

"What is it?" I shake her shoulders as she giggles.

"Open it!"

One by one, I pull them from the bag. My go-to vanilla scented lotion, a new *Breakfast Club* t-shirt, dark chocolates and a clear wine glass with my name etched on the side in rose-gold lettering.

"Dakota Jade." I look up at her with new tears forming in the corner of my eyes.

"Will you be my maid of honor?" she asks, the question ringing in my ears.

"Really?" I'm giddy, rocking back on my feet and my smile stretches across my face. I place the glass back in the bag and set it down. I'm overwhelmed by excitement and gratitude for her.

"I wouldn't want anyone else there by my side!" We hug each other one last time.

"Of course! I'd love to!" I think of how far my friendship with her has come. From meeting for the first time at our coffee shop job, to all of the laughs and tears we've shared in between. Dakota is an amazing friend and I know she's going to make an incredible wife one day.

"I love you," she says as she pulls away from my embrace.

"I love you, too."

Callan waits for me in his car, in the parking lot of my complex. I come down the stairs and see him sitting in the driver's seat of his fancy red car. He jumps out and meets me at the passenger door. I get a whiff of his cologne, woodsy with a hint of peppermint. It intoxicates me and I already want this dinner to be over so we can go straight to bed.

"Happy birthday," I say as I climb into the car.

"You don't have to do this," he says to me as he closes his door shut and pushes the start button.

"I know, but I don't mind." I buckle my safety belt.

Callan had explained to me that he attends dinner at the same restaurant every year for his birthday with his family, but this year they had to cancel. He said he was going to skip out on it all together, but when I saw the disappointment in his eyes my dumbass spoke up, involuntarily as usual, and offered to go with him. I know the feeling of family bailing on you.

But as I look over at Callan now, he looks slightly uncomfortable. His gaze is hard and barely focused as he clips his seat belt in place. Maybe I misread his reaction, maybe he wasn't disappointed.

"Oh, crap," I whisper. "You don't want me to go do you? This is too much isn't it?"

"What?"

"I'm sorry." I unbuckle and start gathering up my purse. "I just kind of invited myself. I'm sorry. I don't have to go." My cheeks feel hot and red.

Callan and I have this undeniable attraction towards each other, and I try not to overthink things when it comes to whatever is going on between us. Instead, I try to focus on being in the moment, feeling the freedom of being sexual with someone, and not feel bad about it. It's addictive.

Though inevitably, every high comes with a low. Callan doesn't do relationships; he's said it more than once. I like to believe that I'm okay with that, but I can't help but notice how full my heart feels when I'm around him. It's getting harder to not want him, to not want more. And the more time we spend together, the more my feelings grow.

Do we keep this a secret?

Am I even allowed to go to a personal dinner with him?

What are the rules to fucking your boss?

Oh yeah...don't.

I also can't get what Dakota said to me out of my head. He kissed another girl. Then hit her. At least that's what she heard. I mean, I really don't think he would do that. And I'm not sure how, or if I'm even going to say anything about it. This is all unfamiliar territory to me.

"Sterling." He grabs my wrist, obviously seeing me run circles in my brain. "Don't overthink this. Sure, this is new to me as well, but I invited you because I want you to come. I just don't want you to feel obligated is all." He brings his fingers up to my face to swipe a strand of my hair back into place.

I relax a little under his touch.

"Sorry," I say, as I sigh in relief.

"And you need to stop apologizing for everything." He pulls the car out of the parking lot.

"Sorry," I say again, and he laughs.

"Why couldn't your parents make it again?" I ask as we each scan our menus.

Callan sits across from me in the dimly lit restaurant. I can't believe how hot he looks. His deep chestnut hair perfectly accents his warm hazel eyes. Tonight, he's wearing a dark green suit with a cream-colored button up underneath, paired with a dark purple tie. Every day, Callan looks like he's dressed to be someone's best man, or the groom himself; the image sends thoughts of marriage to my head.

I've spent more time with him than I have any other man before and yet it's still way too early to even think about the idea of getting married, but I can't control the way my feelings grow when I'm around him. It's dangerous to say the least.

He once told me he wasn't a good man, but I am finding it so hard to understand why, when I can clearly see how perfect he is. This man runs a multi-billion-dollar company, treats his employees, business partners, and clients with the utmost respect and composed professionalism. He definitely treats his pretty little assistant the best.

"Sterling?" Callan's voice catches me off guard.

"I'm sorry, what did you say?"

"You asked me about my parents."

"Right." I pull my attention back to him.

He looks like he's contemplating. Before he can form the words to explain, I decide to chime in, hoping to make him feel more comfortable.

"I'm not sure what happened but I know all-too-well the shit shows that can ensue when it comes to family." I take a deep breath, knowing I'm about to share, for the first time, the one thing I've tried to avoid since leaving home.

"My dad left me and my family several years ago. He had an affair, pretty much decided that this other woman was more important than his wife and kids," I start. Sometimes talking about it hurts, but I know holding it in can only make things worse. "My mom was struggling mentally, and he decided that cheating was the only way out, instead of being there for her and supporting her."

"I'm so sorry, Sterling," he whispers.

"When he left, my mom didn't handle it very well. Most nights she'd drunkenly stumble through the door after two a.m. and sleep past noon the next day. It got to the point where she stopped paying bills and buying groceries. I tried to look after her, but I was only in high school at the time. I didn't know how to be a mom for my mom, and eventually it became too much. As soon as I turned eighteen, I left."

I'm surprised by the tear gliding down my cheek. It happened so long ago, yet it still affects me to this day. Seeing my parents drift apart, eventually leading everyone to heartache, was the hardest thing I've ever experienced. It's something I've never taken the time to process because it has always been too painful. I'll never understand why my dad chose this other woman over his entire family. Or why my mom chose alcohol over me and my brother. Or how my brother chose to deal with it differently than I did.

"Leaving was the most painful part, even though I knew it was the right choice. I love my mom so incredibly much and I never wanted her or Graham to think my leaving meant that that love went away. I tried to reach out after I left, but they never responded. I was hoping they'd understand, but they couldn't, and I had to be okay with that. I wasn't prepared to give up my life, like my brother Graham had to, to look after the mother I didn't even recognize anymore."

Callan gives a few moments of silence, but never breaks the soft eye contact he's maintained while I've shared my story. He gently reaches out his hand to hold mine, giving a soft squeeze. His gesture says a million words at once and eases all the tension I'd been holding onto

"Where is she now?" he asks.

"Honestly, I don't know. Last I heard, Graham moved them both to Utah for a new job opportunity. I don't even know if she's doing any better. She said some really hurtful things to me the day I left.

She wasn't the mom I remembered or needed." Tears continue stinging in the corners of my eyes.

"Have you ever wondered if she said those hurtful things because you choosing to leave triggered something in her?" Callan's words don't quite sit right with me as I attempt to register what he's trying to say.

"What do you mean?" I try to contain the ping of anger brought on by his question.

"I mean, your dad left because your mom's mental health was deteriorating, right? Well, maybe all of those feelings came flooding back for her when you left. Maybe it brought back bad memories. I'm sure she didn't mean to say those harsh things to you." I can tell Callan is trying to help, trying to understand my situation. But I don't like the way he's going about it.

"I'm nothing like my father," I say behind clenched teeth.

"I didn't say you were, I just..."

Is he trying to be a dick?

He takes a deep breath.

"I didn't mean it like that, Sterling, I'm sorry I even opened my mouth." I can't even look in his eyes. Everything about that time floods me with memories, feelings, finger-pointing, the long nights spent awake hearing my mom cry. It was an awful time for me. One I really don't want to relive, and especially don't want to be blamed for.

I was hoping that my vulnerability would make Callan comfortable enough to share his own story. I wasn't expecting him to psychoanalyze my trauma and side with my mom after the way she has hurt me.

"It's hard enough for me to open up about this kind of stuff. The last thing I need is for someone to tell me that my feelings are invalid," I whisper-shout as I push myself out from the table.

"Sterling, wait." Callan reaches for my wrist. "Please, stay. I really didn't mean for any of what I said to come out the way it did."

I watch him with cautious eyes, his posture is sorrowful as he waits for me to respond. I notice a few people at other tables are watching us, and I'm suddenly embarrassed by my reaction.

"Maybe I overreacted," I reply gingerly as I sit back down in my seat. "I wanna be honest with you about these things Callan. Some people just have unresolved trauma that maybe they aren't necessarily trying to figure out, but talking about it helps."

"I don't usually know how to converse with people when it comes to emotional stuff like this, I'll admit that much. I was always taught to show and feel no emotion. And just know that I'm not defending your mom, or your dad, or anyone for that matter."

I want you to defend me, I want to say, but the idea is ridiculous because we're just starting to dive in to a deeper territory here.

"But I just thought that maybe there might be a reason why your mom acted the way she did, just as you had a reason to make the choices you did. That's all."

Callan speaks with such conviction, maybe even from experience. A side I've never seen from him. And here I am practically screaming at him – on his birthday – about how he can't possibly know what it feels like to have deep-rooted issues. I can tell he's being genuine when he says he's learning from me, because I'm learning from him, too.

Maybe he's right. Maybe I've been the one so caught up in my own world, my own sorrows, my own need for happiness, that I didn't even take the time to stop and figure out why my mom acted the way she did when I decided to leave.

My entire personality changes when I'm around this man. But the more time I spend with him, I realize that it's because I'm just learning how to find myself. Be my true self. Allowing myself to go through the motions of everything that I felt like I had to suppress because I never felt good enough to be myself.

"You're right, and I'm sorry for getting angry with you."

"What did I tell you about apologizing too much, Sterling?" he jokes, his genuine smile making my body crave in the best way possible. "You're allowed to feel the way you do. You have those emotions for a reason and they're yours to feel." He sits back looking almost shocked at his own words and trust me...me too. *Who is the man?* Cuz it's not the Callan I met nearly a month ago.

But he's being hypocritical.

"What about you, then?" I ask, letting my body loosen a little as I lean back into my chair, allowing this conversation to grow between the two of us.

"What about me?"

"You said you were taught to live without emotions and feelings. But right now, it doesn't sound like that. It sounds like you have this whole *emotions* thing down to a science. So, why don't you follow your own advice?"

I can see him trying to form the words in his head, as his pupils dilate and darken.

"Come on. I shared my screwed-up family trauma with you. Spill." I take a sip of my wine, watching him with curious eyes.

"Well, for starters, my dad is the absolute fucking worst." We both laugh. I love seeing this relaxed, yet sincere version of Callan. "Growing up, he was always so strict with me, and only me. I hated it when my mom left for work because it meant I was stuck with him. When my sister was born, I'd thought, *Great. Now he'll leave me alone and pick on her.* But I was wrong. It felt like he only got harder on me from there."

"That must've been so hard," I empathize, and I swear I see a small ocean pool in his eyes, like this is the first time anyone has taken the time to really listen. He nods softly and sucks in a deep breath.

"It really fucking sucked. But then I felt like a total asshole for hating him when he told me he has cancer. It was like, the dam holding back all of my emotions broke open and flooded my mind all at once. It enraged me at first and it's not just about the way he has mistreated me. He mistreated my mom even worse."

"What do you mean?" Callan swallows hard at my question. I gauge that he doesn't really want to explain, so I wait for him with patient eyes and a small understanding smile.

"I mean, for as long as I can remember, he's treated her like anything but his wife. Like a roommate. He was more devoted to his work than he ever was to her. And last week, we went over his last will and testament. He pretty much cut her out of it, leaving everything to me and my little sister."

"That's why you wanted to bid on that vacation for her," I mumble under my breath, slowly putting the pieces together.

"My mom cheated on my dad." Callan's tone is stiff. I can tell he's still struggling to process what he just said out loud.

"Callan, I'm so sorry."

"She must've felt so neglected, her husband pouring every ounce of his energy into his work, leaving nothing for her. So, she looked for comfort in another man's arms." Callan fidgets with his wine glass, and a look of pain crosses his face. I've never seen him so disheveled in this way, vulnerable and on edge.

"Well, obviously they worked it out right? I mean, they're still together." I try to assure him.

"She got pregnant during her affair."

Suddenly, I'm understanding more of his story. The betrayal and the lies. The hurt he must have endured, idolizing his mom, while she was living a secret life of her own.

"Callan, I had no idea that you were going through any of this."

"How could you have? I don't like to show these parts of my life to anyone." He runs his hands through his hair, slightly disturbing the way his waves were slicked back.

"My dad has treated her the way he has, because of her betrayal. He wanted to leave, but he stayed for us. Me and my sister. Virginia found out months ago, when she was looking for her birth certificate for cheer camp and saw that there was no name under *father*. I was so confused when she started treating my mom so disrespectfully, but my mom always explained it away as 'classic teenage behavior.' They were all keeping this massive secret from me."

He takes a beat, trying to make sense of what he wants to say next.

There's no way I can deny the way I feel for him in this moment. I really care for this man. When I look at him, I see someone who is just as broken as I am. Fragile. He's just faking it because he has to.

I now understand why he is the way he is. Why he exudes power and passion in everything he does. Why he claims dominance and pride all while being closed-off and unavailable. It's because he's just as afraid as I am that he's not good enough. But he is, he's more than enough for me.

Callan goes on to explain that he feels like he misjudged his dad. He now understands why his dad was angry for so many years and why his mom stuck around anyway. She could have left, and he could have left, too. But they came to an agreement to make the family work.

"I don't want to be like my dad. But I also fear that if I let anyone in, I'd experience the pain he felt. I think it's why I stay away from feeling shit in general." His admission is a deep one, an eye-opening one.

"It's not good to keep it all bottled up, Callan."

"That's why I'm starting with you, Sterling." Something pulls at my heart strings. But I try not to overthink that statement. I don't want to ruin this moment.

It all makes sense. But I hate knowing he's living his life this way. No one deserves to feel like they can't be trusted, or like they're not good enough to be treated with love and care.

Suddenly, it hits me. That's the same way I feel.

Callan hands a credit card to the waiter as we agree we're ready to get out of here. Having shared so much between the both of us, I'm desperate for a different kind of release.

"I have to use the ladies' room, first." I get up and head toward the hall.

I wonder if he feels it like I do. Like it could be more than sex. I wonder if he'll want more with me. He's already broken his rule, *only once.*

As I enter the bathroom, I take a much-needed deep breath, allowing myself to let go of all the anger, sadness, and nervousness I was feeling over the last hour and a half.

I step out of the stall and toward the sink to wash my hands, when I'm startled by a woman's voice coming from behind me.

"Has he fucked you yet?" I'm greeted with a snarky voice. I'm not one hundred percent sure she's talking to me, but we're the only ones in here.

I peek up from the sink and look into the mirror, my eyes meeting her reflection. She has long black hair and beady brown eyes. She's wearing a black button-down blouse with the restaurant's logo embroidered on her shirt pocket. She's leaning up against the wall directly behind me with her arms crossed and one foot holding her balance as the other is kicked up behind her.

"Excuse me?" I question quietly, drying my hands on a paper towel to keep myself busy from turning to face her.

"Callan. I saw you with him. God, he looks fucking sexy tonight, doesn't he?" She looks at me up and down.

"Do I know you?"

"You don't, but Cal does. We've fucked a couple of times. Usually, right where you're standing." She points behind me and laughs a little under her breath as she notices how uncomfortable I am. I don't know what to say. I pretend I'm still drying my hands on the same used paper towel because I don't want to face her to throw it away.

"I'm guessing you're the reason why he's not tearing my clothes off right now." She moves closer to me. Either she's crazy or I'm missing something.

"He usually likes a little role-play with his dominance. Adds a little sugar to the spice." She brings her index finger to her lips and tilts her head as if thinking about something. "Just kidding. No sugar, all spice." She closes her eyes as her head falls back into laughter, I take this as my opportunity to escape, turning quickly toward the door.

"Does he make you beg like he makes me beg?" She jumps at me, not violently, but enough to stop me in my tracks, backing me up against the counter.

Now we're face to face as someone enters the bathroom, a mom and her toddler son.

"Does he bend you over and fuck you *hard*? God, I like it like that." I'm so disgusted, my skin crawls at the way she talks about Callan.

Still, I don't respond or move. I'm trapped between her and the counter.

I don't want to believe that Callan fucks this girl in this bathroom. I don't want to imagine him fucking her, or anyone else, ever.

But I can't act like I didn't have some inclination of what he meant when he said he likes it rough, that he uses women, and there are rules.

"Did you know that today is his birthday? He likes rough sex on his birthday. Hope you're prepared." Her tone is devious. I suddenly feel ill. "Or maybe I'll go out there and get things started, just like I have, every year before." Her laugh is evil, like she knows just what kind of game she's playing.

I can't breathe. Knowing his name is one thing, he's Callan David. Even Dakota knew of him before I did. But knowing his birthday...

Was he going to fuck her tonight?

Even after all that we shared with each other?

Maybe that's why he didn't want me to come.

Before I give her another chance to speak, I push past her, glancing at her name tag as I go, *Desiree.*

I rush out into the hall, stopping right before I enter the restaurant's main dining room. I look over and Callan is still sitting at the table, the waiter handing the check back over. I watch him sign it and all I can think about is how he might have pulled her ponytail the way he pulled mine in his office. How he's come here every year and fucked her in that bathroom.

Suddenly, I'm brought back to what Dakota told me, about Callan and the girl at her party.

It's true, it *has* to be true.

Can I even be mad? I don't know, but I do know that I'm hurt.

My feet start to move beneath me like I'm walking on hot rocks. I push my way through the waiters, and I accidentally bump into one with a tray full of food.

"I'm so sorry," I say as I frantically try to get out of the way. Glass sounding as it crashes to the floor, and everyone stares at me as I run toward the exit.

"Sterling!" I hear a familiar voice in the background, but I don't need to look back to know it's Callan's.

My whole body floods with fury and humiliation. Desiree's words buzz in my ears, Dakota's story layered on top. My eyes begin to water against my will. I know I shouldn't have expectations here and I know that I might be overreacting, but my heart is telling me to run.

TWENTY-SIX

Callan

What could have possibly happened that would've given her a reason to run out of the restaurant

We were having an amazing conversation just minutes ago. Some deep shit I would never catch myself dead speaking to another human. But I trust her. It's different with her. But part of me wonders if she realizes it's a mistake to get involved with someone like me and is trying to run away from everything we just put out in front of us.

I chase after her outside, looking around to see where she could have gone. I drove her here so I know she couldn't have gotten far. I try to remain calm as I walk over to the valet and ask for my car keys, handing him a hundred as I shake his hand.

He pulls the McLaren around a few minutes later, but still no sign of Sterling. There's a bus stop across the street but as I scan around, I see no sign of her.

I stop for a second and take a breath. Everything from our conversation still sits inside of me heavily, like I swallowed a dumbbell. As I start to relive the moments we shared over the last couple of hours, I hear a small, muffled cry coming from around the corner.

I ask the valet to hold the car for a few minutes, passing him another hundred as I walk toward the back alley of the restaurant. She's sitting with her back against the brick of the building with her knees pulled into her chest, burying her face into the palms of her hands.

I take a minute to prepare myself, not knowing what to expect, but I approach her delicately.

"Sterling, what's wrong?" I adjust my slacks to give me room to lean down and match her level, reaching my hand out to touch her elbow.

"Don't touch me!" she shouts. She swats her hand at me, and I'm thrown off balance, catching myself right before I fall on my ass. I stand back up and study her face, it's tear-stricken and red. Her mascara is streaming down her cheeks in waves of black.

"Was it something I said?"

"Try something you *did*," she snaps at me.

She steadies herself to get up from her crouching position and dusts her palms off on her blue velvet dress, leaving a light gray residue behind.

"I can't fix it if I don't know what's broken."

"Broken, is that what you think of me? I'm broken?"

"God, Sterling don't be ridiculous, of course not."

"Don't act like you weren't going to fuck that pretty little waitress in there. Is she why you didn't want me to come?" She shoves past me after the last word leaves her mouth.

I stay in my position, dumbfounded, and confused. I slowly turn around to face her and she's standing in the alley with her arms crossed firmly.

"Desiree," she adds. "Sound familiar?"

Desiree.

God damnit.

How could I be so stupid?

"Sterling, please let me explain." I reach for her hand, but she swings it around and swats me away.

"No!" Her face is red, and worry overcomes me as I can only imagine what Desiree could have said to her.

This is why I don't get involved with women who seek attachment. Though I never anticipated I'd be here with Sterling and that some crazy ex-fling of mine could have the potential to ruin it.

"You know what?" She runs her fingers through her golden, wavy hair before wiping her face free of mascara and tears.

I wait for her to finish, wait for her to speak. But I don't expect the next words to leave her mouth.

"You and I, this stops here." Sterling's reddened eyes meet mine. "It was fun while it lasted, Callan. But I can't trust myself to not feel anything for you. And this is getting too real, too fast and that only leads to heartbreak." She pulls out her phone.

"What are you doing?" I question, feeling a few drops of rain fall from the sky.

"Requesting a ride. This was a mistake." Her tone is sharp as glass as she lashes out at me.

"Sterling, can we please just talk about this? This is all just a misunderstanding. Let me take you home." I don't know how to explain this to her, because I never imagined myself in a situation where I would ever need to.

"Callan, there's nothing to explain." She looks up from her phone at me and takes a deep breath. "You don't do relationships. You're a big boy. You can fuck whoever who want, whenever you want. I know that you have a past, but I just don't think I can do this casually anymore." I'm surprised to feel hurt by her words. I know she's trying to downplay how she really feels. Feelings that she doesn't think she can have because I made her believe this could only happen once.

And then it happened *more than once.*

On my bed.

In my office.

This is all my fault. I never wanted to string Sterling along. She doesn't deserve this.

I knew it from the moment I touched her, I knew how fucking real this was. I let my obsession for her get out of control and now, she's hurt, because of me. And this is exactly what I wanted to avoid.

"Were you going to fuck her tonight?" She sounds so broken. *I did that to her.*

The lack of trust she has in me hurts. I wish she knew that I would never do that to her, she's all I think about morning to night.

"Sterling, I haven't seen her since last year." I'm defensive, I hate that I have to explain this to her, that she even *needs* the explanation.

"That's not what I asked," she demands.

"No, Sterling." I'm short with my answer. I want this night to be over. Or to start over completely so I could tell Sterling to avoid delusional Desiree. But part of me realizes Sterling is right. The connection between us is coming too close, and we're both going to continue getting hurt if we carry on.

"Why even bring me here?" I know what she wants to ask me. *..why even bring me here if you were just going to fuck that waitress?*

But I wasn't even thinking about anyone else tonight. All I ever think about is Sterling.

"She means nothing to me. I honestly forgot about her completely, let alone the fact that she works here. If I had remembered or was even worried in the slightest that this would have happened, I would have never brought you here." I try to be sincere with my words, but I also don't want her to latch on to anything that will upset her more or give her hope otherwise.

She takes deep breaths as she watches me carefully. Her sadness begins to fall from her face. I find this the perfect opportunity to let her down gently.

"Sterling," I whisper to her as she wraps her arms around herself. I can tell she's cold, so I take off my suit jacket and lay it over her shoulders.

"Listen, I told you I have some demons I'm not proud of. And the last thing I want to do is hurt you." I shock myself at how mature I sound. I've never had to end things with someone in this way, especially not with someone who I have feelings for.

Did I just admit that to myself?

I have feelings for Sterling.

Of course, I do.

How could I not?

The time we've spent together may not seem like a lot to someone looking in from the outside, but it feels real and genuine. And different. When you know, you know.

Sterling is real.

But if that's not more of a reason to break this off, I don't know what is. Suddenly I'm stuck with the realization that Sterling might not be the only one who could get hurt here.

"Maybe you're right, this needs to end here," I finish, trying to search her face for any reason *not* to end this. But all I see is a broken heart when I look at her. And that hurts me more than anything.

"Unbelievable," she breathes. "I can't believe you, Callan. You know what, fine. You're probably right. This was never going to work anyway."

She turns to leave but stops in her tracks and faces me again.

"You know, I thought for a brief second that things could be different with you. I thought you could be good for me. I guess I was wrong."

"Wait!" I reach for her as she leaves again, and I'm immediately irritated with myself. I am unbelievable. I'm fucking with her feelings and it probably doesn't feel good to her either.

This girl drives me insane, and I can't seem to make up my mind. Do I let her stay and risk hurting her, risk getting hurt myself? Or do I let her walk away and risk regretting not giving whatever this is a shot?

I remember what she said earlier at the table. About me taking my own advice.

"Hear me out, Sterling." I lead her back over to the brick wall of the building, away from any prying eyes.

"I need your full honesty right now. I can handle the fact that you've slept with other women before me. I'm not naïve to the fact that you're a wanted man, Callan. But I need to know the truth..." Her lashes feather over her rosy cheeks as she breathes in, shivering.

"Ask me anything."

"At Dakota's party, when you came to pick me up. Dakota said you kissed another girl."

"What?"

"Is that true, Callan?"

"Sterling, I-"

"No. I need an honest answer. Did you kiss some girl at her party before you came up to the room to take me home?" I feel the accusation hit me like a semi-truck. I can see the worry in her eyes, that I'm some kind of player. And truth be told, I am...*was*. I was that way. But Sterling changed that. Still, I need to figure out a way to explain this to her if I want a real shot at this. I need her to believe me.

"That's why your friend glared at me..." I realize she must have seen what happened between Stephanie and me. But she obviously didn't see the whole thing play out.

"Callan, please."

"No. I didn't willingly kiss anyone. That girl is another girl I used to fuck around with." Sterling cringes at my admission. "Just once. But she found me at the party and threw herself on me."

"And then you hit her?" Her tone sours when she asks me this and I know immediately that everything was relayed to her out of context.

"God, no, Sterling. I didn't hit her. She forced herself on me, she *bit* me, so I pushed her off. She basically threw a temper tantrum when she stumbled backwards and hit the floor. I swear I'd never lay my hands on a woman like that." I'm angry that this information made its way to her the way it did. False and accusing.

"Someone said they-"

"I don't give a fuck what anyone *said* they saw. You believe me or you don't. I didn't hit that girl. And I haven't been with anyone else since the day I met you." I close the space between us, lift her chin up so that her eyes can't escape mine. The fucking power this girl has over me consumes my whole being as I try to prove to her that I have never wanted anything more than I want her.

"Let's be honest, Callan. You've said it yourself, this is never going to work." Her tone is cold and pained as her words whisper over my thumb gently grazing the supple skin of her bottom lip.

"This was never going to work because I didn't want it to," I explain, letting go of her chin to take a step back. Her body shifts uncomfortably against the brick wall. "I did warn you, Sterling. I gave you a chance to run. But you insisted that you like playing with fire. I only gave you what you asked for. I told you this was a bad idea." I look into her eyes to see if she's even listening to me, rage taking over in passionate waves as I desperately try to make this girl understand. She had a chance to back out. And she chose not to. So now, she's mine. I've made up my mind.

"I don't like being told what I can and can't have. I know what I want. But you told me this could only be a one-time thing and I was okay with that. You made me believe I was another hit and run. But I don't believe that now. I know there's something deeper here."

"Then what do you want? Right now, what do you want, Sterling?"

"I'm not sure, I think I want this. But-"

"Well, I know what I want. I want you. All of you. All. To. Myself." I grab her face and hold it in my hand, swiping my thumb eagerly at the curve of her soft, bottom lip wanting to take it in between my teeth as my other fingers press against the sensitive skin under her earlobes, creating the slightest bit of pressure.

"I don't know, Callan." The look of defeat spreading across her delicate face deflates me inside. I know I did this to her, I played with her emotions and allowed this to go as far as it did. "It hurt, hearing that girl say things about you that-"

"Fuck this." I pull her into me and crash my mouth onto hers. I kiss her with so much force, so much passion, that it hurts to know she could let go and walk away.

But she doesn't.

She tugs at my hair with her fingers, pulling me in closer as her tongue slips its way into my mouth. I groan as she deepens the kiss, rough then soft.

All-consuming.

I pull away first, feeling too much all at once as I look into her eyes. I can sense that she feels the same way I do, *claimed.*

I swallow down the feeling building in my throat, trying to control my own emotions.

I see the war in her eyes as I rest my hand on either side of her head against the brick wall she's backed into. We both unloaded a lot of personal stuff earlier, and I'll admit, it felt really nice to be able to let those feelings out, especially with her. I'm not ready to let that go.

I look at her once bright blue eyes, now clouded and exhausted. I hate that this is where the night led us. I hate myself for allowing this to happen. I worry that this won't be the last time my past will get in the way. I am fully prepared to battle each demon that pops up, for as long as she'll let me.

"Let me take you to my place."

"You can't just deflect the rest of this conversation using sex, Cal." Her tone is sarcastic as she rolls her eyes, the air seeming calmer now.

"Who said anything about sex? It's getting dark and cold out here, I thought my living room would be a better place to talk. I can turn on the fireplace and we can put on a movie." She looks up at me cautiously. I know this conversation isn't over. We've both just said in separate ways that we need to end this. But neither of us wants to walk away.

"But we will talk about this," she insists.

"Whatever you want, whenever you want."

We stand awkwardly next to each other as the elevator climbs up the building to my penthouse. The ride here was quiet, knowing we've both said too much, and not enough, all at the same time.

When I'm around her, my mind spins in circles with *what-ifs* and the only logical thing I can be certain about is that I want her.

I *need* her.

I'm done pretending that I don't know what I want, and I'm done holding myself back from what I deserve to feel. From what we both deserve to feel.

It's so quiet in the elevator, the only thing I can hear is the hum of the motor as it lifts us up, seemingly slower than normal. Her breathing is hitched and erratic, like she's nervous and excited all at once. There's no way I'm going to be able to last through something as civil as watching a movie with her, not when all I can think about is worshiping her the way she deserves.

I watch her out of the corner of my eye as she stares straight ahead, her fingers running circles over her elbow as she holds her arm gently.

The elevator comes to a stop and the wait for the *bing* as the doors open seems to take forever. As soon as they slide open, I waste no time doing exactly what I want to do.

I whip her around before she has a chance to step out of the elevator and hoist her up into my arms, carrying her into my living room. My lips crash on hers before we even hit the couch and I can't help but notice the way she tenses around me as my tongue traces the seam of her lips, begging them to let me in.

She tugs at my belt as I lay her down on the couch and steady myself over her, never letting go of her mouth as my teeth grasp her bottom lip and tug gently. A wanting whimper escapes her mouth when I finally break free.

While I kick off my slacks, she gets up from the couch and turns her back to me.

"I need your help," she sighs innocently as she reaches for her zipper at the base of her neck.

"I thought we were just gonna watch a movie," I quip, pulling her into me, flush against my hardening cock. I touch feathery kisses to her neck and shoulders before taking my time zipping down the length of her dress. When the dress slips off, she turns around to face me.

Underneath, she's wearing a sheer, red lace bra with a matching thong. My breath hitches as she scans her crystal blue eyes up to mine, which are now probably dark with desire. *God, this woman.*

She reaches up to my chest slowly to start unbuttoning my shirt. It feels intentional, like every movement of her fingers is meant to tempt me. But I steady her patiently until my shirt is free.

I pull her into my arms, she clenches her legs around my torso as I carry her to my bedroom and kick the door shut behind us. I'm blinded by the beauty of this girl, everything about her has me feeling so full, so *intoxicated.*

I lay her carefully on my bed and reach down to land a passionate kiss against her soft, pink lips.

Something feels different about this. As I stand back and admire the stunning woman in front of me, I replay the events from earlier. The things we shared, the things we said, the things *I felt.*

It's freeing to know that I have power over my feelings, to give in to my wants, forgetting about the rules and what everyone else might think.

But she's right, we can't deflect with sex, though I do really want to fuck her, make love to her, worship her body till the sun breaks over the mountains; I can tell she wants it too. The red lacey set she has on almost distracts me enough to let the wrong head take over, but I need to do this right.

As if she can sense the war in my head, her sultry voice speaks out.

"Something the matter?" She leans up higher on her knees to meet my eye level.

"I just-" I start, "I want to make sure you know this is more than just sex to me. That I don't want to touch anyone else, see anyone else, fuck anyone else. All I want is you."

We're within inches of each other, almost naked, and breathing in time with one another. I watch the *rise and fall* of her chest, the way she reaches to brush her hair behind her ear, the way she pulls her lip between her teeth before returning to my eyes with a blue wave of passion. The intricate details that I've grown so enthralled with.

She responds softly, "I want to make sure you know I feel the exact same way." Sterling reaches her fingers out to trace circles on my abs. "And right now, I'd like to make you feel the same way you make me feel."

"And how's that, sweetheart?"

She lets out a greedy sigh, "Wanted."

Her hand trails lower, past my Adonis belt and closer to my dick. She reaches into my briefs and grabs the base of my length, never breaking eye contact. The fucking air gets knocked out of me at her touch, so delicate and soft.

She slides her hand from the base to the tip as I groan. Her touch feels like fire and ice all at the same time.

"You don't have to do this, Sterling." I reach my hand down as she lowers herself to level with my center.

"I want to." She yanks at the hem of my briefs and pulls them all the way down so that I can step out of them. My erection springs free.

"Just tell me to stop if it's too much?" I tell her, my thumb tracing her lips.

"Mm, hm," she hums at me as she positions herself onto her knees.

She applies a little pressure at the base, then, she rubs me gently. Fisting my sensitive skin up and down. Precum makes its way to my tip which rewards me with a beautiful sigh and quickening motions of her hand. I rock into it a little, the feeling of her hand on my dick is amazing. Her body rocks with her hand as it jerks me off, her breasts bouncing in her sheer bra.

Euphoria.

"Eyes up here, baby," I groan, wanting her to see what she's doing to me. I look straight into those pretty sky blues.

But it's the feeling I'm overwhelmed with when she doesn't let go of our stare as she parts her lips and pulls me in to fill her mouth. The feeling of her tongue gliding under my cock almost sends me over.

I've been struggling to take control of my feelings in this situation because I am obsessed with Sterling. But she allows me to lose control, craves it.

I wrap my fingers around her hair as I help her find her rhythm, wanting to keep her as close to me as possible. There's no way I'm ever letting her go. She bobs back and forth, giving me a little nibble with her teeth with every suck and the feeling has me entranced.

She still has her hand wrapped around the base of my length. And I can tell she's afraid she'll gag because she doesn't push me into her too far. But it's enough for me. *Sterling is enough for me.* I throw my head back as I tug on her hair, a moan leaving my mouth.

I can see the finish line coming into view and as much as I want to spill every ounce of my cum into her pretty, willing mouth, I am just as desperate to give her everything her body craves. I look down at her as the feeling approaches and her eyes are now shut, a lone tear escapes the corner of one eye.

"So. Fucking. Sexy." I murmur breathlessly as her tongue rakes up the length of my erection. "But I need you to stop, I don't want to come just yet," I say under a deep sigh. She opens her heavy eyes up to me and parts her glistening lips to speak.

"You told me whatever I want, whenever I want. So, shut up and let me finish what I started." Her eyes sparkle up at me and my dick throbs in her hand. *Fuck.* I definitely did not expect those words to come out of her mouth.

She pulls me back into her mouth, her tongue hitting every sensitive nerve. My ejaculation meets her taste buds, and my eyes roll to the back of my head. I grip the fuck out of her hair, thrusting faster as I fall apart inside of her. She lets out a wanting whimper to meet my growls when she tastes me.

I'm not sure she's fully aware of what she just did.

She *claimed* me.

I'm hers.

And I'm going to spend the rest of the night doing the exact same thing, *claiming* her.

TWENTY-SEVEN

Sterling

Callan takes his time with me. After I sent him over the edge, he laid me down and slowly, sensually undressed me. Now, we're body to body, naked, his cock softening against my inner thigh.

"What are your plans this weekend?" Callan asks me as he swipes a warm cloth from my stomach down to my thighs. This is one gesture that I thoroughly enjoy after we have sex, his intentional movements as he cleans me up, making me feel special.

"I have to go apartment hunting." My admission brings me back down from the high Callan gave me. "I have to find a new place to live."

He gets up from the bed and makes his way to the bathroom.

"How come?"

"Well, honestly, I can't afford to live there on my own. I need to find something cheaper. Maybe even a new roommate." I feel slightly embarrassed as I admit this to him. Here I am in bed with a man who can afford anything life has to offer and I'm still struggling with the simplest of life's necessities.

He makes his way out of the bathroom and leans against the frame, now wearing a pair of sweatpants. His eyes are low and focused.

"What's wrong?" I ask him as I sit up, covering myself with his comforter.

"Nothing."

"You're lying," I accuse. I can definitely tell his demeanor has changed and I'm not sure why.

"Stay here." He walks over, reaches down to the end of the bed, picks up my clothes and lays them nicely on the night stand next to me.

"What do you mean?"

"Can you please get dressed? I find it really distracting that you're naked in my bed." I jump up as quickly as I can and get my clothes on before following Callan out to the living room.

"Callan, what did you mean?"

The sky is now dark, I notice the time on the clock reads nine p.m. It's been only a few hours since our fight, if we can even call it that.

"All I'm saying is that you can stay here," he starts as he cracks his knuckles together before placing them in his lap.

I heard what he said. But I don't think I'm registering what he's saying.

Callan gets up from the couch and heads into the kitchen, grabbing two glasses out of the cabinet. I watch him fill each glass with water before taking a deep breath as he walks back over to the couch, setting the glasses of water on the coffee table.

"What do you mean?" I lean over to grab my glass and take a big gulp of water, trying to push down the lump in my throat.

"I mean..." he trails off for a second, taking a breath before continuing, "I like having you here."

Call it a knee-jerk reaction or maybe utter shock, but I spit my water out in the direction of Callan. Water drips from his chin and onto his pants as I stare at him in complete confusion.

He looks upset as he leaves the couch, once more, to grab a towel to wipe himself off. I still haven't registered what he said.

"Well, that's not quite the reaction I was expecting." He leans against the kitchen counter facing the window.

"You want me to move in? With you?" I stand from the couch and face him.

"It was just a thought. You don't have to." I walk over to where he's standing, only stopping a few feet in front of him. I see his biceps flex as he tosses the towel into the kitchen sink, and I'm so tempted to throw out all rationality and give him whatever he asks for right here and now.

"Callan, do you remember that conversation we had just hours ago outside of the restaurant? The one about feelings and complications? We practically both said out loud that we needed to end whatever this was," I mention, trying to place my words carefully but too confused to know how.

"I get it, Sterling. I do. But I'm pretty fucking sure I've established that that is definitely *not* what I want." He focuses his gaze on me, which brings even more heat to my skin. "*This* is what I want. I'm done playing these stupid games." He pulls me into him, eyes low and piercing.

"So, you just decided, within the last hour, that I should move in with you?" I look up at him, then to the spot where his hand barely holds on to mine, then back at him again.

"No. I've been thinking about it since the moment you told me about your eviction notice, as more of a roommate situation until you can get back on your feet. But nothing is ever that simple with us as it seems." His eyes are on the floor as I let go of our brief contact and start to pace in front of him. "But now, I feel like we can make it more than just a roommate situation. I'm not lying, Sterling. I want this, and I won't be going anywhere."

But would we be dating?

What do we call each other?

What if we end up hating each other five days from now?

What if this is all just some crazy fling that we had for a few weeks and it all goes up in flames?

Nerves and thoughts of what-if consume me as I watch this man patiently begging – unintentionally – with his gold-flecked green eyes.

"What made you change your mind?" I ask.

"You." His eyes bore heatedly into mine.

I let out a much-needed exhale and stop fidgeting around Callan's living room. I steady myself back in front of him.

"I can't possibly afford half of the rent for this place." I throw my hands around me.

"Sterling, I own this place. You'd be paying nothing." His eyes bore into mine. He's really fucking serious about this.

But why? I find it really hard to believe that this is a real conversation I'm having right now.

He reaches for my wrist and pulls me gently to him, then lifts me up and sits me on the counter. I position my legs around his torso and look up at his beautiful dark eyes. He lowers his voice and wraps his hand around my waist.

"You don't have to call it *moving in*. You can just call it *crashing with a friend* or whatever you feel like calling it. You can stay here until you feel comfortable enough to find a place of your own or you can stay as long as you'd like. I even have the spare bedroom over there if that makes you feel more comfortable." He nods his head past the kitchen. "But if you don't want to, I get it. The invitation has been extended so it's up to you. But I'd really like it if you stayed."

I let his eyes wander over my face, noticing that I've never seen Callan so expressive and sensitive before. So vulnerable. His fingers squeeze a little tighter into my hip like he's trying to pull me closer, and his eyes wrap me in a warm hug.

"If I stay here, hypothetically, what do we tell everyone at work? How do we explain whatever this is to someone who asks?" I push him back a little, giving myself space to breathe while I try to process my thoughts. "We'd be spending pretty much all of our time together."

"We can tell them the truth," he states.

"The truth?"

"Yeah."

"And what's the truth, Callan? That me and the boss are exclusively fucking and living under the same roof? That sounds like an HR field day." I roll my eyes.

"I am HR, Sterling."

"How convenient," I say, and he chuckles a little, lightening the mood a bit. Some tension lingering still, but the air feels a bit more breathable around us.

"We don't owe anyone anything. But we do owe it to ourselves, to explore this." He leans into me, pursing his lips before he blows air onto my neck, the warmth of his breath encasing me so seductively that my body tightens with need. "I want you to know that I won't throw around your feelings anymore, I won't hide from you. So if it helps, you can say that you're living with your boyfriend."

"What?" I pull back, searching his expression. It's serious. He's actually serious right now. *Boyfriend.*

"I want to give this a shot."

He's right. We both clearly want this. I don't know what's getting in the way of me saying yes. Maybe I'm still anxious about getting hurt. Falling too deep. Burning alive with the fire that Callan has set inside of me.

He presses a pillowy kiss to my temple as his hands gently caress my back.

I bring my hands up to the sides of Callan's face, my thumbs gently stroke his cheeks as he leans in to kiss the palm of my hand. In an instant, his lips are on mine. It's a kiss laced with fear and hope and reassurance.

A kiss that scares me and claims me all at the same time.

A kiss that tells me that he's got me and he's not going to let me go.

TWENTY-EIGHT

Sterling

"So, what *can* you tell me?" Her sweet little voice sounds up at me as I watch her pack clothes into a suitcase.

"I can't tell you anything, Sara," I laugh at her as she rolls her big brown eyes.

I've missed Sara so much these past couple of weeks. I was so relieved when I got a call from Mrs. Chen moments after Callan offered me to live with him. Moments after I told him that I wanted to take it slow and that I needed time to think. I've never had a boyfriend before, and I want to make sure I won't regret this.

"You've got a boyfriend, don't you? It's about time you old hag. I thought you'd die alone." She tosses one of her stuffed animals at me.

Being here with Sara gives me the space I need, the space to step away from such a hectic weekend, despite the bliss I felt not long ago. I don't mind finishing my Sunday night off by listening to cringy pop music and putting on a fashion show with my favorite 12-year-old. When Mrs. Chen called earlier, she said it was an emergency, and was practically halfway out the door when I got here. I'm trying not to worry too much about it, but it was a little unsettling seeing her so frazzled, when she's always been so poised and put-together.

From the moment I arrived about an hour ago, Sara's been begging me to fill her in on the latest things happening in my life. She said she could *sense a change in me.*

"It's your boss at your fancy new job, isn't it? Did he ask you out or did you ask him?" She smiles and looks right up at me.

Brat.

I reach across her bed and grab a flower-shaped pillow to toss at her head.

"What the heck!" She jumps up and tries to fight back while I laugh at her.

"What are you packing for anyways?"

"I don't know. Mom just said to pack a bag, I hope she surprises me with a fun vacation for my birthday," she giggles.

"Oh yeah. Don't remind me. You're going to be thirteen soon." I jokingly roll my eyes.

"Don't be jealous because I'm a cool thirteen-year-old and you probably weren't," she deadpans.

"Oh, get over yourself," I joke. "I just can't believe you're growing up." I pretend-sniffle while she throws a swimsuit in her suitcase.

"Well, your birthday is also coming up and you're probably dreading becoming...*old,*" she says it like she just realized she stepped in gum and it's hot and sticky as she pulls her foot away from the pavement.

"You know I actually did miss you, brat? Don't ruin it," we laugh.

"Anyways, back to my birthday. I'm registered at Target, Amazon, and Bath and Body Works," she smiles with amusement as we stare at each other for a few moments before both breaking out into mad laughter.

"Sterling! Sara!" I hear Mrs. Chen call from downstairs. It startles me because she'd only just left an hour ago. I wasn't expecting her to be back so soon.

We both look at each other very confused, I gesture to check my wrist for the time on my fake watch, before we both start running down the steps.

Mrs. Chen stands in the middle of the kitchen, frantically shoving clothes and hygienic necessities into different suitcases spread across the kitchen island. It's a panicked movement, like she can't stuff the suitcases fast enough.

How long has she been down here doing this?

"Mom, what's going on?" Sara asks, looking at her mom with a worried look, noticing the urgency.

"Did you pack your bag?" she asks, not looking up from her own bags.

"Almost. I just have-"

"I need it packed, now!" she shouts, causing both of us to jolt back in shock.

I've never heard Sara's mom raise her tone, ever.

"Mrs. Chen. Is everything okay?" I decide to step in, noticing that Sara is utterly shocked.

"Sterling, I will be writing you a severance check. Tonight will be your last night caring for Sara." She looks up at me for a brief moment with a look of pain in her eyes that says *sorry* before returning her attention to everything strewn out across the countertops. I blink, unmoving. Almost as if I'm stuck in the space of her words.

A severance check?

My last night?

Mrs. Chen moves her head up slightly to peer at me from under her lashes and that's when I see it clearly .... the black eye.

Her right eye is bruised with purple and dark gray colored abrasions and her skin is raised a bit, making her entire cheek look swollen.

"Wait, what? Mom, what's happening?" Sara's small voice is laced with confusion and panic as she looks between her mom and me. "What happened to your eye?" Sara's jaw drops as she stares straight at her mom.

"Mom?" Walking over to her mother, Sara places her hand on top of hers. "What's happening?" Mrs. Chen looks down to her daughter, and suddenly, she's crying.

"I'm so sorry, Saralee." Her mom sobs into her palms. "I tried so hard to be forgiving. Please understand that I tried."

"What do you mean?"

Sara's mom looks over at me and gives me an apologetic look before turning back to her daughter.

"Daddy's been absent a lot. Have you noticed that?" she asks, wiping tears from her face.

Sara nods.

"Saralee, you are beautiful and loved. And nothing will ever change that," she begins.

"Mom, please."

The air is stale with confusion and tense with fear. Mr. Chen hasn't come home with Mrs. Chen in months, I've noticed that. But I thought it was just because he'd been busy after date nights or maybe had other things going on at work. But Sara's mom is obviously about to break some really upsetting news to her daughter, and I take a deep breath as I prepare myself for what she's about to unload.

"Your father and I have been fighting a lot and tonight he..." Her breath hitches as she tries to compose herself. "He hit me," she announces as she gently brings her fingers up under her eye to graze the damage. The look on her face when she looks into Sara's eyes at the admission is one of a failed mom. She thinks this is her fault.

"Hit you?" She blinks up at her mom. Her face displays traces of skepticism, tears begging to break free from her coffee-colored eyes.

Watching Sara carry so much pain in this moment hurts me just the same. It feels like we're stuck to the ground as an earthquake shatters everything around us.

"You're lying!" Sara shouts, tears streaming hot down her face.

"No, I'm not, Sara. Look at my face." She turns back to her suitcases. "We need to leave. He's drunk and I don't want him to come home and hurt you. That's why I needed you to pack a bag. That's why I have to let Sterling go. We're leaving, we're moving in with Mimi." She sucks in some much-needed air as she searches my face for a reaction.

"Why would he do this?" Sara steps back from her mom. "Why?" She demands. I watch her as she takes small steps backwards, like she's trying to put space between her and her mom's words. She doesn't want to believe that someone she loves could do something so horrific.

"I don't have an answer for you, sweetie." Her mom tries to stay calm, and I notice that she looks to me for help as Sara is on the verge of losing it.

"Sara, why don't you head upstairs, and I'll meet you up there in a minute. Okay?" She wipes tears from her cheeks before nodding and running back up the stairs.

Mrs. Chen waits for her daughter to be out of sight and earshot before turning to me.

"How could he do this, Sterling? How could he?" she questions in between sobs and sighs.

"I don't know how to answer that question," I whisper as she pulls me in for a hug.

I know that they aren't my real family, but I feel heartbreak from this as well. The all-too-familiar feeling flooding its way back into my heart, crashing and breaking. Shattering into a million tiny pieces.

I can remember exactly how I felt when I got similar news. *Dad has betrayed us.* No little girl should have to feel hate in their heart for their father, or anyone they love for that matter.

This is exactly what scares me the most about commitment. Getting hurt, or betrayed, or abandoned all over again.

The product of family trauma.

The solution is to put up a wall, let no one in. Because as long as they're only looking at you from the outside, they can't destroy what's inside. They can't break your heart.

But choosing to live that way could be just as damaging.

The product of self-destruction.

There's no way out, no way to win the war. I've been so determined to guard my heart from pain, but what if it no longer needs guarding? What if my heart is finally safe, with Callan?

"I just feel like you're wasting your time here with me when you could be out there exploring your heart's desires."

Sara's old words find their way from the archived conversations I keep in the back of my mind. I think about how silly she sounded at the time but now it's like she knew I was going to need to hear it. Except the part where she said I was wasting my time with her. Every moment spent with Sara has healed the parts of me that so desperately missed being part of a family.

I've made up my mind about what I'm going to do with my life, with my heart. But first, I have to go say good-bye to the little girl who probably has no idea that she changed my life.

TWENTY-NINE

Callan

I'd been waiting for what felt like years, for Sterling's call last night. When she finally did, she said she wanted to talk, but needed sleep first, which made me nervous as hell, but she insisted everything was going to be fine.

I practically begged her to come back to my house, but when she told me about what happened with Sara, I understood why she was exhausted. She said she needed to get into a better headspace.

But now, I sit here in my office waiting for her to call or text or even show up for work, for fuck's sake. She's late and I hate that she hasn't even called to explain her unexcused tardiness. There's a knock at my door, and disappointment washes over me when I see Cora standing in the doorway instead of Sterling.

"Yes, Cora?" I raise a brow in annoyance to meet her flirty smirk.

"I just wanted to check in. You seemed-" I raise my flat palm out in front of me.

"Just stop. It's none of your business. Please get back to work."

If Cora put as much time and effort into her job as she has into trying to get me alone in my office these past couple of weeks, maybe she would've actually gotten the assistant position she wanted. I'm so glad she didn't, though. Otherwise, I may have never met Sterling.

My undoing.

The woman of my dreams.

The woman who is still late to work right now and is totally getting away with it.

I'm hesitant to reach for my phone to text her first. I hate not knowing where she is or what she's thinking. These past few days with Sterling have really heightened everything. Especially after yesterday. Since coming to the realization that I don't have to be ashamed to have actual feelings, I've been able to let down my highest walls, to be my full self with her. It has been so freeing.

But it also feels daunting to open myself up. I just hate that I'm subjecting myself to the possibility of getting hurt, how I imagine my mom did to my dad. But after spinning all the thoughts in my head over and over, I tell myself that I'm okay with that risk because Sterling is worth it. If she'd ever be ready to take the next step, I'll be right there by her side, a proud and changed man.

After a few long minutes pass by, I give in to the urge to send her a text message. But just as my fingers hover over the send button, a familiar voice presents itself at my door.

"Mr. David. I was wondering if I could have a word?" She's staring up at me with those beautiful ocean blues that lock me in a trance.

But her perfect eyes don't excuse the fact that she has a job to do, and I want to be mad at her for being late to work.

"You're late," I snap, not harsh enough to make her think she's in any serious trouble, but enough to tell her that she can and will be punished.

"I know, I just had to wrap up a few things with the moving company. They kept me on the phone way longer than I expected and-"

"Movers? You found a place?" I interrupt, trying to hide the disappointment in my voice. I hate that I'm affected this way, that I'm jealous of the new place she's moving into.

"Yeah, some guy asked me to move in with him and at first I didn't think it was a good idea, but then I thought having a roommate could be nice."

Sterling stands near the doorway only inches inside the office. She's wearing the sexiest ripped jean shorts and an oversized graphic t-shirt. Nothing near work appropriate. *Did she just say she's going to live with another guy?*

"Who is he?" I ask with as much restraint as I can gather. I mean, I just asked her to be my girlfriend the other day and she has the audacity to walk in here and break this news to me?

Sterling walks into the room and closes the door behind her quietly before turning back to me. She walks directly up to me and places both hands on my face. I feel heat everywhere. Heat from desire because I haven't been able to stop thinking about her, but also heat from vexation that she would announce this news so nonchalantly to me. And now, she's moving in with some random guy that I've never even heard of.

"Callan." Her voice is my vice. Her eyes are like sirens, pulling me into the ocean that is her deep and drowning gaze.

"It's you, silly," she whispers, a smirk curling on her pink lips.

My heart jumps.

"What?"

"You're the guy. The movers will have all my things into your place by this afternoon," she speaks with amusement, as if she knows what she just did to me. I don't know if I should be pissed or relieved. "I hope that's okay," she adds.

I can't move fast enough. I lift her into my arms, straddle her around my torso and kiss her with as much force as I can. The way she riled me up just now somehow ignites the most passion I've ever felt, in this kiss. I thought she was leaving me, and I never want to let her go.

"I don't have a lot of stuff, I promise," she says behind a sly smile, letting go of the kiss as I set her down to sit on the edge of my desk. I stand between her legs, my hands still wrapped around her waist.

"Sweetheart, I wouldn't have been mad if you brought fifty boxes or wanted to say fuck it all and left everything behind. I could have taken you to buy anything you wanted." And I would have. *Anything for her*. But she just shrugs her shoulders and giggles silently.

"Come on, let's go." I pull her by the wrist to guide her out of my office.

"Where are we going?"

"First, to breakfast. Then, we'll spend the rest of the day moving you in."

"We might want to skip breakfast and go straight to your house. The movers are kind of waiting to be let in," she laughs, which makes me laugh too.

She wasn't lying when she said she didn't have a lot of stuff. She mainly brought over clothes and a few boxes of necessities. I feel excited as I watch the movers drop her boxes into the spare room, though I hope she'll be spending most nights in my bed.

I can tell she feels awkward and maybe even a little unsure about what's happening. I mean, I'd be lying if I said I didn't feel a bit of that too. But I want to reassure her that she is free to come and go as she pleases. I told her this only has to be temporary if that's what she wants.

"And what if I don't want us to be temporary?" she questions, picking up on our conversation right where we left it in the car earlier.

"Then you can stay."

"What if I want to leave next week?" she asks.

"Then I'll help you pack." At my answer, she looks at me with a sense of ease. "I wouldn't want that to mean that you and I stop seeing each other, though. If you decide that living here is too much or too soon, you're free to go. But I won't stop seeing you." A small smile perks up on her beautiful face.

I walk her into the spare bedroom, now *her* bedroom. I gesture for her to explore her new space as I watch the wonder fill her eyes.

"Holy shit!" she shouts from across the room.

"What?" I hurry over to where she's standing, not sure what I'm about to find.

"This closet is bigger than my apartment." She looks around with wide eyes, and I can't help but let out a laugh.

I haven't seen her smile so wide in a while. I make a silent promise to myself to do whatever it takes to pull that smile out of her as often as possible. I follow behind closely as she admires the walk-in closet. A round vanity sits in the middle, with glass drawers perfect for jewelry or makeup or whatever accessories she might like. I'd be overjoyed to fill this closet with anything and everything that brings this smile to Sterling's face.

"It's all yours," I say and just as she turns to look at me with thankful eyes, the movers interrupt us by knocking gently on the bedroom door.

"We're all done here. Miss. Cooper, we'll need a signature and an email to send the invoice to."

"Yes, it's-" Sterling walks past me toward the movers to oblige but I stop her in her tracks, holding her gently by the wrist as I step forward.

"I'll take care of it." I scribble a signature on the electronic device and hand them my credit card.

"What are you doing?" Sterling speaks up from behind me, trying to fight her way through.

"I'll take care of it, Sterling," I repeat. The mover hands back my card and with a nod, they step out of the room and let themselves out through the elevator. As soon as the doors slide shut, I turn to face her.

"You didn't have to do that," she says.

"One thing you're gonna need to know about me, sweetheart, is that I don't do anything I don't want to do."

"Yeah, but if we're going to make whatever this is work, you really need to stop stepping on my toes, Callan." My name glides off her tongue with a little bit more sarcasm than the rest of her words.

"You think I'm stepping on your toes?" I ask as I lean against the door frame.

"Well, yeah. Kinda." Her lips curl into a small smile.

"I thought you liked it when I get bossy." I want to touch her, kiss her, everything with her. But this feels like unfamiliar territory to me. I'm so overcome with emotions, I don't know which to feel first.

"Well, thank you for taking care of the moving expenses for me, Mr. David," she speaks in an exaggerated fancy voice, verging on British. "Now if you don't mind, I have to run to the store for a few things."

"Well, I'd be happy to escort you, Miss Cooper," I offer, in a tone that mocks hers.

I see the gears twisting in her brain as she looks at me behind a curious but nervous smile.

"Actually, I think I should go by myself." Her voice shifts back to normal. She places the palm of her hand over my chest, pats it a few times and smirks at me. I love playful Sterling.

"Okay, but I actually need some things too," I mention, wondering why I can't tag along on her shopping adventure. "We can even make a list and have Gerald run the errand," I suggest.

"Gerald does your grocery shopping?"

"If I ask him to. Sometimes he gets bored."

She looks at me, still curious.

"I didn't mean to overstep," I say.

"You...didn't really," she hesitates. "It's just, I need to get some personal things from the store."

It clicks in my mind what she means when she stretches out the word personal. But nothing scares me when it comes to this girl. And nothing will embarrass me about her either.

It's silent for a second as I watch her eyes waver from mine to the floor. And then she bursts out into laughter.

"What's so funny?" I ask, leaning against the wall, tucking my hands into my pockets as she chokes on every breath with laughter.

"You've probably never even been to the grocery store, let alone to buy a girl tampons." She slows her laugh into a small giggle, her hand on her stomach where she's folded over.

"Are you done yet?" I joke with her in an unamused tone. Even though she's right, I hardly go to the store, and I've definitely never bought menstrual products before.

I walk over to Sterling and grab her by her ass; I have to touch her. She sucks in a breath as I pull her up to me, forcing her legs to spread open to wrap around my torso as I push us into the wall behind her. I can feel her heartbeat. I close any space there could be between us before I take my tongue and trail it over her collarbone and up to her bottom lip.

"My little rose, are you trying to get a rise out of me?" She sighs a deep, lusty sigh as my tongue glides over her lips.

"If you asked me to go to the store to buy you tampons, I would. I'm not a little boy. Don't play with me." I take my eyes off hers to gaze at her chest, I can see goosebumps forming over her flesh and the sight sends blood rushing to my cock. I feel her shiver as she notices it too.

"Prove it." She tempts me, pushing her pelvis into my torso harder.

"Excuse me?" I cock my head at her.

"You heard me." Her smile goes dark as she gazes at my mouth.

"You'll regret that," I growl as I lower her down to her feet, take my hands to the inside of her t-shirt and rip the piece of fabric down the center.

She gasps as she looks up at me. I give her a rough, promising kiss as I unbutton her jeans and slide them down her legs. She looks at me with a look of unfairness, so I pull my shirt over my head.

I see her eyes go from innocent blue to feral grays, like ocean water tainted with waves of desire.

I don't waste a single second getting down on my knees for the stunning woman in front of me. I feather my fingers over the band of her thong as she writhes against the wall. She's already wet, I can smell her arousal as it presents itself on her red panties. I gently slide the piece of fabric down her legs, and she lets out a longing sigh as the frigid air hits her glistening pussy.

I am so eager to taste her but take my time spreading burning kisses from her knees back up to her bellybutton. As she wiggles greedily, I slowly slide my fingers over the apex of her thighs and I revel in the way her knees buckle at my touch.

"Callan," she whispers heavily as she digs her fingers into my hair. "Please."

"You're soaking wet, my little rose," I groan into her heat as she hums in approval. I take one of my hands and reach behind her back, she arches just right for me, and I unclasp her bra exposing her beautiful breasts. I push my middle finger inside of her with one hand, the other plays with one of her nipples, she sighs heavily with pleasure.

"I need...more...proof." She looks down at me, breathless, as she rocks her hips into my hand.

"You do?" I look up at her teasingly.

"Mm, hmm." She nods as she bites her lip. My cock throbs with want for the way she looks at me, begging me to be inside of her.

I let my index finger join my middle finger deep inside her pussy as I curl my digits against her walls, and she lets out an unholy moan. I give her more of what her body is craving and pump my fingers in and out as I let my tongue find her clit. I circle it relentlessly, soaking in the way she tastes.

"More," she begs behind whimpers of pleasure. I stand up and crash my lips into hers, lusty sounds escape her mouth at the taste of her arousal on my lips.

"You're such a good girl for me, sweetheart." I grip her chin with my hand and tilt her head up to meet my eyes, holding her lips just close enough to barely touch mine.

She reaches for the waistband of my briefs and teases gently, pulling them down just enough to let her fingers graze my hardness.

I kiss and lick and suck feverishly on her neck, my hand encompassing her throat with enough pressure to arouse her even more. She can't keep her hands to herself anymore, and I before I know it, she's pulling my briefs down and guiding my cock into her entrance.

"An impatient one you are," I whisper into her ear, and she inches me closer, trying to get me inside. The heat between us is undying, sweat dripping down both of our bodies as she begs for more friction.

But before I can let her go any further, I pick her up and carry her to the other side of the room, kissing her neck as her legs squeeze my torso. She gasps as I press her back against the cold glass. I slowly let her down, holding her hips in my hands, kissing her the entire way down. She sighs even deeper when I spin her around and press her against the floor-to-ceiling window, putting us on full display. The view faces the city. Though no one can see us from twenty stories up, we can see everything from here.

"Callan," she whispers against the glass.

"Yes, Little Rose."

"We're so high up." Her gasps are a little heavier, and I remember her admission of being afraid of heights.

I take a fistful of her hair and yank her head slightly, pulling her back into an arch; her nipples perk up as they graze the cold surface of the glass.

"Do you trust me?" She gives me a hesitant nod. I know that nothing can happen to her from in here, but what if I take her out on the balcony and attempt to test that trust? I decide I'd rather fuck her right here, watching our reflection in the window.

"I've got you."

I take her neck under my lips and suck hard enough to leave marks. She's begging for more, wriggling her ass into my core and I can't take it anymore.

I push her head forward into the window, and I feel her tense as my cock finds its rightful place, letting my slickness mix with hers before thrusting myself into her from behind as she falls into oblivion. Every ounce of her body is quaking under my thrusts as I fuck her hard. The sound of our bodies meshing echoes off the walls and entangles with her lustful cries.

"Oh, fuck." She manages to get out. I focus one hand on her hip, digging deep into her skin, pulling her closer every time I pump into her, and the other is gripping her hair. She steadies herself against the window with one hand as the other reaches behind her to grip my hip.

"What do you think they could see if they could look up at us right now? They'd see my pretty girlfriend getting fucked by her boss, needy for more." I feel her contract around me as I feather the words onto her skin, her moans louder and louder as she approaches the edge. my little rose, about to jump off the cliff.

Both of us reach our climax at the same time, falling over the edge together. Our guttural moans meet as one as her orgasm suffocates her and my hot cum jets inside her.

"So beautiful," I murmur in her ear.

Sweat drips from the both of us, our breaths are short and heavy. I release my grip on her as she catches her breath. She turns around, pulling my dick out of her warm pleasure as she faces me. I lean over her with one hand up against the window behind her.

"Did I prove myself?" I ask as she forces her gaze to mine. And I'm sure that I did. But I didn't know that she could be so naughty, her next words striking another fire in me.

"This was a decent start." She smiles deviously before licking her lips, pleading for round two.

THIRTY

Sterling

We spend the next few weeks christening his apartment. *Our* apartment. It feels nice to say that.

Work isn't awkward. Except for the time when Jax almost walked in on us again in Callan's office. That man has impeccable timing.

My time with Callan has been eye-opening. I feel like I can be myself, like I finally have a shot at this thing called life. It's refreshing. And who knew that all that stupid arguing about what we wanted out of what was supposed to be just a work relationship would turn into us dating each other.

And I won't lie, I feel some kind of pride fall over me when I think about how I brought this man out of his shell as well. And I'm falling head over heels for him.

I show up to work a few hours late today. I haven't been feeling well for the last couple of days; probably food poisoning from the hole-in-the-wall burger joint across the street.

And no, I'm not pregnant. Dakota made me take several tests. Plus, I'm still on my birth control.

Callan woke me up softly this morning and told me to take my time, leaving with a kiss on my temple which definitely helped me feel better. When I felt strong enough to get up and get ready, I took it slow in hopes of keeping the vomit down.

I get a few stares as I walk in, probably because I look as bad as I feel, but I don't let it bother me too much. I notice Callan's door is closed, and I hear his voice along with another man's voice, so instead of greeting him, I continue to my office, not wanting to bother the meeting he might be in.

I get settled in my office and log into my computer, taking slow sips of the coffee I poured for myself in the lobby. Two new tickets need to be filed today and some business expenses need to be approved by finance, so I get to work and catch up on emails. After about an hour and a half, there's a knock on my door. The sound nearly splits my head in two, though the knock itself wasn't even that loud.

"Come in," I rasp.

"Hey there, sunshine." Jax peeks his head through the door and smiles that classic bad-boy grin before his face warps into horror.

"Whoa, you look like you got hit by a car." His words take me back to a couple months ago, when I actually *did* get hit by a car, which makes me giggle a little. Weirdly enough, I've almost entirely forgotten about the car accident. Everything is so good now, and honestly, I'm glad it happened because it led me here, to this dealership, to Callan.

"I should have just stayed home. I feel like garbage," I admit as I rub my fingers over my temples. He gives a small chuckle before sliding into my office.

"Are you preg-"

"No." I hold my hands up abruptly at him. "People can get sick and not be pregnant, okay?" He laughs at me.

"Callan just asked that I check in with you." He fiddles with some pens in a jar on my desk.

"Why couldn't he just check in on me himself?"

"He's been in back-to-back meetings today. Texted me that you weren't feeling well and wanted to make sure you were okay." He smiles. "What have you done to my alpha-hole of a friend, Sterling? Have you whipped and tamed him?" His smirk deepens as he leans against my desk, his slight southern accent coming out a bit.

"I cannot confirm or deny if I've had any part in this," I laugh, holding my palms out in front of me. "But hey, enough about me. I heard you're leaving the dealership?" I ask, remembering that Callan mentioned a conversation between him and Jax a few weeks ago.

"Yeah, nothing is official yet. I just kind of want to figure out my life. I've been away from my family for a while. My brother is supposed to be coming home from deployment soon. Which I could honestly care less about. I like this job, but I feel like there's something else out there for me," he admits and his boyish smirk dissipates slowly as he ponders. And I know exactly how he feels...or I did at some point.

"Where's home?"

"Dallas."

"Oh, so he *is* a southern boy," I quip and his smirk deepens. "Well, I think you need to follow your heart." It's all I can say.

Though I think he senses that I'm probably not someone who's in the best shape to be giving out advice as I'm half-awake with my head resting on one hand. He gives me a grateful and sympathetic smile.

"Thanks, Sterling. Well, I'll leave you to it, and I hope you feel better." As he turns to leave, I hear the click of a door being opened down the hall. He looks out. "Looks like Callan's meeting just left if you'd like to go see your boy." He smiles again before disappearing into the hall.

"Thanks, Jax. See ya." I throw my head down on my desk and groan into my forearms before getting up and smoothing my hair down. I know Callan will either tell me to go home or give me the remedy, so I decide to head toward his office.

I knock on his door gently and his sexy voice answers in return.

"Come in."

"Hey," I mumble as I close the door behind me.

"Hey sweetheart. Are you feeling any better?" Callan gets up from his desk immediately and walks toward me.

Today he's wearing a dark maroon pants-suit with a black silk tie on top of a white button down. My breath hitches at the realization that this is the man who fucks me when he comes home from work.

"Actually, I think I'm going to head back home. I really don't feel well." My head aches as I talk to him, the lights seem too bright, and my stomach is twisting like I just got off a rollercoaster.

He turns towards his desk and digs in one of the drawers before coming back to me. He reaches out his hand and gestures to me to open mine.

"What's this?" I hold my palm open as he drops a single key in it.

"Your new car," he announces.

"What?"

"Sterling, you couldn't possibly think that I'd own a dealership, let you live with me, call you my girlfriend, and not get you your own car, did you?" He smirks his all-consuming grin at me as I blink in bewilderment. "Especially when you've been such a good girl." His grin turns nefarious as he winks his stupidly gorgeous eye at me.

My own car?

I'm speechless.

"But seeing as you're pretty out of it, I'm going to have Gerald take you home today. We can test run this bad boy another day." He saunters back over to his desk to call Gerald.

"Callan, I don't know what to say. Thank you." He smiles at me as he waits for his call to be answered.

My own car.

I don't know how to process this.

God, could this man be any more perfect?

He finishes his conversation then walks back to me, still seated with my head in my hands.

"Do you need to go to urgent care?" I wince at the mention. Even though I'm in a better place now, I am still paying off the hospital bill that Callan has no idea about and I still don't have health insurance. The dealership offers coverage, but I missed the new hire deadline and now I have to wait for open enrollment. *Ugh, my head hurts so fucking bad.*

"No, I think I'll be fine. I just need more rest." Callan leans against his desk, his thigh brushing against my arm as he leans down and presses a sweet kiss into my hair.

"Gerald should be here soon." He presses another kiss to my head before pushing himself off his desk. But he redirects his path from his desk to his door when a knock raps against it.

"Come in," he hollers as he makes his way over. I know that as his assistant, I should probably make myself presentable, but I don't have the damn strength, so I bury my head further into my arms against his desk.

I hear the door creak open as an unfamiliar voice greets Callan.

"Hey, Dad. What are you doing here?" Callan asks and my whole body freezes.

His dad?

As in former owner of this dealership?

Play dead.

Please don't notice me.

"You haven't answered our calls since the family meeting and your mother was getting worried, so I decided to come check on you. Wanted to see the dealership too, see how things have been since I've left," his dad explains. Maybe it's because I'm super out-of-it, but I feel like there's something familiar about his voice.

I slowly lift my head from the desk and look over my shoulder. Callan is blocking his dad's view into the office; I can't see him, and he can't see me.

"Well, that's nice of you dad but I'm fine. Business is fine. Why don't you head back home? I promise I'll call when I'm ready," he speaks confidently to his father. It makes me hot when he talks like that, all bossy and powerful.

Suddenly, and shamefully, I feel a sneeze rising in my throat. It tickles the back of my nose and I try to pinch my nostrils to suppress the urge, but I can't stop it. It comes out full force. And I feel my face burn bright red when Callan's dad realizes that I'm in here.

"Do you have company?" his dad asks.

"Yes dad, but now's not a good time."

"There's always a suitable time for business. Introduce me. Don't be rude." I hear his dad's words and can pinpoint exactly what Callan meant when he'd said that his dad always has to make it about himself. Not to mention, he speaks like he's the most important person in the room.

As Callan attempts to reject his father access to the office, I get up from my chair and smooth myself over in an attempt to look somewhat decent. But my skirt is wrinkled, and my hair is now a tangled mess of waves.

I turn to the door just as Callan's dad pushes his way in. I look at Callan and his nod gives me a knowing apology.

"Dad, this is Sterling. My assistant. Sterling, this is my father, Richard."

"So, *this* is Sterling. Well, aren't you a sight for sore eyes," his father says as I bring my eyes up from the floor to his neatly pressed slacks, his single-buttoned blazer, his crisp tie, and his barely-shaven face. But... *his face.* I've seen that face before. I've seen...

"Sterling?" Callan's voice is weak in the background as I stare at the man in front of me. If I wasn't sick before, I am now. I know this man.

"Someone I love could be ruined if you speak about this accident."

"Take the money and never speak of this again, or else."

"You hit a deer and that's all anyone needs to know."

The words from that night filter into my head, like a memory I've lived over and over again, but tried to forget. I was groggy and on pain meds and I couldn't remember what the stranger had said to me, the one that gave me that envelope...until now. Until he's standing in front of me, locked onto me with his beady little eyes.

My body goes numb. All my organs suddenly act like they don't know how to work, and it feels like I can't breathe.

It's him.

The man looks at me and his face is sharp. I'll never forget his face.

The hospital.

"Is there something else I can help you with, dad?" Callan's mouth moves but the words are silent. I don't think he notices my reaction.

My head feels dizzy, as I'm flooded with this memory that I tried so desperately to forget.

The car accident.

Fire, snow, smoke.

The ground feels unsteady underneath my feet.

"Your assistant doesn't look so good," the old man speaks.

"Yeah, I was just about to send her home for the day until you so rudely interrupted."

"Why are you calling him *dad?*" I finally speak through hyperventilation. Callan's eyes fill with fear as he notices the panic in my voice.

"Sterling, are you okay?" Callan reaches over for my arm. His dad's eyes are studying me sharply. The walls feel like they're caving in.

"This is- this is-" I can't get the words out.

"Son." The man looks at Callan and I know he remembers me.

He has to.

The money.

The inconvenience.

"Sorry about the accident."

"Callan." I try to grab on to something, anything. I feel like the room is going black as I fall backward, catching myself on Callan's desk.

"Sweetheart, what's wrong?" Callan tries to hold me up and the touch of his hand on the small of my back sends adrenaline up my spine. Suddenly, the room stops spinning for a minute and I take a deep, long breath.

"Sweetheart?" His dad looks between the two of us.

"Callan," I attempt to speak as calmly as possible. "Is this man your dad?" I ask, afraid of his response. Even though I already know the answer.

"Yeah. Why?" He looks confused. But he had to have known the whole time. There's no way he didn't know. There's no way he...wait. If his dad is the man who bribed me, that has to mean...

"Someone I love..."

"You?" I seethe in question at Callan. "It was you!?"

I look over at the man who seems slightly uneasy now, as if he's just now realizing what I am just now realizing.

"So, this is *her*?" He asks Callan but is still staring at me. My body feels numb again, like I might faint.

"What the fuck is going on?" Callan demands.

"I can't believe you've been lying to me this whole time!" I shout at Callan. "And you!" I point to his dad. "You're a piece of shit, you know that?"

His dad snickers a small, sad, laugh laced with the roughness of a cough. Callan's eyes blink heavily, the hazel turning black, and his chest collapses harder with each exhale.

"Sterling, what are you talking about?" His concerned tone doesn't sound angry, but I can tell he's muddled and irritated. "Someone tell me what the fuck is happening!" Callan tries to lean into me, but I push him away.

"Don't touch me!" My mind goes blank, everything replaying in my head.

I try to form the words, my mind flashing between the night of the crash, and now.

Flames that beg to be put out, but the betrayal I feel only sets the fire free.

Lighting everything in its path.

Angry and vicious.

"You were the hit and run who wrecked my car, who wrecked my life," I start, trying to control my breathing. "You hit me, and then you just took off? You left me out in the cold? I could have died. And you-" I take in a hard, cold breath. "You had your dad bribe me to keep quiet? As if money is just the solution to everything, huh?"

It's all making sense to me now, as I pull all of the details together in my mind.

"He planted the idea of me using the money to buy a new car, which led me here, to you. You thought that this was the way to shut me up. You two came up with this little plan together?" My eyes dart feverishly between Callan and the man I remember in my hospital room that night, handing me a thick envelope of hundred-dollar bills, the *inconvenience fee.*

"You both knew? You gave me a job. You paid my rent, so you'd have something to hold over my head. You asked me to move in so you could keep tabs on me, and you told me-" The gears in my head are spinning, it feels like everything is spinning. "So, this was your plan? To string me along so you could continue to protect yourself? To keep me from telling your secret?" I'm disgusted. Every moment I've spent with Callan reruns in my head.

"Sterling..." Callan's words are quiet and small, barely a whisper, in the roaring chaos that fills the room. "I had absolutely no idea that was you." Callan finally speaks. His words hit me like hail. How can he continue to lie like this? He had to have known.

"Dad?" He looks over to his father.

"Wow, Callan. Run to daddy, why don't you? See how far that's gotten you?" I can't help it, the hatred I feel in this moment. The sob story he fed me about his family, was that a lie too? Was everything a lie?

"Callan, you should have known she was going to find out at some point." His dad speaks, coughing loudly after every few words.

"You really bribed her?" Callan's eyes turn from anger to sadness to confusion and then all three at once. "This wasn't supposed to happen. I never should have listened to you!" Callan fires back at his dad, but it feels insincere to me.

"Sterling, baby. You have to believe me." Callan reaches for my hand as I try to press my back against the wall, wanting to melt right into the paint. *I need to get out of here.*

"You! Stay the fuck away from me!" I demand as I hold my hands up between us.

"Maybe you should go, Sterling." Callan's dad addresses me.

"Don't talk to me. Either of you. I'll call the police," I threaten, not really knowing what the police could even do at this point. I'm crying so hard, shaking even worse, I didn't even realize it at first, but I feel like I'm drowning.

"Sterling, please." Callan doesn't move any closer as he speaks. He just stands in the middle of his office looking at me with pleading eyes. The ones I used to love getting lost in, but now I can't trust them.

"There's no fucking way this is a coincidence," I hiss at him, trying to keep my composure. "I don't want to be a pawn in your fucked up little father-son game anymore. Just stay away from me." I throw my words at Callan, and I can tell they strike, as his eyes glaze over and tears begin to fall.

I can't take this anymore. I sidestep Callan and his dad, keeping my head down as I speed walk out of the building. I need to put as much distance between me and them as possible. My feet finally hit the pavement outside, and I stop in my tracks, staring at the clouded sky above. Nothing feels real.

Was he telling the truth? Did he not know? Surely, he had to have known. Tears stream down my face as rain starts to pour from above. Perfect. Just fucking perfect.

Who do I call? What do I do? Where do I go? I can't call Dakota. I can't go to Sara's. I still have a couple of days left in my apartment before the new tenants officially move in. And I certainly don't want to go to his house. I can't believe this is happening.

I look down, remembering the key from Callan is still in my palm. I release the grip, realizing I've been squeezing so tight that I left an imprint on my skin.

I click the unlock button frantically and hear the beep echo from afar. I walk toward the noise, still dizzy with anger. My feet drag as I weave through the cars, and the sound finally pulls me into a red BMW. *Prick.* I know nothing about cars, but I know that this will get me to where I need to go.

Far, far away from here.

THIRTY-ONE

Callan

"I told you not to fuck this up," My dad speaks to me, his tone controlling and demanding.

"None of this would have happened if it weren't for you!" I shout. My head is pounding. The woman in the driver's seat, the blood, and the smoke. *That was Sterling?* How have we gone all this time without her mentioning the car accident once? I could have explained everything to her sooner, avoided this whole situation. It doesn't help that I had no idea about the bribe.

"Why the fuck did you have to ruin this?" I yell at my father.

"Ruin what? Who knew that the girl you hired was the one you almost killed with your reckless driving?" He finds this comical. "And it seems as though you're involved with her, romantically? Bad call. Didn't I teach you to not mix business with pleasure?"

"Fuck off!" I go to walk past him, but he blocks me.

"Son, I didn't come here with the intention of this happening. But maybe it's best it did. She was going to find out one way or the other."

"Oh, like you care."

"Cal. I don't have much time. I came here to apologize." He grabs me by my elbow.

"Are you fucking crazy?" I shake him from me. "You just blew up my whole fucking life. Sterling is never going to forgive me." I grip the door frame with one hand and fist my hair with the other.

This is not happening.

How can Sterling be *that girl*? I've allowed myself to finally feel, I let this girl infiltrate my heart, my life. And this one stupid fucking mistake is going to ruin it.

"Do you love her?" My dad asks in a monotone voice.

"What?"

He chokes out a couple of coughs before speaking again, "Do you love her? Really?"

"Why the fuck does that matter to you?" This feels unreal. I have to go after her.

I turn to grab my car keys and my phone.

"I'm sorry, son. I'm sorry that I turned you into this monster of a man who doesn't feel emotions. I should have led you down a different path." I choke out a laugh as he speaks. The words seem so insincere coming from his mouth.

"Fuck you. Lucky for everyone I wasn't too far gone, and Sterling was able to crack the broken surface you created. She uncovered the real me, the one you tried to bury."

"It was for your own good," he states. "Or at least I thought. I just didn't want you to get hurt like I did."

"What the fuck does that mean?"

"Your mom-" He tries to speak but the cough stops him from continuing.

Then I remember the family meeting, the news my mom broke. The reason why my dad is a pain in the ass. Because he was hurt by a woman he loved.

"Just because you got hurt, doesn't mean you had to scare your only son into living an emotionless life," I respond, looking down at my phone as I type out a text to Sterling.

A thud to the ground radiates to my feet like an earthquake and my eyes dart up. My dad is on the ground, hand thrown to his chest as he cries out in pain, coughing and trying to breathe. I panic and move toward him, not knowing what to do.

I swing my office door open, looking for someone, anyone, to help.

"I need someone to call an ambulance. Now!" I shout down the hall. I reach down and stare at my dad, realizing the severity of his condition.

"Fuck, dad. Hang on. Help is on its way."

THIRTY-TWO

Sterling

Tears stain my cheeks as I weave down the winding road toward my old apartment. I use one hand to wipe my eyes, the other hand gripped anxiously on the steering wheel. Halfway through my drive, I realize this is the same road that started it all.

The car crash.

I'd never noticed it before because I was always sitting in the backseat of Gerald's car, probably too busy overthinking. But being the one in the driver's seat, the memories smack me in the face so hard, I have to pull over.

When I step out of the car to look around, it's like a time warp. I can perfectly envision his car coming around the corner at an ungodly speed as his headlights blurred my vision. I remember myself trying to start my car, frantically attempting to prevent the inevitable. Then, black.

A tight lump forms in my throat as I picture it all playing out in my head.

I picture Callan getting out of his car, assessing the damage. Then getting on the phone, presumably calling his dad. Then within minutes, he's gone.

I squeeze my eyes shut and look away, hoping maybe I can force the memories to disappear if I try hard enough. I inhale slowly, trying to catch my breath. I can't do this to myself.

I get back into the car and speed away, knowing that being there, reliving that moment over and over again, would only make me feel worse.

The apartment is cold and dark and empty with only a couch that we left behind when I moved out. The whole situation seems strange. Of course, I don't want to stay here tonight, but the thought of going home, to *our* home, makes my stomach churn. I feel a wave of regret wash over me as I think back to how quickly I agreed to move in with Callan. *Do I really even know him?*

I don't know how to process this. The mess that's laid out so cynically in front of me.

I only know that I want it to stop.

The pain.

The heartbreak.

I lower myself to the worn-down couch and curl up, wishing I could bury myself in a blanket. It's a bad nightmare and maybe when I wake up, it'll all be over.

I'm awoken by my phone violently buzzing. The late afternoon sun peeks through the small window, the harsh rays making me squint as I try and shake the sleepiness.

A text from Callan sits at the top of my notifications, along with the several missed phone calls before that.

> My dad is in the hospital. He had a heart attack.

I'm still reeling from the shock of what I found out a few hours ago, I definitely don't know how to react to this on top of everything. This can't be happening right now.

And then another one comes through.

> I'll leave you alone if you need space. You can have the penthouse to yourself, I'll find somewhere to stay. But please let me know when I can come talk to you. I promise I can explain.

My heart sinks.

I'm sad and torn apart. I never should've gotten my hopes up for a future with him. This whole time, it was Callan. All I can think about is how much time I've wasted with this person, with this monster. How could he live his life with this kind of secret hanging over his head?

I wipe the sleepiness from my eyes as I walk to the bathroom. I run cold water from the sink, splashing my face in hopes that it'll wake up my brain and give me all the answers. I look in the mirror. Even when I was at my worst before, I was at least able to recognize myself. But now, I see a stranger.

The product of a broken heart.

But I still care about him. Those feelings won't go away overnight, no matter what.

I start to dial Callan's number, my fingers hesitating over his name. I feel numb, especially as I hit the call button and the phone starts to ring. It only rings once before Callan's voice comes through on the other line.

"Sterling?" His voice is raspy and deep, and desperate. "Please talk to me."

I sit quietly, looking out the window as the sun starts to set behind the mountains. I take a second to calm my breathing and think about what I want to say. I hate how just the sound of his voice can elevate my heart rate so quickly.

"I care about you, Callan, so much. And it scares me how quickly that's happened. I think that's why we need space," I whisper into the phone and my heart breaks a little more.

"Space?" I hear the waver in his tone, he's scared. He knows he messed up. "Don't do this, Sterling. I'll pay for your medical bills. I'll turn myself in. I had no clue that was you, I swear. It was a mistake. I need you Sterling."

I pull the phone away from my ear, not wanting to hear his begs and pleads. I can't take any more pain right now and I definitely don't want to feel sorry for him.

"I don't want your money, Callan," I say as I bring the phone back up to my ear, tears involuntarily streaming down my face.

"Then what do you want? What can I give you right now? Name it. I'll give you anything. Just tell me what to do Sterling." His voice is shaky, like he's on the verge of crying.

"Give me space," I whisper lightly as my heart races in my chest.

"I don't want to give you space," he responds.

"I just...I need time."

"Sterling," Callan whispers, and the way he says my name hits me like a ton of bricks. The pain in his voice sounds sincere, and I want to believe him.

"I'll stay at the penthouse, but I need time." I hear him sigh with what almost sounds like relief. I'm half tempted to hang up the phone, but I wait for his response.

"I'm sorry, Sterling. Please call me when you're ready." And then the phone clicks to silence.

The tears hit relentlessly, attacking my face all at once. It's too much. The feelings are too much, I just want to shut them off.

At least he didn't lie about one thing.

He did ruin me.

THIRTY-THREE

Callan

I have cancer.

The words played on an aggressive loop in my head as I drove down the winding, snow packed road. Speeding. Drunk. Pissed.

Who the fuck springs those words on someone over the phone? I know who, my father. He's the true definition of asshole. He acts as if he's so professional and such a "family-man" for an audience, but behind the curtain he's an inconsiderate, cowardly prick. And now, an inconsiderate, cowardly prick with cancer.

I was just leaving a company party when he called. We were celebrating a record-breaking year, my first year as owner of the dealership. When I stepped outside to take the call, he didn't even give me a chance to be eased into the news. Just casually dumped it on me, like it was a weather report.

He might as well have said, "Oh hey, son. So, tomorrow's weather is going to be a bit snowy with some light wind chill. Oh, and a one hundred percent chance of me having cancer."

And to say that I walked my ass right back into that party, accepted my award and then downed a whole bottle of Don Julio, would be an understatement. I wasn't expecting that phone call. But then again, I'd never expect anything less from him.

I knew I needed to get out of there, I didn't want my business partners to see my drunken meltdown.

I traveled down the winding road that led from my dealership to my penthouse, speeding, drunk, pissed. I wasn't thinking straight. My head felt fuzzy and even though the buzz numbed some of the emotion, I was still filled with confusion and anger as I kept driving in the raging blizzard.

Next thing I knew...

Headlights.

Then a crash.

The sight of snow and smoke blurred my vision as I struggled to get my seat belt unbuckled. My Aston Martin took the collision head on, but my vehicle wasn't nearly as bad as the other's.

I panicked. I was so wasted I didn't know who else to call and before I could decipher what I was actually doing, my dad's voice answered the phone.

"What's going on, Callan?" His annoyed voice stuck in my head proving how much of an inconvenience I was to him.

"I just got into a fucking wreck."

"A what?"

"A car accident you dumb ass!" I yelled at my dad.

"Watch your tone with me, son." His voice was stiff and tense, his poor attempt at speaking like a man with power.

"What the fuck do I do? It's bad. It's really bad."

"How many others?"

"Just one, I think."

"Are they breathing?" he had asked.

I attempted to get closer, but I chose not to. I didn't want to have to see the damage I'd done. I saw steam escape her nostrils in the freezing air, an indication that she'd been breathing.

"She's alive. But fuck, it's so bad."

"I'll take care of it."

"What do I do?"

"Wait there for Gerald. I'll have a tow truck come for your car and I'll take care of the rest."

"What about the girl?" I questioned.

"I said, I'll take care of it."

Everything after that was a blur for so long. I blocked out the memory of that night because it's always been too painful. I've hated myself every day for hitting someone and driving off. Now knowing it was Sterling, the torment is a thousand times worse. I have to face what I've done, and what I allowed my father to do.

My driver, Gerald, dropped me off and I walked through the double glass doors of my all-too-familiar childhood home. I headed straight to the bathroom, turned on the faucet and noticed that my hands were shaking for the first time in my life. I splashed cold water over my face and looked in the mirror. I didn't even recognize the person staring back at me.

I gripped the sink with my hands as I took a deep breath. I never felt so out of control before. My whole life had been made up of rules and regulations, like a damn contract handed over by my father.

I have cancer.

As I stared back at my reflection, my eyes clouded with dark circles and my deep brown hair was a scrambled mess. I thought about why I acted out when my father called me and told me he had cancer, why what he said angered me so damn much.

I have cancer.

He said it like it didn't matter to him. Like it didn't matter to me. And maybe it didn't. Maybe I didn't care, and I got pissed because he knew we were celebrating a big night, my first since I'd been in control of the company and as usual, he needed to steal the spotlight.

I looked back down at my hands, unable to stop them from trembling. How could I have been so fucking stupid? Why did I call my dad for help? Why did I seek answers from a man who caused me to react that way in the first place? I was so pissed off that the situation took a turn for the worse. But what pissed me off the most, what caused me to throw my fist into the mirror, was that I listened to him.

The glass shattered, spilling all over the counter, shards glistened with the running water. It didn't shock me when I looked up and saw my dad standing in the doorway, staring at me behind unamused eyes. He turned back into the hallway. I reached over for the hand towel and cleaned up the blood from my knuckles before joining him.

"What's your problem?" My dad took a seat at his desk and motioned for me to do the same, as I followed him into his office. The dark cherry wood of his desk seemed darker as the blackout curtains were pulled shut, leaving only the sconces stuck in the wall that provided dim lighting around us.

"Are you fucking kidding me?" I shouted in question without thinking.

He shuffled his position in his chair.

"Don't play dumb. You know what you did." I tried to keep it together, but I couldn't control my irritation. This was exactly what he wanted to happen. He wanted me to need him for something.

"Callan. I understand this may seem-"

"Fucked up," I finished his sentence.

"Yeah, sure. But you have to understand-"

"Fuck that. Don't tell me what I have to understand. Do you have any idea how fucking selfish you are? I was on that road because of you! I was under the influence because of you!" My father was always one to try and weasel his way out of owning up to anything. And even if there wasn't a bigger picture here, I'd still make a big deal about it. He was always trying to make everything about him; springing his illness on me on one of the biggest nights of my life is a prime example for starters.

"Are you mad at your carelessness or that I have cancer?" His question ticked in my ear. "Son, I didn't ask for this disease. But you sure as hell didn't need to lose control like that. You could have killed someone. You better be fucking thanking me for-"

"For what? For being a fucking hero and saving the day?" I leaned in my chair and loosened the tie around my neck as I huffed in frustration.

"Everything is taken care of," he'd answered as he lit a cigar that he pulled from his stash.

"That's all you're going to give me?" I questioned, getting up from my chair.

"Your new car will be delivered in the morning. Everything is taken care of. Be lucky she didn't die. A dead body is a lot harder to cover up." He stopped as he dragged the cigar to and from his mouth,

blowing a cloud of smoke into the air. "Callan, this can't get out to anyone. Me being sick is bad enough. But you're the CEO now, the owner of the business. If this got out..." He trailed off and it took me a second to process what the fuck had just happened. I started to realize that all I was able to do was to move on. What's done was done, and the sooner I accepted that, the quicker I was able to get the hell out of here.

Sure, my dad's audacious act of covering a hit and run was ludicrous at best, but better a hit and run no one knows about rather than a drinking and driving charge that could destroy my career.

The doctors confirm that my dad had a heart attack, a common complication of lung cancer, likely due to being in a state of distress.

My drive home from the hospital is emotional; I'm so incredibly furious with my dad, and yet, I hate seeing him sick. I want him to be okay. And above all else, I'm desperate to talk to Sterling. She's the one person who I'd want to run to at a time like this, and I've completely fucked it up.

It's highly likely that she'll move out of my house, and I'll never see her again. But she asked for space, and I want to respect that.

I think back to that night. How my dad called me and delivered his death note. And the way I drowned myself in alcohol before attempting to drive myself home.

Then I hit her.

I was so incredibly selfish that night.

Tears fill my eyes at the memory.

As I pull into the driveway of my family's estate, shakiness overcomes me, and all of the emotions flood my body at once.

"Fuck! Fuck! Fuck! Fuck! Fuck!" I scream as my fists match rhythm with my words, slamming down into the steering wheel. This is all my fault. If Sterling never forgives me for this, I don't know what I'm going to do, but the only person I can blame is myself.

It takes everything in me not to call her or go see her. Minutes turn into hours. The hours turn into days.

It's been the longest four days of my life, since I've last spoken to Sterling. Going into work without her feels meaningless. But there's really nowhere else for me to go. If I'm not at work or my parent's house, I'm at the hospital. And though I'm pissed at my dad, he's still my dad. The downfall of opening up my heart is realizing that there's a part of me that still cares about my dad and wants him to somehow overcome this.

I pull into the hospital parking lot for the third time this week and every time it gets harder. I know this is where they took Sterling. To know that she was here struggling after what I'd done makes me sick. But I find a way to suppress the feeling as I enter the emergency unit and sign in to go visit my dad.

"Heard he's doing better today," the receptionist says to me as she prints a visitor sticker.

"That's good to hear." I take the sticker from her.

"Visiting hours end in about forty-five minutes."

"Thank you," I say before turning to head to his room.

I walk around the corner to see Virginia sitting on a chair just outside of the waiting room down the hall.

"Hey, Ginny," I offer as I approach her.

"Hey, Cal."

"Oh, she talks today," I attempt a joke, but I instantly regret it when she shoots daggers at me with her sharp brown eyes.

"It's been four days, Cal. Is dad going to get to leave soon?" She looks up at me, water begging to break behind her lashes.

I sit down in the chair next to her and wrap my arm around her back and pull her into me. As soon as she's huddled in my embrace, she cries. I feel for her. She has also been affected by so much these past few months. Finding out at fifteen that your dad isn't actually your dad has to be life-altering. And as close with him as she was, I'm sure it only became more painful when she learned that he's sick.

"Listen, Virginia. I'm not sure things will get better. But I promise I'll always be there for you. No matter what." I press a kiss into her hair.

"I just want this all to end. I want everyone to be happy again." She pulls herself out of my embrace and swipes at the tears on her cheeks.

"Me too, sis."

"Hey, kiddos," Mom's voice breaks through the air. "Callan, Dad would like to see you." She approaches the chairs and offers me a small smile as we trade places.

Walking into my dad's room feels different this time. Because even though I've been here every day since the accident, I haven't actually talked to him.

I turn the corner and enter his room. His bed is angled so that he's sitting up slightly, watching the evening news on TV.

"Hey," I murmur.

"Son," he responds, groggy and tired.

"How you feeling today?" I walk into the room a little further.

"Better. But not my best."

The room goes silent.

What is there to say?

Sorry you had a heart attack because the new assistant I hired and started seeing found out that you bribed her not to tell anyone about the car accident I caused with my drunk driving because you told me you had cancer?

Yeah, let's not.

"I'm sorry for everything," my dad speaks quietly from the other side of the room.

That's a start.

"I didn't mean to cause this much turmoil in your life, really. I only wanted what was best for you, Callan." I look over to see my dad struggling to get the words out, like it's taking everything in of him to apologize.

"I have fought a war in my mind every single day, trying to cope with how you treated me," I start, "I tried to build a relationship with you when I was young, wanted to look up to you. But I never felt worthy of your attention. Do you know what that felt like as a little boy?" I feel myself choke up as I admit what I've been holding onto for years. But if I never took the chance to tell him how I feel, I'm not sure I'd ever be able to forgive him.

Or myself.

"I do know what that feels like. My dad did the same thing to me. Pops was a real dick," we both chuckle, remembering what an even bigger asshole my grandpa was. The angriest old man I've ever known.

"Doesn't mean I needed to project that onto you and I'm sorry," he finishes.

There's so much unsaid that I can't force myself to bring up. It seems pretty meaningless at a time like this. He was there for Ginny and that's all that matters. I will move on from this. But I hate that all of this has affected the woman I love.

The woman I love.

I love her, so much. And it's just dawned on me that I may never get to tell her. And though we're no on the best of terms and the timing might absolutely suck, I have to tell someone.

"I do think I love her," I tell my dad.

"Love is tricky, son. It's messy and it hurts. But when it's not messy and when it doesn't hurt, it's the best feeling in the world," he coughs before he can finish, "I loved your mom with every ounce of my being. Still do. She was always there for me, till she wasn't. And even though she made a mistake, I still loved her. But it was never the same. The biggest heartbreak of it all was finding out that Virginia wasn't mine." His voice begins to break as he forces out the last sentence. He clears his throat and adjusts in his bed.

"Listen," he begins again, "I know it's not ideal timing, but I think you need to go to her, to Sterling. You'll never know if you don't try. I'd hate for you to look back wondering what could've been all because I was the worst parent on the planet."

I take in my dad's words carefully. This is the first meaningful conversation I can remember ever having with him. And though he's stuck in a hospital bed, it's nice.

But I don't know how I feel taking advice from him now or ever. I do know that my heart craves Sterling right now.

"I told her I'd give her space," I answer.

"When women say they need space, it means they want the opposite," he replies.

"I highly doubt that's what they mean," I scoff. He's clearly delusional.

"You're probably right. But you still need to go to her. Don't give her any more time to know what it feels like to be without you. I'm sure she needs you right now as much as you need her." He waves his hands to the door.

I nod my head at him knowingly.

It won't last long, this bridge building we have to do to get back some sort of semblance of a relationship, because soon his time will run out. And honestly, something like that will take more time than he'd have even if he wasn't dying. But it means something to me now, in the moment. "Thanks, dad."

"Now tell the nurse to get in here, I need a cigar and a sandwich." I let out an annoyed laugh as I turn to the leave the room.

As I step into the hallway, I'm stopped dead in my tracks.

An illusion.

It must be.

I blink my eyes hard and when I open them, she comes into focus once more.

"I heard through the grapevine that you may be in love?" Her voice fills my chest, like a breath of fresh air I didn't know I needed.

"Sterling?"

"He's right, you know." She takes a few slow steps towards me from the other end of the hall, but I don't want to move, in fear that this daydream will end.

"About what?"

"About women asking for space. Usually, we say that because we're angry or upset. But we're too stubborn to admit that what we really want is the opposite." She smiles that beautiful fucking smile, and every part of me aches to have her in my arms.

"You heard that?" I ask.

"Every word." She bats her lashes at me, pushes her hair behind her ear and then says, "And I think I love you too."

I don't hesitate, I track my way toward her to close the distance with such eagerness, I almost collide with her. But just like in the movies, she jumps at just the right time, and I pull her into my chest, wrapping her legs around me. I brace her with one hand on her bottom and the other in her hair and the crash of our lips is like fitting the last puzzle piece to reveal the final image.

An all-consuming kiss.

Lightning and thunder.

My girl in my arms.

"You're here?" I break the kiss reluctantly.

"You'd think I'd let you deal with this all on your own?" Her fingers run through my hair, the feeling of longing settling in me.

I set her back down, and she plants her feet on the ground in front of me.

"Sterling, the car acci-"

"Callan."

"No, I need to apologize." I hold up my hand to my chest. Sterling's eyes catch mine, they look just as tired as mine probably do.

"I know, Callan."

"Well then hear me out," I plead.

"No, I mean I know. I got here before you did and talked to Richard. He explained everything to me."

"Richard? As in my father? You talked to my *dad*?" I'm in shock. And I'm now understanding the conversation with my dad even more. He had his heart softened by Sterling, just like I did. She dug the emotion out of him just as she's done with me. It just secures the way I feel about her even more, heightens the way I need her.

"Yes, that would be the Richard I'm referring to." She lets out a small chuckle, then her expression turns serious. "I'll be honest, Cal. When he got a hold of me and asked me to come, I was prepared to let all hell break loose on him. But I chose to listen to him first and when he explained what had happened, how he dropped the news of his cancer on you so abruptly, everything made sense. He told me about the bribe, told me how completely unaware of anything he did. Told me how upset you were at him and at yourself that you didn't do the right thing after you hit me that night. It doesn't excuse what happened, but it gives me enough to go off of. Enough to understand that you are not the monster I assumed you were in that moment. I know you were in a bad place, and I know that you never intended to hurt me, or anyone." Her soft voice is so sincere. Tears gather in the corners of my eyes just as hers start to stream down her cheek.

Both of us take a much-needed breath before she continues.

"I want you to know, I'm going to be mad at you. But I don't want to hold this against you forever, and I want us to move on." Her lashes fan the tops of her cheeks as she looks down to the ground and then back up to me. In this moment still, I've never seen anything more beautiful than the woman standing in front of me.

"I'm so incredibly grateful for you, Sterling. And I will spend the rest of this life and the next, doing everything I can to show you how sorry I am, if given the chance."

"This is something I want to work through with you. Together." Her blue eyes hold me hostage.

"I don't deserve you," I whisper as I reach out to run my thumb along her cheek.

"We all make mistakes. Yours are just really big and hard to ignore and probably deserve some jail time and a couple of AA classes." We both laugh, lightening up the mood a tad. But her laughter does more than that to me, it brings me back to life. "But nonetheless, you deserve a second chance. I see you for who you really are. Kind, hardworking, and willing to be better than you were the day before. And I'm not ready to let that man go."

My heart beats for this girl. Every ounce of me is alive for her.

"Can I take you home?" I ask, feeling too overwhelmed to keep standing here.

"I'd like that."

I take her hand and lead her down the hallway.

I'm not wasting any more time. I'm going to make this right.

THIRTY-FOUR

Sterling

The assault of butterflies happens all too quickly as the elevator doors open. Though I've been staying here the past few days, it feels different now that we're both here, together.

I know my heart isn't going to heal from this overnight, but I know that with Callan it will feel full again. His willingness to work through this with me proves that. Love isn't always perfect, but with him it feels right.

Callan kicks off his shoes as he drags me by my hand deeper into the living room. When he pulls me closer into him, he holds my face in his hands as the browns and greens in his eyes search mine. Everything I've been feeling these past few days is overcome with so much more emotion. The ache in my heart turns to passion.

"I've missed you so much, Sterling." Callan pushes my hair behind my shoulders and the mere touch of him gives me heart palpitations, heat racing to my cheeks.

"I missed you, too."

He leans in and spreads kisses from my lips to my neck and back up to my lips, his hands passionately grazing my skin under my shirt. The ache in my core grows increasingly with every brush of his lips.

We kiss for what seems like forever, just standing in the center of his living room. I think he's hesitant because it feels unreal. I feel it too. So, I decide to lead the way, breaking the kiss to take him into his room.

We get to the edge of the bed, and in a frenzy we're both pulling at each other's clothes.

"God, I've fucking missed you," he repeats again as he gently glides my pants down.

He trails kisses up my legs on his way back up, taking his time so he doesn't miss a single spot. I moan when he reaches the apex of my thighs, his lips teasing me at the top of my thong, and I throw my head back as I feel all the pleasure he's bringing to my body.

"Everything inside me burns for you, my little rose. You've ruined the fuck out of me and if you don't mind, I plan to do the very same to you." He stands up to meet me, our eyes searching for each other's deepest desires. It's all too much and he gently pulls my face up to his and he greedily takes my mouth into his, kissing me roughly and passionately.

"I'd very much like that, Mr. David," I whisper, and he lowers me onto my back. His mouth moves to my collarbone then slowly makes its way to the top of my bra with delicate kisses, my skin pebbling as he does.

"But one more thing, Callan." I hold my hands to his chest before I let him continue.

"Anything."

"No more secrets. We tell each other everything from here on out," I manage to say. I don't want anything like this to happen to us again, we all make mistakes, but I want us to go through them together.

"Promise." He kisses my temple gently.

"And I do want a label," I admit rather playfully.

"A label?" he asks with a classic Callan smirk curled on his lips.

"Yes. I want to be-"

"My girlfriend." He cuts me off, and I can't hide the massive smile that spreads across my face.

"Yes."

"Sterling Rose wants to be my girlfriend." He licks his lips as his fingers trail from my waist to below the curve of my breast. "Did you think that you were gonna make it out of this any other way?" He unhooks my bra in one swift motion. I let out a breathy sigh as he swirls his tongue around the bud of my breast. He uses one hand to grip the back of my neck, squeezing lightly as he sucks.

I moan as I arch my back with his touch.

Greedy for more.

He dips his hand into my panties and finds the heat of me.

"Fuck, baby. You're so fucking wet for me."

"I told you I missed you." I take my hands to his back and dig deep into his skin with my nails which rewards me with a reverberating growl against my breasts.

"I can't wait to show you how much I've missed you too." His fingers slide up and down, gliding confidently like he knows me better than I know myself. I grab his hand and lean in to lick my arousal from his fingers. He growls as he leans back into my breast, sucking on my skin.

I guide his head down to my core. He splays his palm on my belly as he uses the other to take my underwear off. His tongue meets my clit and electricity shoots up my spine, my whole body lifting off the bed as I moan.

"Damn, you did miss me," he whispers as he inserts two fingers into my entrance.

He looks at me with his hungry hazel eyes, his fingers pumping inside of me as I grip the bed sheets.

"I want you inside me, Cal," I say to him very impatiently. And he wastes no time giving me what I want.

He stands up and pulls down his pants, his erection freeing as his boxers hit the floor. My stomach growls at his length, almost forgetting how large he is. He rips off his shirt and hovers over me, but I take control as I stand up and press my palms to his chest, pushing him down to the bed to lay flat on his back.

"Who's the bossy one now?" He laughs as I climb on top.

I pull my mouth over to his and kiss him softly before taking my mouth to his dick. I give him one long lick up his shaft and swirl my tongue around his tip, tasting his pre-cum. I pull back up and position myself, my knees on either side of his thighs. I grab the base and guide it in, slowly and steadily. Callan bites his lip so hard, I'm afraid he's going to bleed. I work my way over him as he thrusts his hips gently into me.

"I was made for you," I tell him, pushing his dick deeper inside of me.

"Yes, you fucking were, my little rose," he growls as he digs his fingers deep into my ass.

Now, he's all the way in and the way he fills me up makes me go dizzy. I take his hands in mine, lacing our fingers together. At first, we move slowly, speeding up as we find the perfect rhythm with each other. The feeling of my walls gripping his cock is exhilarating. I speed up my pace, needing to let go of his hands to lower myself into him. He grips tightly around my waist as I take control. The sound of our breathing gets heavier.

"Atta girl," he groans. "Keep it up, baby." I lean into his neck and allow myself to lick the lobe of his ear which makes him pull me deeper into him.

"Oh, fuck, Sterling. You ride me so fucking well."

I can feel myself about to cross the finish line. And I know he's close too.

I sit up and lean back a little, arching my spine as I continue riding him.

It's overwhelming. My heart beats faster as the intensity spreads through my body, tingles and goosebumps taking over my skin as I look into his eyes.

I can feel it.

"You are so breathtakingly beautiful." He praises me and I feel myself contracting, tight with pleasure as he thrusts into me and whispers his affirmations to me.

It's consuming.

"Callan." His name is a whisper on my lips.

"I know, baby." He leans in to kiss me. "I know."

Love.

What I feel is love.

Home.

It's funny how the universe brought us here. Creating love in a way we never knew we needed. Sharing passions and secrets and deep desires that make us stronger, connecting us.

We may have been led down the wrong road at the right time, or maybe it was the right road at the wrong time. Regardless, we traveled down that road, and it led us here, to find what our hearts truly desired, *to feel loved.*

Colliding.

But regardless of the path we took to get here, it was always meant to be us.

Callan and I, we were made for each other.

Together, we crashed. Forever, we'll burn.

THE EPILOGUE

Callan

SIX MONTHS LATER

"I can't find it anywhere. I swear I left it right here." Sterling frantically runs around the bathroom, hair half curled, half pulled into a clip on the top of her head. She's wearing my personal favorite pair of skinny jeans she owns, and a red lace bra. She hasn't even put her shirt on yet as she scours the bathroom.

"Baby, I'm sure it'll turn up somewhere." I stand at the doorway knowing damn well that I have what she's looking for. Her promise ring. The one I gave her a few months ago. It was to establish my promise to her, to always keep her smiling. It was perfect for her, a little rose on a golden band and a small diamond in the center.

I know she said no more secrets but, this one doesn't count. I mean, some secrets have to be kept.

"I just don't understand how it grew legs or something. I put it right here." She spins around to face me and sighs out frustration, her hair lifting in front of her face as she huffs. *God, she's fucking beautiful.*

"It's not funny," she rasps.

"You look like a crazy person, Sterling," I joke, and she reaches out to backhand my chest.

"Ow, that hurt," I say sarcastically as I pull my palm to my heart.

"You're an ass," she sneers. I walk up to her and plant a soft kiss on her temple, but she playfully tries to wiggle free.

"Finish getting ready, sweetheart. You're gonna make us late. We'll look for the ring later." She turns back to her curling iron. "And put a shirt on before I say fuck dinner and take you to bed instead." She smirks at me in the mirror and disappears into the closet.

About a half hour later, we show up to the restaurant. It's nothing too fancy, but it's a nice and quiet little place that overlooks the city. We're guided to our table by a waiter and take a seat near the window.

"Why the hell did they seat us at a table with eight chairs?" Sterling's face is filled with confusion as I pull out a chair for her.

"Maybe it was all they had left?" I lie, knowing damn well that I made the reservation and I specifically asked for a table of eight.

"Whatever, at least the view is nice." She's looking out the window, and I'd have to agree, only, I'm not looking out the wi ndow...I'm looking at her.

"Drinks?" The waitress asks and I let Sterling order her own drink first, the same way I have ever since the lesson she taught me with that damn strawberry daiquiri. She smiles as she orders a dirty martini and I order my usual whiskey neat.

"This is nice, we haven't done this in a while." She reaches over to me and grabs my hand but with my nerves so on edge, I accidentally pull away slightly. I don't want her to feel how badly I'm shaking.

She gives me a worried look and I pretend like I had to reach for my phone. *Just one more secret. This will almost be over with.*

"I know, we've both been so busy with work," I smirk as she looks into my eyes. Knowing damn well that *busy with work* means *fucking in my office* most of the time. But really, she does work hard, and the dealership is running great.

"Here you are. Are you ready to order?" The server places our drinks in front of us before pulling out her notepad.

"Not quite, we're still waiting," I gesture to the table, and she smiles and walks away.

"Waiting for what?" Sterling questions, but before I have time to come up with an excuse, a voice shouts her name from across the restaurant.

"Dakota?" Sterling gets up from her seat and walks toward her friend. They share a big grizzly hug before turning back to the table. "What are you doing here?"

"I was invited to dinner, so I came." Her friend looks over at me and smiles before pulling out a chair across from us.

"You were?" Sterling looks between the two of us and I'm nervous she's going to work it out before I want her to. "You came all the way from North Carolina for dinner?"

"I needed to come down anyways, Asher and I need to work some things out. But you're what's important right now. I've missed my bestie." She smiles as she tilts her head down to her shoulder and Sterling returns the gesture.

"Right this way." We hear another host walking three more people toward our table. This time, they're for me.

"Boss man! What's up?" Jax's voice reaches us first, followed by my mother and sister.

"Hey honey," my mother greets me as she approaches us, Virginia in step and Jax right behind them.

"Hey mom." I stand up to kiss her on the cheek then reach to hug Ginny. Sterling is now eyeing Dakota with a stare that says *what the fuck* and Dakota just shrugs her shoulder.

"So nice to see you again." Mom reaches for Sterling as she gets up from her chair and hugs her.

Sterling met my mom and sister at my dad's funeral a few months ago. It wasn't how I wanted them to meet but nonetheless they did, and my mom has gushed on and on about how much she loves Sterling. She's had an effect on Virginia as well. They occasionally go to get their nails done on the weekends and Ginny has even opened up to her about the new girl at school that she secretly has a crush on.

"You too, Cait," Sterling says before turning to me with a slightly uneasy glare. I start to feel guilty, hiding this from her when she was just expecting the two of us to go out for a dinner date.

"What about me?" Jax pipes up as my mom and sister take their seats. He pulls my girl into a hug before turning to me to do the same. Jax sits next to my mom, who both sit across from us. Sterling looks to her left and there are two more empty chairs next to her and I know she's trying to put something together in her head.

"So, who else is joining us?" She turns to look at me, trying to seem unaffected but I know she senses something's up.

Everyone smiles politely at each other before the server comes back and asks the others what they'd like to drink. I reach my hand under the table and squeeze Sterling's thigh which elicits a small moan out of her. She seems a little on edge but soon, I'll be able to tell her.

"Do you want any appetizers?" I ask her as I try to calm my nerves.

"Did someone say appetizers?" A little voice speaks up from beside Sterling and everyone including the waitress looks over. But the look on Sterling's face when this particular guest shows up is the one I was anticipating the most.

"Sara?" Sterling rushes out of her seat and picks up the thirteen-year-old girl, swinging her in her arms. "Oh my gosh, what are you doing here?" Sterling looks up behind Sara to see Miss Nguyen, formerly Mrs. Chen.

"Well, someone's boss called and asked if I would be down to come eat some bomb food while he asked you to-"

"That's enough Saralee." Her mom nudges her, and I slide my hand down my face thankful that she didn't continue any further.

Sara giggles as she slides in next to Sterling.

"You did this?" she whispers to me as everyone requests drinks and appetizers from the server. I simply smile and reach over, feathering a knowing kiss to her lips. *Of course, I did this. I'd do anything for you,* I want to say.

For the next hour, we all share stories and life updates and talk about future plans as we enjoy tasty food, drinks, and company.

I look around and I love seeing how happy Sterling is. This is what I've been missing in my life. And I know she feels the same. I wish I would've been able to get in touch with her brother and her mom, but I knew there was a chance I wouldn't be able to, and honestly, I'm not sure if she'd be ready for that right now anyways. I just wanted to make sure she was surrounded by as many loved ones as possible for tonight.

"Did we leave room for dessert?" the waitress asks as she clears plates from the table.

"You got one of them cookie skillet things?" Sara speaks up from beside Sterling and everyone breaks into a laugh.

"Can we get one of them cookie skillet things?" I ask as I lean over to wink at Sara, "And the other dessert special that you guys are having." The server nods at me knowingly but Sterling looks around confused.

"The other dessert special?" she asks, and suddenly everyone leans in and is attentive. Those were the code words.

It's time.

I get up from my seat and pull Sterling over to my chair, at the edge of the table. Dakota gets her phone out and my mom already has tears falling from her eyes.

Sterling looks at me like I'm crazy, but then I get down on one knee and level with those gorgeous blue eyes I fell in love with months ago.

"Callan," she whispers, and I give her a smirk before I begin my speech.

"Sterling, I am so in love with you. Everything that you are and all that you do is everything I never knew that I needed. You have brought out the best in me, even on my worst days." My hands start to get clammy as I reach into my pocket. "I was not in the right headspace when we first met, but I knew without a doubt that you were all I could think about. And now, I'm sure that I never want to live this life without you." Nervousness begins to wash over me as I feel everyone's eyes burn into us, but I relax when I remember that the only ones that matter are hers.

"I made a promise to you." I pull out her promise ring, the one she was frantically searching for earlier. She gives me the most devilish smirk and it awakens something in me, but I adjust myself and continue with my speech. I put the ring back in place, on her right hand.

"This promise meant the world to me. It's what I hold on to every day when I wake up. But it's not enough anymore, Sterling. I need more." I reach into my other pocket and this time, when I pull out the rose-gold band, there's no mistaking that Sterling knows what this is.

She immediately stands up in her chair, her mouth falls open with an audible gasp and a tear escapes her eye. Dakota and my mom are quietly crying and Jax is silently cheering me on.

"I want to do more than make promises to you, Sterling. I want to vow. And I can't wait to honor those vows for the rest of our lives, if you'd do me the honor of being my wife." I take her shaky hand in mine and hold out the two-carat princess-cut diamond ring, waiting for her to answer.

"Callan," she whispers again, and every ounce of me begs for her to say yes. If she says no, I'd be wrecked. But a few seconds go by, and she doesn't say anything. She doesn't look at anyone else but me. My heart starts to hammer harder in my chest.

"Sterling." I shake her hand gently.

"You did all this for me?" she asks, and it's not what I want her to say. But I stand up from my knee, still holding the ring in my hand and using the other to swipe my thumb across her lip.

"I'd do anything for you, my little rose. I love you." I pull her into me, and I feel a tear stream down from her eye and meet where our lips are pressed together.

She pulls away and I miss her already.

"Callan Greyson David," she breathes, only loud enough for me to hear. "There is nothing I want more than to be your wife. Of course, I'll marry you," she says, and my brain can hardly process it.

"Really?" I ask.

"Yes!" she shouts, I place the ring on her left hand and claps begin to erupt from all around us. Not just at our table, but from the whole restaurant. She jumps up into my arms and kisses me frantically. "Yes," she murmurs into my lips, and I squeeze her tight, never wanting to let her go.

"Special dessert delivery." The waitress lowers a cake to the table with a topper that says *She Said Yes* on top and she gives me a warm smile as I lower her to her feet.

"You're incredible, Mr. David." Sterling takes her seat and I follow in next to her.

"Anything for you, my beautiful fiancé." It feels so good to say those words.

Fiancé.

Everyone starts bantering again, reaching for cake or asking to see the ring. It's perfect for her. She's perfect for me. This night went better than I expected.

I can't help but feel so full of love and life as I look at what I have in front of me. I'm not sure what I did to deserve any of this. But I do know one thing and I'm reminded of it every time I look into my beautiful girl's eyes...

It was always you.

ACKNOWLEDGMENTS

I think I've anticipated writing these acknowledgements more than I've anticipated writing the book itself. Okay, that's a lie but I can't believe we've made it this far.

For everyone who made it this far and took a chance on my debut novel, thank you. Your support means the world to me. It may not be perfect; I'm still learning along the way but it's incredible I've come this far. This book is about passion and the power of physical, mental, and emotional connection, and how strong a love can burn even when faced with hardships and imperfections. This story took a while to perfect. I changed a lot as I listened more to what my characters wanted to say... yes, they talk to me. Lol. And I put all of my passion for love into this book as I will with all my others. I hope you enjoyed reading Sterling and Callan's story as much as I loved writing it.

Jared. You know, there are days where I wish I could give you back to your mom but there are days where I'd be truly heartbroken if I ever went through with it. The only person I ever need in life is the one who bounces off my "that's what she said" jokes and someone who thinks I'm pretty even if my hair is stuck to my forehead from sleeping like a wild animal. Or someone who thinks that I can do no wrong even when I am wrong, which is a rarity if I may say. Marriage isn't easy, but being your wife is. I'm lucky to have someone to celebrate this with. I love you.

Before I continue, I want to give a little love to a few people in my life who didn't get the chance to see me make my dreams come true. Grandpa and Grandma Rice, I miss you both more than you'll ever know. Grandad Eugene, I hope you know how much I love and miss you. Michael Beck, the use of curse words I've used in this book was inspired by you, you were always saying the word fuck and I'm one hundred percent convinced that my obscene usage of curse words is because of you. And lastly, to my little sister, Emily Sue. Life isn't the same without you. But sissy is thinking about your beautiful smile every single day and I know you were looking over my shoulder while I was writing this book. Sara is how I imagined you would talk to me if your beautiful voice ever had a chance to be heard. I love you always.

I'd like to move on to the one person who made this whole thing so much more manageable and honestly, who helped me make this a reality, my editor Paige. I owe you a suffocatingly, ginormous hug. Everything you did for this book is beyond what I could have asked for and I'm so grateful to have you in my life as a friend and my forever book editor, so long as you don't mind me texting you in the middle of the night asking for advice on the next best sex scenes and brainstorming plot ideas with you. And also, thanks for putting up with all the spelling errors and strange ideas I threw at you and for sacrificing your google search. I'll never be able to repay you for the time and effort you put into this project with me and for pushing me through the finish line. I love you endlessly.

Cindy and Terry, you two are my biggest supporters even though I was super worried (and still am) that you will forever judge me after this. But that's okay, because I know you love me, and I appreciate your cheers for my success even if it may seem like a bad idea. I love you both with all of my heart.

Shoutout to Haylie, Chy, Jackie, Sydney, Bex, Jordan, Ryleigh and all the other MAU girlies who had to put up with my constant convos of this book, even when you literally would rather be doing anything else. Your support has been the greatest to receive and the hype you all provided for this book will forever keep a smile on my face.

Mom, life hasn't dealt us the best of cards. But I hope you know how much I love you, even if we don't share those words every day.

Uriah and Jolynn, boy do I hope you two never read this book. At least not till you're thirty lol. Being your mom has been the greatest adventure in my life and everything I do I do for you. Uriah, you amaze me with how smart you are and how big you grow each and every day. I'm so proud of all your hard work and dedication to everything you put your mind to. Jolynn, your love for reading makes my soul happy and I can't wait to see what you do with your future. Your constant ability to make me feel loved and happy even on my bad days as me pushing forward in life. I'm so blessed to have you both as my minions. And thanks for always asking "Mom, is your book done yet?" because it definitely gave me the push I needed.

For my Alpha and ARC Readers, you da best! Thanks for all the time you put into making this book the best it can be.

Now let's be honest, I saved the best for last. BOOKTOK, where you at? I started writing this book before I discovered #booktok, actually I didn't even have a TikTok at all. My amazing editor suggested it and it was the best decision I made for this journey because through that platform alone, I have met some pretty incredible people and friends. And this book was hyped up through all the lead-up and teasers and it's all because of you, my good girls. Power of social media and word of mouth is real and for any and everyone who spread word of this journey of mine, thank you.

Well, this has been fun. I can't wait for you to meet the next couple for book two in the series. I hope you love them as much as I do. Stay smutty, babes!

About the Author

AJ Nicole lives in Colorado with her two kids, her puppy daughter, and her husband. She is a Capricorn through and through and above all else, has a passion for creating. She runs on coffee and music and is an avid reader as much as she is a writer. When she's not plotting her next spicy romance, you can find her embarrassing herself on TikTok, reading all of the romance books, or binge watching The Vampire Diaries. (BTW, she's team Damon but Kai Parker is King.)

Want to stay updated on all things AJ Nicole? Like when the next book is coming out and where you can find her signing? Visit her website or follow her on social media for more!

Visit my website:

www.booksbyajnicole.com

Instagram and TikTok

@booksbyajnicole

Join My Patreon for all the dirty details...

www.patreon.com/authorajnicole

THE PAIN & PLEASURE SERIES

An interconnecting standalone series that is messy, spicy, fun, and swoon-worthy.

He's her boss and he's obsessed with her, but he's keeping a secret.

He's the single dad who makes all of her dreams come true.

He's her old best friend who broke her heart but tries to win her back.

After you've read them all... find the novella. Where happily ever after is just a kiss and a vow away.

ISA
ion can be obtained
ng.com
0424
040B/381

9 798869 235831